Political Thought in Ireland Since the Seventeenth Century

Edited by

D. George Boyce, Robert Eccleshall and Vincent Geoghegan

London and New York

First published 1993
by Routledge
11 New Fetter Lane, London EC4P 4EE

Simultaneously published in the USA and Canada
by Routledge
29 West 35th Street, New York, NY 10001

© Editorial Matter D. George Boyce, Robert Eccleshall, Vincent
Geoghegan. Individual contributions © Individual contributors

Phototypeset in 10 on 12 point Times by Intype, London

Printed in Great Britain by T. J. Press (Padstow) Ltd, Padstow, Cornwall

British Library Cataloguing in Publication Data

A catalogue record for this book is available from the British Library

Library of Congress Cataloging in Publication Data

A catalogue record for this book is available from the Library of Congress

ISBN 0–415–01354–2

Contents

Notes on contributors

D. George Boyce, who took his BA and Ph.D. at the Queen's University of Belfast, holds a personal chair in Politics at University College, Swansea. Among his recent publications are *The Irish Question and British Politics 1868–1986* (1989), *Nineteenth Century Ireland, the Search for Stability* (1990), and *Nationalism in Ireland* (rev. edn, 1991).

Robert Eccleshall, who received his BA and Ph.D. from Hull University, is Professor and Head of the Department of Politics at the Queen's University of Belfast. His recent publications include *British Liberalism* (1986) and *English Conservatism since the Restoration* (1990).

Richard English, who was educated at Keble College, Oxford and the University of Keele, lectures in Politics at the Queen's University of Belfast. He is author of *History of Ireland* (1991) and co-editor with Cormac O'Malley of *Prisoners: The Civil War Letters of Ernie O'Malley* (1991). His Ph.D. thesis is to be published by Oxford University Press as *Radicals and the Republic: Socialist Republicanism in the Irish Free State, 1925–37*.

Vincent Geoghegan, Reader in Politics at the Queen's University of Belfast, received his BA and Ph.D. from Newcastle University. He is author of *Reason and Eros: The Social Theory of Herbert Marcuse* (1981) and of *Utopianism and Marxism* (1987), and has recently written articles on Golden Ages, the Irish Owenite Community at Ralahine, and the Irish Jacobite, James MacGeoghegan.

Ian McBride is a graduate of Jesus College, Oxford and University College, London, where his doctoral thesis was on Ulster Presbyterianism in the late eighteenth century. In 1992 he was elected to a research fellowship at the Institute of Historical Research, University of London.

Breandán Ó Buachalla, a Member of the Royal Irish Academy, took his MA and Ph.D. at University College, Cork. Formerly a lecturer in Celtic at the Queen's University of Belfast, he is now Professor of Modern Irish Language and Literature at University College, Dublin. His publications include *I mBéal Feirste Cois Cuain* (1968), *Peadar Ó Doirnín: amhráin* (1969), *Nua-Dhuanaire II* (1975) and *Cathal Buí: amhráin* (1976)

Margaret O'Callaghan, who lectures in Politics at the Queen's University of Belfast, was educated at University College, Dublin and St John's College, Cambridge. Formerly a Fellow of Sidney Sussex College, Cambridge and university lecturer in Modern British History, she is preparing her doctoral thesis, *Crime, Nationality and the Law: The Politics of Land in Late Victorian Ireland*, for publication.

Jennifer Todd, who received a BA from the University of Kent at Canterbury and a Ph.D. from Boston University, is a lecturer in Politics at University College, Dublin. She has written articles on aesthetics and politics as well as the Northern Ireland conflict. She is completing a book on the Northern Ireland conflict and preparing another on political ideologies in Northern Ireland.

Acknowledgements

Robert Eccleshall and Vincent Geoghegan wish to acknowledge the financial support of the Nuffield Foundation, and would also like to thank Gerry Fitzpatrick for his invaluable assistance during the preliminary stages of this volume. The editors are grateful for the advice and encouragement of Claire L'Enfant.

Introduction

The history of political ideas in Ireland is largely unwritten. A fairly standard canon of 'major figures' has emerged, including Jonathan Swift, Henry Grattan, Edmund Burke, Thomas Davis and Arthur Griffith. But these all too often set the boundaries of such attention as the subject receives. 'Lesser mortals' are usually ignored; and some political traditions, conservatism for example, are regarded as either of no great importance as a subject for analysis, or as (in the case of socialism, at any rate before James Connolly) marginal to the political development of Ireland.

One reason is that Irish historiography has been little affected by recent methodological developments in intellectual history. From the perspective of the classic texts approach – the search for the Irish *Leviathan* which, once found, is to be carefully dissected in the hope of discovering the essence of the human condition – Ireland, along with many other societies, has comparatively little to offer the historian. During the last two decades, however, there has been a move away from regarding political texts as embodiments of eternal truths to a more contextual approach: one in which political theory is regarded not as the rarefied speculation of isolated individuals, but as a social activity conducted by numerous people using a variety of linguistic conventions. The effect has been dramatically to extend the canon of works to which attention can be legitimately devoted. In Ireland political thought is to be found in myth, law, literature, theology, folklore, in ballads, newspapers, parliamentary debates, pamphlets and sermons, as well as in the conventional texts. Furthermore, Ireland's political thinkers have displayed great heterogeneity, encompassing, for example, seventeenth-century bishops and poets; professors and conspirators in the eighteenth century; improving landlords, urban artisans, journalists in the last century; and politicians and *literati* in this. Yet Irish historiography has remained largely unaware of the rich pickings offered by a more contextual approach to political ideas.

Instead, emphasis is still placed upon men or women of action. Attention focuses on the origins and development of political movements; on

struggles for power, rather narrowly conceived; on the doings of government, especially British government; on the administrative process; and
on political violence and its consequences. All of these are of course of
great importance, but Irish history – more charged than that of most
countries with the ferment and clash of ideas – is then seen as a struggle
to seize or for that matter retain power. And so the search is made
for those who organized, brought pressure to bear on government, and
established themselves in the place of British administration.

Yet the study of power-seeking cannot be separated from the study of
ideas. And not only of the ideas of those who followed the great banners
of unionism and nationalism – important though these are – but of those
who sought ways of justifying what they were doing, even if they failed
in the end to do it; and of influencing others, even if in the end they
failed to achieve this purpose. Peripheral individuals, failures, even what
in retrospect look like eccentrics, all are the stuff of the historian of
political thought.

An exploration of the thinking of these latter figures exposes a common
assumption about political ideas in Ireland: that they are all too frequently
written about, and are all too easily understood. Caricature is an ever-
present danger. Protestants are unionists, or at least crypto-unionists, and
have always been so. Roman Catholics have been nationalists without
qualification, and always will be. Seventeenth-century Catholics were
separatists in the making; eighteenth-century Protestants were all 'Colonial Nationalists'. An investigation of Irish political ideas reveals their
complexity and their constant ability to surprise. Moreover, when the
dominant ideologies are examined more closely, they show a tendency
to defy easy categorization. Unionism cannot be reduced to a simple
basis of fundamentalist religious belief, nor to a bourgeois ideology aimed
at saving unionist businessmen from the consequences of class conflict.
Nationalism cannot be simplified into ultramontane Catholicism, nor into
Ireland's version of nineteenth-century liberalism. Ideologies varied
according to time, circumstance and place: the view from nationalist
Dublin was not the same as the outlook from nationalist Skibbereen;
unionist North Down did not necessarily share the same outlook as
unionist Dungannon.

Irish political ideas were shaped by the circumstances of Ireland's
geography, history and society. That is obvious and applies to the making
of any country's political traditions. But Ireland is an island behind
another island, separated by a few sea miles from Great Britain. And
this proximity and distance help explain both the similarities and the
remarkable differences between the political ideas of the two places.
Ideas which took their root in England, or in continental Europe, found
their way to Ireland quickly enough. Issues of political obligation, a state
church, legitimacy of the sovereign or of the state, democratic reform,

social equality, political sovereignty, personal liberty, all were debated as hotly in Ireland as elsewhere in the British Isles.

But Irish history and society invited a different response. Ireland never discovered the settled constitution that her neighbour evolved after the revolution of 1688. There was a fundamental difficulty in translating the benefits of revolution – a balanced constitution, religious toleration, a religious establishment, personal and political freedoms within the law – into a country whose history was marked by the growing realization of the fact that one party's hope must encompass another party's despair. This of course applied, though to a lesser degree, across the water, but the difference was that England sustained a very different social structure. Her Anglican establishment was more numerous, more secure than its opponents, whether Roman Catholic or Dissenter. Ireland's political and religious establishment had to remember that its fight for life was only narrowly won; Catholic and Dissenter might try another contest. Moreover, the events of 1688–90 reinforced Protestants in their belief that Irish Roman Catholics were a threat, not only to the Anglican ascendancy, but to the whole stability of the two kingdoms of England and Ireland. Irish Jacobitism held that the Catholic nation might yet be restored to power and prosperity. England might, over time, forget this – at least until the 1715 and 1745 risings in Scotland reminded them that such threats could indeed occur again, albeit from a different quarter. Protestant Ireland could not forget its narrow escape. And relations between Catholic, Anglican and Dissenter were characterized by divisions deeper and more dangerous than those across the water.

This sense of danger was not allayed by the events which immediately preceded the Act of Union of 1800, and the union itself. Radicalism in England might threaten the monopoly power of the political establishment. In Ireland radicalism might, indeed almost certainly would, necessitate a renegotiation of the whole question of who constituted the 'Irish people' in the first place. Moreover, this constitutional change revealed another aspect of the different contexts in which British and Irish political thinkers worked. The question of the state involved matters to do with getting or losing power, and of winning or failing to win the attention and support of a government under which Irishmen and Irishwomen lived, but over whose conduct they had only a very imperfect influence. How could the state be manipulated? How could it be opposed? How could it be transformed into an Irish state? How could such a transformation be frustrated? What if it were removed; what would replace it if it were removed? Irish political ideas were deeply influenced by the peculiar institution of the Union Parliament, in which Irish members sat, but whose government they could never constitute, and hardly ever substantially modify.

This produced an anxiety which at times came near to desperation in Irish political thinking. If the purpose of political writing is to persuade

– and it is hard to see why else it was ever written – then the task confronting the Irish theorist was a formidable one. Irish thinkers had not only to persuade their own constituency (and perhaps, if possible, other Irish constituencies); they had also to respond to their powerlessness in the British state, and seek to catch and hold the attention of a busy and often oblivious British public. This resulted in a kind of schizophrenia, as Irish political thinkers used words, terms, concepts that were in common use in England – obligation, public opinion, democracy, establishment – but which in Ireland carried a very different meaning because of the intense suspicion and tensions which existed in a country where the numerical majority did not, until 1921, constitute the political nation.

Irish thinkers also engaged in a debate aimed at creating new relations between these groups of people, and establishing new social and political constructs. The divided nature of Irish society and the alarming prospect, which reared its head from time to time, of outright sectarian war, pushed thinkers into seeking alternative ways of creating political consensus in Ireland. Indeed, the search for consensus is as significant a part of the Irish political tradition as the quest for differences. Some socialists, for example, sought to create a nation out of the various classes in Ireland, and to reconcile them to each other. Then there was the search for national unity: this might be found, as in the late eighteenth century, through political radicalism, with its strong Protestant overtones and its affinity with the European Enlightenment. Or it might be sought through the creation of an elite-led public opinion, anti-democratic in tone, but seeking to give Ireland the kind of political leadership that only her educated Protestant middle classes and gentry could supply. The working man might be integrated into a political movement, which would smash the Protestant and Catholic middle classes. Tenant farmer might combine against landlord, irrespective of religion. Or perhaps a Jacobin state might be created in twentieth-century Ireland, if only republican socialism could get it right. Or a cultural revival might be inaugurated which would eventually encompass all Irish people, encouraging them to seek common ground in their great historical and literary traditions. All might be possible; all might not. Yet the thinkers who explored these possibilities have a right to our attention, even in failure.

Irish historians could not avoid interrogating the past, or versions of it. Ireland was a country where conquest created a deep and lasting tension, sometimes dormant but never far from the public mind. The ruling Anglican elite of the eighteenth century had to repudiate the accusation that they had in some sense disrupted the continuity of Irish history. They responded by claiming that they had brought a barbarous society to civility as well as restoring the apostolic purity of the Celtic Church. But the ideal of a Celtic past would be put to other uses. The Romantic movement exerted a deep and lasting influence on Ireland, emphasizing as it did cultures and traditions that were supposedly authentic in a way that modern, especially Anglo-Saxon, civilization was not. The past might be recalled to help shape the future. Ireland could be re-made, and some, like Douglas Hyde, even hoped that the new Celtic nation could be interpreted in such a way as to give Irish Protestants their due place: for, after all, had not the Celts inhabited Ireland long before the Roman Church won the battle for religious and cultural hegemony throughout the British Isles? History was a political weapon throughout Europe in the nineteenth century, but there can have been few places where it was deployed more persistently than Ireland: indeed, the prefix 're' is one of the most potent in the Irish political vocabulary.

Another peculiar characteristic of Irish political thinking is that issues had to be addressed in what was almost a laboratory atmosphere. Ireland lacked a settled society, a deep-rooted constitution, and a defined culture. It seemed, indeed, that Ireland could be re-made, the political system changed radically, and society recast in new moulds or in ones that could reverse the verdict of some previous historical contest such as the Battle of the Boyne or – since 'recent' had a different meaning in the Irish context – the Plantation. To make mistakes, to lose an argument, to fail to establish a point, all might have profound and immediate political consequences in Ireland. Isaac Butt, when debating with Daniel O'Connell in 1843 the advantages or otherwise of Repeal of the Union, was not merely seeking to win his case; he was endeavouring to save his people from the weight of Irish Roman Catholic populism and the end of Protestantism as a religious, political and social force in Ireland. In the background of Irish political ideas lurked a fear that the country might slip back – and quickly – into a state of nature, with political institutions toppled and the rival populations at each other's throats. The history of seventeenth-century Ireland proved as much. This gave an urgency to Irish political thought: there was always the suspicion that contingency plans were needed, that in the end each side must look to its own survival.

The result was that Ireland asked searching questions about the issues that engage the attention of political thinkers. Concepts such as 'civility' as against 'barbarism', nationhood as against sectionalism, radicalism as against conservatism, socialism as against all other 'isms', gathered a cutting edge in the world of Irish politics. In Ireland the role of political thinkers was as important as it could be, even when their ideas were swept aside. Debates about power, sovereignty, political obligation, freedom, the use of force, were not matters of abstraction: they shaped the behaviour of ordinary people, justified what they did, helped them to win, or lose, in a political world where winning and losing could bring with them the most dire consequences.

The following chapters do not constitute a comprehensive history of Irish political thought. Instead, they explore some features of a largely untrodden intellectual terrain. The hope is that these pioneering essays will show that there has long been a vigorous tradition of political thinking in Ireland, even if until now ignored by academic students of political ideas.

1 James our true king

The ideology of Irish royalism in the seventeenth century

Breandán Ó Buachalla

I

The notion of change pervades seventeenth-century Irish literature. From the opening decade of the century to the last, even a superficial reading of the literature – particularly of the poetry – reveals common themes enunciating again and again that Ireland had changed, that old ways were being forsaken, that new fashions and new classes were in the ascendant, that Ireland was under attack, in danger of being submerged, her future uncertain. It was such common sentiments which led and which still lead modern scholars to interpret the cataclysm of the seventeenth century solely in terms of despair and terminal decay. A typical illustration is the last chapter of Flower's *The Irish Tradition*, significantly entitled 'The end of the tradition':

> By the beginning of the seventeenth-century Ireland lay exhausted and panting and what seemed the final blow to all her hopes and to the old order of things under which the poets had flourished was dealt by the mysterious flight of the two Northern Earls, Tyrone and Tyrconnel in 1607, an event that led directly to the plantation of Ulster and as an inimitable result to the rising of 1641. . . . One of their poets has expressed all that this fateful moment meant for those to whom the old Irish order was the only way of life they had known and who were now to see that order crumbling into ruins about them.

> This night sees Ireland desolate
> Her chiefs are cast out of their estate
> Her men, her maidens weep to see
> Her desolate, that should peopled be.

> O'Donnell goes in that stern straight
> Sore stricken Ulster mourns her fate
> And all the Northern shore makes moan
> To hear that Aodh O Neill has gone.

> Her chiefs are gone, there's none to hear,
> To bear her cross or lift her from despair,
> The grieving lords take ship
> With these our very souls pass overseas.[1]

The fact that the poet to whom that elegiac poem is generally ascribed (Fear Flatha Ó Gnímh) received a royal pardon in 1602 and was subsequently patronized by Martha Stafford, daughter of Sir Francis Stafford, an English official in Ireland, and wife of Sir Henry O Neill,[2] suggests, at least, that the poem should not be taken as being totally representative of his *œuvre* as a whole nor of his attitude to contemporaneous affairs.

That the seventeenth century in Ireland was an era of unprecedented upheaval cannot be gainsaid. It was, undoubtedly, a watershed and for the hereditary learned classes in particular the beginning of the end of their priviliged position in Irish society, as the socio-economic system on which their status depended slowly gave way. The end of the bardic order should not be interpreted, however, as the demise of a culture, language or society. In socio-cultural terms that order represented but the tip of an iceberg which, ironically, revealed more and more of its variety and complexity over the next two centuries. As the professional hereditary class of literati gradually lost their privileged status in society and their control of literary tastes and canons they were replaced by other types hitherto unknown in Irish literary annals – the gentleman-poet, the priest-poet, the amateur poet, the prose writer – and by a new class of semi-professional literati who had to adapt their traditional training and attitudes to changing circumstances. New metres, new themes, new poetic surnames, new literary classes, new modes of writing – in prose and verse – emerge. As a consequence, the seventeenth century was also a major period of literary diversification and of reorganization: it must be placed with the twelfth and seventh centuries among the great periods of creativity and literary renewal. A paradigm of change alone will not suffice in dealing with the seventeenth century; the apposite framework is change within continuity – the central pattern of the Irish cultural tradition. There is, moreover, another perspective which cannot be ignored: the general European background. For Europe as a whole, the seventeenth century was also one of upheaval; of social, political and religious strife of such proportions to warrant the title 'the General Crisis of the Seventeenth Century' in the historiography. The origin of that crisis was not in essence political, although it had political implications, but intellectual, what Mousnier labelled 'an intellectual mutation', one which essentially redefined the relationship between people and the state.[3] Since religion underlay all political ideologies in Western Europe, it subsumed not only practice and belief but also matters of state. The application of the principle *cuius regio eius religio* not only determined the denominational/sectarian character of the emergent centralized mon-

archies and states but for many of Europe's peoples it inextricably inter-
twined religion with national consciousness. In England and Ireland, in
particular, religious allegiance and national identity coalesced, Protestant
and Catholic being perceived as synonymous with English and Irish
respectively. There was a fundamental difference, of course. In England,
Protestantism (the Anglican variety) enjoyed the privileges and status of
a state-church whereas, in Ireland, Catholicism, the religion of the
majority, was denied legal rights or official recognition. In rejecting the
Reformation, the Irish found themselves in an anomalous and unique
situation in Western Europe in that a Catholic majority was ruled by a
Protestant sovereign. Therein lay the kernel of the politico-religious
nature of Ireland's problem and the ultimate source of the major changes
that ensued. Of all the changes evidenced for seventeenth-century Ireland
one of the most far-reaching and most significant was an ideological shift
among the learned classes, an intellectual mutation which necessitated
the redefinition of an Irishman, the rewriting of Irish history, the reformulation of Irish distinctiveness; above all a rethinking of attitudes and
policies towards the temporal authority. The immediate sources of this
mutation were politico-religious in nature. One is the fact that by the
end of the sixteenth century the Irish upper classes – the equivalent of
the political nation in the English context – had irrevocably aligned
themselves to the Church of Rome. The second is that after the battle
of Kinsale and particularly after the Flight of the Earls the overriding
attitude of those classes was one of accommodation of the new order.
Central to that accommodation was the evolution of a *rapprochement*
with the temporal authority as represented by the King.

The accession of James I to the Crown of the three kingdoms in 1603
was a source of hope and joy to the Catholics of the towns and boroughs
of Ireland. His mother being a Catholic, it was assumed that he would
be lenient and understanding, if not positively tolerant. In this expectant
mood Catholic churches were reopened, Mass was celebrated openly,
public religious processions organized and Protestants banished. In a
letter to the King of Spain, O Neill and O Donnell gave their explanation
of that hope: 'When the Queen died and this King, who was before King
of Scotland, succeeded to her, the Irish hoped, on account of their old
friendship with the Scots, that they would receive from the King many
favours and, in particular, their liberty of conscience.'[4] The same optimistic hope underlies two poems in Irish written by two Ulster poets immediately on James's accession. In one of them, Eochaidh Ó hEodhasa, a
poet from County Fermanagh, who as a 'deserving native' received 300
acres under the terms of Ulster plantation, contrasts the metamorphosis
of Ovid to the changes for the better which James's accession has brought
about. Although the poem's discourse is stilted and rather arcane, the
message is obvious:

Many a thing – need it be said – in the beginning changed to evil;
much more propitious now is the fate that causes everything to turn
for the better . . .

The brilliant sun has lit up, King James is the dispersal of all mist;
the mutual mourning of all, he has changed to glory; great the signs
of change.

More remarkable than that is the fact that we, the troubled people
of Ireland, that each one of us has forgotten the tribulation of all
anxieties . . .

It is meet for us, though I say so, to bid farewell to our yoke of
anxiety; the helping eye of our King supersedes the lasting force of
our sorrow . . .

May no reversal come soon again either from evil or from envious eye
or from reversal of fortune; we have experienced every transformation.[5]

The second poem, by a Donegal poet (Eoghan Ruadh Mac an Bhaird),
is much more concrete and less abstruse. He states clearly the hereditary
basis of James's claim and invokes the twin validatory mechanisms of
genealogy and prophecy to legitimize his unquestionable right to the
crown of Ireland:

Three crowns – 'tis fitting for him – shall be placed on James's head;
the utterance of the books is no secret, every seer confirms it . . .

That young Prince so high of mind, James Stewart, shall have Ireland's
wondrous crown – an honour, I know, he well deserves . . .

For three hundred years – lasting their effect – is it in the possession
of the high-king's ancestors . . . Scotland of the smooth-earthed land
was held by nine of his family before him; I will give you their
names . . .

O prince whose hand gives straight judgments – it will now be said –
talk not of 'taking new territory'; thou hast already a right to red-
sworded Ireland . . .

The Saxons' land has been long – 'tis well known – prophesied for
thee; so likewise is Ireland due to thee, thou are her spouse by all the
signs . . .

There is no high-king's blood, however noble – save that of the Virgin's
son – that surpasses thine.[6]

The emphasis, in both poems, on James dispersing enmity and strife; on
him, in the second poem, giving 'straight judgments' could, obviously,
be applied to contemporary affairs but they also reflect traditional notions

of legitimate and righteous kingship. For Mac an Bhaird to address James as 'Ireland's spouse' was to bestow on him not only an honorific accolade but the ultimate seal of legitimacy; Ireland's spouse in traditional Irish ideology was synonymous with the rightful king who would bring peace, banish strife, and under whom, because of his rightfulness, Ireland would prosper and abound in beneficence.[7] Indeed it is in such millenarian terms that Ireland, under James I, is described in the social satire *Pairlement Chloinne Tomáis*: 'When King James ascended the throne, as a result of his goodness and graciousness, under him Ireland was filled with peace and prosperity for a long time and Clann Tomáis set about sending their children to school and to study for the priesthood.'[8] The adoption of James I by the Irish learned class and his absorption by them into the Irish scheme of things is reflected most vividly in the work of the genealogists. Overnight an impeccable genealogy was bestowed on him; as Mac an Bhaird declared, only the son of Mary had more noble blood than he. James's descent was, in fact, of particular interest to the literati and it constituted one of the causes of dissension in the 'Contention of the Bards', one faction claiming that James was descended from a Munster King, another that he was of Ulster origin.[9] They were not, in fact, conflicting claims as the official genealogy proved conclusively that on his mother's side James was descended from the Ulster King Fergus, the first Irish King of Scotland, whereas on his father's side he was descended from Corc, the fifth-century king of Munster. Moreover, it was subsequently shown that he was also related directly to the kings of Connaught and Leinster: an impeccable unquestionable genealogy.[10]

The accommodation by the learned class of James I and the facility by which an appropriate niche was found for him in the inherited Irish value-system is merely a working out in intellectual terms of a shift which had already been accomplished in the theological and religious spheres. The crucial development was the appointment of Peter Lombard as Archbishop of Armagh and Primate of Ireland in 1601 and the subsequent implementation of his policy of acceptance of the status quo.[11] Lombard believed that the cause of Catholicism in England and Ireland could best be advanced by accepting James as the lawful king. This was not merely a strategic ploy, it was a conscious decision based on a realistic assessment of recent politico-religious developments in Europe; it was moreover based on the new theological formula which had been developed and advanced by the Jesuit theologians, Bellarmine and Suarez. According to their teaching, as temporal and spiritual authority were to be clearly distinguished it was possible for a Catholic people to give allegiance at least *in temporalibus* to a 'heretical' Prince. Lombard, through his vicar Rothe, had this new policy adopted and approved by the clerical synods at Drogheda (1614), Kilkenny (1614), Armagh (1618), Cashel (1624). The official teaching as promulgated at those synods specified unequivocally that James was due, by his subjects, the loyalty due to Caesar.[12] That

was henceforth official Church policy in Ireland and it is well reflected in
the catechismal and spiritual material now being provided in Irish by the
agents of the Counter-Reformation. The general principle is laid down
in the earliest catechisms translated into Irish:

> The fourth commandment: Honour thy father and thy mother. This is
> how one transgresses against this commandment . . . whoever does
> not remain obedient and respectful to his prelates and to his princes
> and to his temporal lords and to those who are in high office over him
> and those who do not yield to the laws and statutes of their place of
> domicile . . .

> Not only are we bound to honour our fathers and our mothers but we
> are likewise bound to give the same honour to every superior either
> of Church or State.[13]

The practical implications of the teaching were spelt out and applied to
concrete circumstances in the spiritual tracts provided by Mac Aingil and
Ó Maoil Chonaire:

> But notice that every Christian is bound not only to keep the com-
> mandments of God and his Church, but he is also bound not to break
> the commandments of the civil authority. . . . Therefore you must
> ask yourself if you have broken, and how many times, the lawful
> commandment of your Prince, your Lord, your master, your father or
> any other person who is lawfully your superior. But if any of those
> superiors were to impose a commandment on you which would be
> contrary to God's law or the Church's it were more proper for you to
> obey God and the Church rather than that commandment. . . . More-
> over, if your father were to impose a commandment on you which
> would be contrary to the commonweal . . . or contrary to the com-
> mandment of your Prince don't take any notice of it and if your Prince
> were to give you a commandment which would be contrary to God's
> commandments do not be reluctant to break it. . . . Similarly if a
> temporal superior commanded you not to frequent the sacraments, not
> to listen to Catholic sermons, not to make confession or communion, to
> listen to the service or sermon of the heretics, not to fast, to violate
> the churches, to insult the statues, understand that these are unlawful
> commandments which are against God or the Church and that you are
> bound to disobey them. However, every commandment which your
> legitimate temporal superior gives you, particularly if he is your Prince,
> and if it is not contrary to the law of God or of the Church, you are
> bound in conscience to obey it . . .

> If the Emperor orders me: be prepared for my service, that is right;
> but not to accompany him to the church of the idols for a higher
> authority has ordered me not to go there. I beg your pardon, you [the

temporal authority] are threatening prison, he [the spiritual authority] is threatening the fires of Hell. Accordingly Caesar is entitled only to his due; he is not entitled to God's.[14]

Ó Maoil Chonaire, Ó hEodhasa and Mac Aingil were not only leading figures of the Counter-Reformation movement in Ireland, they were also typical representatives of it. Their primary aim of winning over the minds and souls of the Irish was achieved by presenting the issue to their followers in apocalyptic terms, applying to the Irish scene the Counter-Reformation polemic imported from the Continent where they had been trained and where they now resided. But behind the rhetorical and polemical language of their tracts a subtle pragmatism can be detected, one which differentiated between the heretics as such and the leader of their heretical Church: James 'our noble King', 'our noble illustrious King', 'his majesty the King', as Mac Aingil calls him, who although not a son of the Catholic Church, neither subscribed totally to the teachings of the blasphemous heretics Luther and Calvin; moreover James was not fully culpable – he had been led astray by 'bad teachers' in his youth.[15] This notion of 'bad teachers' or 'evil advisers' is utilized by other writers as well in their successful attempt to divorce James from the church of which he was head and from the actions carried out by its officers. It is but another manifestation of the lengths to which the literati, both lay and clerical, were prepared to go to rationalize their accommodation of James I. The theological and ideological dimensions of that accommodation are easily established; behind both theology and ideology lay a practical acceptance of the facts of Irish life and of the status quo. James was not only king, he was an absolute king whose writ had, for the first time ever, complete sway over the whole of Ireland; in practical terms he was Ireland's first 'High-King' and the ultimate source of power, favour, preferment and patronage. There was only one choice in dealing with the totally new situation. Lombard had spelt it out in the early years of the century: 'by the King's favour or by arms', and the same bleak choice was repeated by O Neill and O Donnell in their dealings with Philip III of Spain.[16] The hope of armed aid from Spain and a successful recourse to arms never died, but in the meantime reconciliation with the ultimate source of power was the only practical course available.

That attitude and its practical implications are well documented in the contemporaneous literature, the tone and the terminology of the excerpts being as revealing as the actions they describe. According to Red Hugh O Donnell's mother, the leaders of the rebellion of 1608 were guilty of 'treason against their King'; it was against 'the King's ordinance' they rebelled, declared the Four Masters; Rory O Donnell went to Dublin in 1603, according to the poet Eoghan Rua Mac an Bhaird, to parley with Mountjoy 'the deputy of the High King of Ireland'; in another poem, the same poet declares that Ireland was now in the King's 'title'; he assures

Niall Garbh who was then imprisoned in the Tower of London that he will be forgiven his crime 'when the crown remembers him again with favour' and that he will be released 'as soon as King James bends [in forgiveness]'. It was 'with the permission of the King and his writ', an anonymous poet declared in the 'Contentions of the Poets', that the Northern Half would exact tax and tributes henceforth from the Southern Half; Mac Aingil declared that he was addressing those under the Majesty of the King – 'the King's majesty and his people whom I wish to teach'; furthermore he declared that no one should obey any ordinance which was contrary to the 'commonweal'.[17] The most interesting feature of those excerpts is the new terminology being utilized and the new concepts being signified: *réim*, 'writ'; *teideal*, 'title'; *Prionsa*, 'sovereign'; *mórgacht*, 'majesty'; *maitheas poiblighe*, 'commonweal'; *an choróin*, 'the crown'. None of them had hitherto any place in native Irish law, Irish polity, or in traditional Irish ideology. Not all of those terms acquired the same currency, nor are they all attested outside particular texts. Some of them, on the other hand, are widely attested and they became permanent items of a new political lexicon. They all, however, constitute a formal reflex not only of the intellectual mutation in progress but also a literary reali-zation of a central fact of Irish political life: that the overall aim of Catholic Ireland's élites was to come to terms with the King, since they realized that it was only through him that they and their cause could prosper. In the ensuing conflict between Parliament and Crown the Irish aristocracy, and accordingly the Irish learned classes, sided unequivocally with the King. Their redress was always to their own understanding, tolerant King, not to a Puritan Parliament from whom they had no hope of even toleration, let alone preferment. And when they did eventually have recourse to arms – in 1641 – they did so not as an act of rebellion, but in the King's name: 'We are in no rebellion ourselves, but do really fight for our Prince in defence of his Crown and royal prerogatives.'[18]

To the new lexicon of Irish political thought (sovereign, the crown, commonweal) one must add two more central and pervasive elements: *ríoghacht*, 'kingdom', and *náision*, 'nation'.[19] Ireland was now one united kingdom with her own king as titular head; the crown of Ireland consti-tuted one of the 'three crowns' worn by James and to him was accordingly due the loyalty due to Caesar; in the island of Ireland there now resided, a *nation* – the Irish nation which was also a Catholic one.

II

The identification of Catholicism with Irish national consciousness is not reflected in the literature until the early seventeenth century but by that stage it is all-pervasive; a universal understanding permeating both prose and verse, common to the writings of layman and cleric alike in Irish and in Latin. According to Lombard, 'Catholicism is the one unifying factor in Irish life; it is the fact that makes an Irishman'; Ireland alone, according to O Sullivan Beare, of all the countries in Northern Europe was steadfast in her Catholicism; according to John Roche, Bishop of Ferns, 'the very ground the Irish tread, the air they breathe, the climate they share, the very sky above them, all seem to draw them to the religion of Rome'.[20] The war in Ireland, maintained the priest-poet Ó Dubhthaigh, was one between General Patrick on one hand and, on the other, Captain Luther and Captain Calvin; it was tantamount to death for Ireland the manner in which 'her laws and her faith' had been denied, said Ó Gnímh; among the tragedies which had befallen Ireland, according to Mac Marcais, were 'the prohibition of music, the subjugation of the Irish language and neither wine nor mass being held in esteem'; as a result of the death of O Donnell, Mac an Bhaird declares, the true faith had been eclipsed, and a loathsome band of heretics had taken over God's vineyard; religious tracts had to be provided in Irish, Mac Aingil explains, 'because every other Catholic nation has books like these'.[21]

The acceptance by the Irish intelligentsia of the centrality of Catholicism to Irish ethnocentricity is paralleled, of course, in the attitude and actions of the government, particularly under Wentworth. For him and his absolutist policies religion was the overriding criterion of differentiation; as far as official policy mattered only two types existed in Ireland: Catholics and Protestants. The levelling effect of the acceptance and application of Catholicism as a distinctive ethnic feature had obvious implications for the native Irish and the Old-English alike. According to Carew the native Irish, because of their travel abroad, had become more civilized and as a consequence the old enmity and mutual distrust between the Irish and the Old-English was on the wane and accordingly 'under the mask of religion they being then conjoined it is worthy of consideration . . . what more danger to the state their union can now produce'.[22] Another official source blamed 'the pervidious Machiavellan friars at Louvain [who] seek by all means to reconcile their countrymen in their affections and to combine both those that are descended of the English race and those that are mere Irish in a league of friendship and concurrence'.[23] To ascribe to the friars of Louvain total responsibility for the emergent concurrence between Gael and Old-English, would of course be too simplistic. Nevertheless it is obvious that the continental colleges were vibrant powerhouses of new ideas and new attitudes and that they played a vital role in shaping the *mentalité* of the intelligentsia – and most probably other elites – in Ireland. Most Irish colleges on the Continent housed communities comprised both of Old-English and native Irish, and though those communities were often racked by personal and provincial rivalries, that rivalry never diminished the dynamic of their dedication to a new cause. It is accordingly not insignificant that the first poem in Irish which embodies the new thinking on the Old-English was written abroad by Eoghan Rua Mac an Bhaird in a poem of dedication to Hugh O Donnell, son of Rory O Donnell, who was about to set out on an expedition to Ireland. The poem accompanied a war manual, translated by the poet himself, but which included advice not only on how to wage war, but also on how to make peace and prevent evil. In the poem the poet addresses the book, exhorting it to make its valuable learning available to the nobles of Ireland, not only to the native Irish nobility but to the Burkes, the Butlers, the FitzGeralds as well:

> O little book that is dedicated to Aodh, in thee is ample lore, bound for the Island of the Fair, of bright sward, lore that will be sweet to Ireland's hosts . . .

> The Burkes and the Butlers will not be weary of thy tales, nor the Geraldines who won affection beyond the old families of Fintan's land.

> Conceal from the race of Gaoidheal Glas no knowledge that thou hast found, nor from the Old English of the land of the Fair, with whom we, the warriors of Ireland, have united.

> Though I present thee to Ó Domhnaill above all in Fintan's land, go around the land on every side, share with every Irishman.

> Our own Gaels and Fair Foreigners, blessings on them with sincerity. Take my blessing to the land of Fál, a blessing go with thee now, little book.[24]

The significance of the poem lies not only in its attitude and sentiments but also in its terminology. The Old-English families are *Fionn-Ghaill* 'fair-foreigners'; they, and 'our own Gaels' are subsumed in the new common denominator of *Éireannaigh*, 'Irishmen'. Mac an Bhaird's poem is not the only instance of the new terminology nor of the new attitude implicit in it.[25] Philip O Sullivan Beare in his *Zoilomastix* of 1625 castigates Stanihurst for using the insulting term 'Anglo-Hiberni' when referring to the Old-English. There was no such group in Ireland, he declares. Ireland contains only two types: Irishmen who are Catholic and Englishmen who are heretics; accordingly, *Posthac Ibernia dicantur Iberni*.[26] Interestingly enough, in an earlier work O Sullivan Beare had himself used the term 'Anglo-Hiberni'; he now however rejects its validity, blames Stanihurst for putting it into circulation and calls on all Irishmen to unite in the common cause: *Ibernis concordia suadetur, Anglorum doli panduntur. De Anglorum perfidia.*[27] As Séathrún Céitinn pointed out in an elegy on two members of the Butler family, between the native Irish and the Old-English there was 'mutual sympathy of blood, marriage and faith'; to those two brave steadfast groups 'of the family of Banbha' the New English – 'a foreign haughty swarm' – showed nothing but 'envy and fury'.[28] One of the tangible concrete results of the Counter-Reformation movement in Ireland was the involvement, for the first time in several centuries, of the Catholic Church and of individual churchmen in the creation and cultivation of literature in Irish. As a result, a new element was introduced into the Irish intelligentsia – the priest-poet/priest-scholar – who being both Irish poet and Roman priest could invoke two sources of authoritative knowledge and apply them in reconciling the old with the new. Séathrún Céitinn (*c.* 1580–1644) is a fairly typical representative of this new class who by virtue of his training both in native lore and continental Renaissance humanism was able to provide a convincing legitimization of the new ideology in his definitive history of Ireland: *Foras Feasa ar Éirinn (FFÉ)*.[29]

The Renaissance humanists were the first to make a concerted effort to study the past with some appreciation of temporal perspective. By applying an historical technique to different branches of learning, particularly to jurisprudence and philology, a new understanding of history itself and, as a consequence, modern historiography was born. Central to the historiographical 'revolution', as it has been called, was an awareness of evidence which established the primacy of original documents in historical writing.[30] But if the new sense of historicism was the product of Renaissance humanism in general, the specific forms and interpretations of history it generated were shaped in particular by the upheavals of the Reformation and by the national rivalries that ensued. And although partisanship often distorted historical perspective, it did give impetus, organization and direction to historical investigation. Religious rivalry, the burgeoning of the notion of *patria*, the rise of national consciousness, the diffusion throughout Europe of the humanistic national history, as initiated by Polydorus Virgil, all reinforced what Dumoulin taught: the nation was now the 'only intelligible field' of historical study.[31] For a nation to lack a written history, Boudouin wrote, was an incontrovertible sign of barbarism, of cultural childhood.[32] Ireland too, claimed Keating, was 'a kingdom apart . . . like a little world'; it was not fitting that so honourable a country, nor so noble a people, should go unrecorded.[33]

Keating's immediate purpose, in writing *FFÉ*, was to answer the 'falsehoods' concerning Ireland and her inhabitants which were being propagated in the writings of Cambrensis and his latter-day followers, Stanihurst, Spencer, Camden, Davies and others. It is highly significant that in demolishing the malicious falsehoods of those foreigners, writers whose work resembled that of the beetle 'rolling itself in dung', Keating applied to them contemporary historiographical criteria. Naturally, he found them wanting. As regards Cambrensis, 'there is not a lay nor a letter, old record or ancient text, chronicle nor annals' which could support his lie; it was no marvel that Stanihurst did not know what he was talking about since he had never seen the original records, furthermore he was totally ignorant of the language in which those records were written and accordingly did not deserve the title of 'historian'; Campion was more like a player on a platform recounting stories than an historian; Morryson's work could not be regarded as 'history' since he had ignored the rules

appropriate to the writing of history as laid down by Polydorus Virgil;
all those foreign writers were but retelling 'tales of false witnesses' who
were hostile to Ireland and ignorant of her history; he, and he alone,
had access to the primary sources.[34] Keating, it is obvious, had absorbed
the new historical awareness and was accordingly conversant with the
new historiography, but in substituting his own retelling of Irish history
for the falsehoods of foreign writers, he was addressing himself not to the
past but to contemporaneous issues. He was engaged, not in a scholastic
retrospective study, but in a highly relevant political exercise. The Elizabethan intellectual rationalization for both Reformation and conquest in
Ireland rested on one simple premise: the Irish were primitive barbarians,
bereft of either civility or religion.[35] In refuting that thesis, Keating was
demolishing the premise itself and replacing it with the truth, 'the truth
of the state of the country, and the condition of the people who inhabit
it'. Ireland, like every other country in Europe, had its rabble of course,
but the faults and evil habits of the lower orders should not be visited
on Irishmen as a whole. The Catholic faith which Patrick had brought to
Ireland had never lapsed; and the evil, immoral practices which Camden
had ascribed to the Irish clergy arose only after Henry VIII had changed
his faith and were practised only by the schismatic clergy who had dis-
owned their ecclessiastical superiors. If truth were known, the Irish were
comparable to any nation in Europe in three aspects: 'in valour, in
learning and in their being steadfast in the Catholic faith'.[36] It was not
disinterested curiosity concerning the past, then, that led Keating to
provide Ireland with an integral authoritative history of her own, but
rather his own interest and involvement in the politico-religious issues of
his day. Far from intending *FFÉ* to serve as a 'monument to a doomed
civilization', as has been claimed,[37] he envisaged it as a tract for his own
times and for future generations.

For though *FFÉ* in conception and methodology reflects the new
humanistic historicism and is, accordingly, to be placed among the
national histories of sixteenth- and seventeenth-century Europe, the
framework in which Keating presents his narrative to his readers reflects
the socio-cultural and political realities of the 1630s in Ireland. The
ideological mutation which the Irish political nation in general and the
learned classes in particular had undergone is tacitly assumed by Keating
and it is that which forms the basis of his perspective: Charles I is 'our
present King', whose legitimacy, and that of his father, can be confirmed
by the traditional validatory mechanisms of prophecy and genealogy; the
inhabitants of Ireland are now designated as *Éireannaigh* and they com-
prise both native Irish and Old-English; what obviously distinguishes
those from the others – the heretical 'New English' – is their Catholicism.[38] The new politico-religious demarcation of seventeenth-century
Ireland and the resultant alignment of Irish and Old-English is clearly
delineated by Keating in his introduction; he concludes by addressing

himself to the origin of the Old-English in Ireland, in particular to the Norman conquest. He has already pointed out in the introduction that this was a 'christian-like conquest' (since the Normans did not eradicate the Irish language) and that their 'noble earls' had frequently intermarried with the Irish nobility; in his final chapter he stresses the reforming and religious nature of the conquest and, in particular, its legal basis. Since the nobles of Ireland, after the death of Brian Bóraimhe, could not agree among themselves concerning the control of Ireland, in 1092 'they bestowed with one accord the possession of Ireland' on Pope Urbanus. Consequently the Pope of Rome 'had possession of and authority and sovereignty over Ireland from that time' until Pope Andrianus bestowed the 'Kingdom of Ireland on Henry II'. The Irish clergy, having considered the conditions on which the Pope had granted Ireland to Henry, 'they all agreed to them, and they gave their assent in writing'; moreover, at that time, there was 'no king or leader or lord in Ireland who had not submitted to the king of England and acknowledged him as their lord'. Keating challenges the view that it was necessary for Henry to reform religion in Ireland, he castigates the bloody, violent deeds of treachery and tyranny perpetrated by the five principal Norman leaders and he pointedly asserts that it 'was owing to tyranny and wrong and the want of fulfilling their own law on the part of the Norman leaders in Ireland' that the Irish resisted the Norman yoke. In fact, there was not a race in Europe who would be more amenable to the law than the Irish, 'provided the law were justly administered to them'. No less an authority than John Davies is invoked to prove that it was not through evil disposition that the Irish often rebelled against the law, 'but through the rulers failing to administer the law justly to them'. But that was not the complete story. Other Norman lords also came over who, unlike the five principal leaders, were not guilty of any treacherous deeds but on the contrary who did 'much good' in Ireland. In particular they had built churches and abbeys, had supported the clergy and had done 'many other good deeds besides'; in return God had given them as descendants 'many noble families in Ireland today': FitzGeralds . . . Burkes . . . Powers . . . Graces . . . Nugents . . . Dillons . . . Browns [39] . . . Prestons . . . D'Arcys . . . and, of course, Keatings![40]

It is obvious that Keating was not merely retelling in a descriptive and synthetic mode the history of Ireland; he was rewriting it and presenting it anew to his readers. To the received canon of traditional lore he had grafted, in a most sophisticated manner, a contemporaneous perspective which took cognizance of and which was a response to the realities of his own day. Central to that reality was the authority of the Crown and the pivotal place of the Old-English in the political nation. Keating not only reflects that reality, he validates it by presenting it in an appropriate historical framework. The claim that Keating in *FFÉ* provides 'tacit approval for rebellion against the English authority in Ireland'[41] is a total distortion of what he wrote and intended; on the contrary, what he provides is an historical legitimation for that authority, for its acceptance and for the status quo. Accordingly, in Keating's new authoritative history of Ireland there was a definite and honoured place for both Stuart Kings and Old-English Catholics. Ranum has suggested that it would seem that the function of historiography in early modern political cultures was that of legitimator and codifier of the internal and international institutional changes which had occurred: 'History . . . did coherently depict recent institutional and intellectual shifts by changing the "canon" of accepted truths about the national past to reflect new political realities.'[42] *FFÉ* is a classic example of that process. In it Keating provides the necessary rationalization for the general acceptance of the status quo. Its companion volume, the 'Annals of the Four Masters'[43] (*ARÉ*) provides another literary realization of the same process. That popular title has, unfortunately, concealed the importance and significance of the venture, and the fact that it is written in the traditional annalistic mode, as opposed to the narrative mode of *FFÉ*, has likewise tended to camouflage the innovative nature of the project, both in concept and execution. For, notwithstanding the traditional and derived nature of their material, the perspective and frame of reference are unashamedly contemporaneous: they are compiling the annals of the '*Kingdom*' of Ireland, a kingdom ruled over by 'the Crown', a crown which was then personified by 'our King Charles' in whose reign the annals were completed.[44]

Universality, taught Baudouin, was one of the prerequisites of the *historia perfecta* and, to achieve it, the historian would have to synthesize both ecclesiastical and civic history in a single narrative.[45] It would be impossible, Ó Cléirigh declares, to write the history of the Irish saints without incorporating the history of the kings from whom they were descended, and thus the project, although initially conceived in an ecclesiastical context as an Irish contribution to the general European religious controversy, became a major comprehensive thesaurus of extant antiquarian lore – *omnia quae ad sacrum profanumque Hiberniae statum pertinent*.[46] Ó Cléirigh's belief that there was nothing 'more glorious, honourable and august than to bring to light the historical knowledge of ancient authors and knowledge concerning the nobles and chiefs of former times' was an apt and concise insight into the aim and scope of contemporaneous historiography.[47] The exact instructions which Ó Cléirigh received from his superiors – not to deviate from the original texts – was totally in keeping with the contemporary historiographical principle of *ad fontes*; the demanding task he was ordered to undertake – 'to gather from all parties and countryes, and prepare to the printe the ancient histories, offices'[48] – was similar in conception and terminology to the directions given to Leland, Parker, Bale and Foxe in England; to the work undertaken by Haillen in France; and was but part of a vast undertaking being organized simultaneously in Louvain, Rome and in Germany.[49] The motto which Ó Cléirigh invoked on initiating his task – *dochum glóire Dé agus onóra na hÉireann*, 'for the glory of God and the honour of Ireland' – was but one variant of a common invocation practised widely by scholars at home and abroad; a similar justification is expressed by Bale in England and Dumoulin in France;[50] the organizational principle behind the Four Masters work – a group of scholars working in unison on a single project in one location – was that originally developed by the Bollandists in the Netherlands and subsequently applied to other projects in other countries.[51]

To perceive the Four Masters merely as traditional Irish annalists is to ignore the contemporaneous European context in which they must be placed and to underestimate the innovative nature of their work; to label their major work *Annála Ríoghachta Éireann (ARÉ), 'Annals of the Kingdom of Ireland'* a 'conscious appeal from a doomed civilization' or 'a memorial to a lost civilization' is to misinterpret their intention and achievement with twentieth-century hindsight.[52] There is nothing retrospective in their plans to have the annals printed initially in Irish and then translated into Latin and other languages; nor in their decision to have as patrons for their work three members of the Dublin Parliament – Sir Fergal O Gara, Terence Mac Coughlan, Brian McGuire. In particular, there is nothing backward in the Four Masters' attitude to contemporary affairs as is evident from entries dealing with events after 1601. Those entries not only abound with references to 'the King' and 'the Crown' but there is an explicit acceptance of the King as the source of power:

O Neill . . . and most of the Irish of the Northern Half . . . came in under peace; for a general peace and a restoration of his blood and territory to every one that wished for it from his Majesty King James had been proclaimed, after he had been anointed in the place of the Queen over England, France and Ireland.[53]

In subsequent entries, it is evident that the sympathies of the authors lie completely with those who had come to terms with the King, not with those who were still in rebellion. Accordingly Niall Garbh (who claimed the Lordship of Tyrconnell after Rory O Donnell accepted the Earldom) is criticized for proclaiming himself O Donnell 'without consulting the King's representative or the Council'; when he rebelled in 1608, it was a rising 'against the King's law' from which 'innumerable and indescribable' evils emanated:

Alas! although it was no wonder that this noble chieftain should have avenged his dishonour, innumerable and indescribable were the evils that sprang up and took root in the entire province of Ulster through the warlike rising which he undertook against the King's law. It was indeed from it, and from the departure of the Earls we have mentioned, it came to pass that their principalities, their territories, their estates, their lands, their forts, their fortresses, their fruitful harbours, and their fishful bays, were taken from the Irish of the province of Ulster, and given in their presence to foreign tribes; and they were expelled and banished into other countries, where most of them died.[54]

Even in the terse account of the Geraldine rebellion, the attitude is one of disapproval. In chronicling the death of the Earl of Desmond's son in 1582 they regret that 'were it not that he was opposed to the crown of England, the loss of this good man would have been lamentable, on account of his liberality in bestowing jewels and riches, and his valour in the field of conflict'.[55] Their regret on the death of the Earl of Desmond himself is no less palpable and the subsequent general demise of the once all-powerful Geraldines is, at once, explicable and acceptable:

> Were it not that he was given to plunder and pillage (as he was) this Earl of Desmond would have been one of the great stories of Ireland. . . . It was no wonder that the vengeance of God should exterminate the Geraldines for the opposition to their Prince whose predecessors had granted to their ancestors as patrimonial lands from . . . [56]

ARÉ concludes with an account of the death in Rome of O Neill in 1616. It is expressed in the verbose register of traditional encomium: 'A powerful mighty Lord endowed with wisdom, subtlety and profundity of mind and intellect; a warlike valorous predatory Lord . . .' The jargon is traditional; not so, however, the interpretation of O Neill's actions: 'a warlike valorous predatory enterprising Lord in defending his faith and fatherland against his enemies'.[57] In conjoining the hitherto disparate notions of *faith* and *fatherland*[58] into one synonymous cause, the Four Masters not only reflect – for the first time in literature – the new and persuasive rallying call of Catholic Ireland but they also provide a highly relevant reinterpretation of its history. Their achievement, and likewise that of Keating in writing *FFÉ*, was to provide a new and appropriate origin legend for the emergent Catholic nation. Both texts, significantly, subsumed the earlier national origin legend *Leabhar Gabhála Éireann*[59] and had built on it, to furnish in different, but complementary, historiographical modes the supreme literary realization of the new orthodoxy in Irish political thought. Central to that orthodoxy was the unassailable position of the Stuart kings and their unquestionable right to the Crown of Ireland. It was, I stress, an orthodoxy. There were other voices which from time to time questioned the orthodoxy, only to be dealt with as heretics. Thus when the Jesuit Conor O Mahony published his *Disputatio Apologetica* in 1645 urging the Irish to reject Charles I, since he was both a heretic and a foreigner, he was denounced from the pulpits and his book publicly burned by the Council of Kilkenny and subsequently by a national synod of the clergy. A similar fate was meted out to Richard

O'Farrel who wrote a pamphlet in 1649 blaming the Old-English for Ireland's misfortunes.[60] Significantly enough those voices of protest against the new orthodoxy are not reflected to any great extent in Irish sources. In Irish political poetry (particularly from 1630 down) the Old-English nobles are no longer differentiated from the native aristocracy: they are all Irish who are to be contrasted with the New English and in particular with the Cromwellian 'scum' who after 1650 were in the ascendant. As one poet put it, they could understand being conquered by a group of nobles descended from legitimate kings or of noble strong Grecian blood, but to be vanquished 'by the odorous remnants of churlish craftsmen descended from harlots monsters and rebels of whom nobody in Europe knew what dog had excreted them' was rather unacceptable. He hastens to add that he is not referring to the *Gaill uaisle*, 'the noble foreigners' (= the Old-English) who are without blame and who, though they also had to yield to force, habitually support Charles; he concludes the poem by lamenting that in the death of 'propitious bountiful Charles', Ireland had lost her head.[61] Similarly with the other Stuart Kings, their position in Irish literary sources was unassailable. I know of only one contemporaneous poem in which the cause of Ireland's misfortune is attributed to Stuart misrule and in particular to Charles I's guile and duplicity.[62] Its significance is that it constitutes an exception. To the poet's contemporaries Charles I was still their rightful King – 'this good tho' unfortunate King', the Irish were *sliocht Shéarlais*, 'Charles's people'.[63]

Henrietta Maria, Charles I's wife, expressed her surprise to him that the Irish 'do not give themselves to some foreign King: you will force them to it in the end, when they see themselves offered as a sacrifice',[64] but their anger and disgust were turned not against the King but against the Parliamentarians 'who had betrayed King Charles' and voted to have him beheaded, against the unfaithful Scotch who had 'sold the King for gold', against the heinous regicides 'by which Crumwell and the rabble of bloody rebells murthered the good King Charles the First'.[65] John Lynch encapsulated their common sentiments in a succint couplet:

Scotia vendiderat, mactaverat Anglia regum
Astra rege sua semper Ierne stetit![66]

Not surprisingly then, the Irish, on Charles's death, turned neither to a foreign king, as foreseen by Henrietta Maria, nor a native king, as urged by Conor O Mahony, but rather to Charles's legitimate successor – 'The Prince', according to Ó Bruadair, 'it were proper to love'.[67]

III

The sanguine hopes of the Catholics of Ireland on the accession of James I in the beginning of the century were replicated by the hopes of their descendants on the restoration of his grandson Charles II in 1660. They

were similarly disappointed. 'We expected some toleration and conniv-
ance when our King would be crowned', complained Edmund O'Reilly,
Archbishop of Armagh, 'but no such thing took place: those who hoped
for such were disappointed.'[68] The disappointment of the Irish was of
little consequence, argued John Lynch, compared to their overwhelming
joy at the happy restoration of their own king.[69] As the title of his book
implies, *Cambrensis Eversus* is a spirited denial by Lynch of the false
and unwarranted accusations made against the Irish by Cambrensis, but
its writing afforded the author an opportunity of dealing authoritatively
and comprehensively with the moral and legal basis of the Royal writ in
Ireland. Lynch establishes the sovereign right of the Crown to Ireland
since the time of Henry II, although he admits that it was not generally
accepted by the Irish until the accession of James I. The legitimacy of
James's claim is conclusively proved, as is his unquestionable right to the
Kingdom of Ireland and to the allegiance of its people.[70] It was the
extent of that right which 'The Loyal Formulary or Irish Remonstrance'
endeavoured to establish. Presented to the King in 1661 as an attempt
by a group of Irish Catholics to convince him of their independence of
'all foreign power, be it either papal or princely',[71] it re-opened a debate
among Catholic churchmen which was only resolved at a general synod
convened in Dublin in 1666. After a prolonged acrimonious discussion,
the overwhelming majority of the clergy rejected the Formulary as initially
proposed, but adopted instead a modified one which was based on the
Gallican principles as formulated by the Theology faculty at the Sor-
bonne:

> We do hereby declare, That it is not our Doctrine, that the Pope hath
> any Authority in Temporal affairs over our Sovereign Lord King
> Charles the Second; yea, we promise that we shall oppose them, that
> will assert any Power, either direct or indirect, over him in Civil and
> Temporal affairs.
>
> That is our Doctrine, That our Gracious King Charles the Second
> is so absolute and independent, that he acknowledgeth not, nor hath
> in Civil and Temporal affairs any Power above him under God: and
> that to be our constant Doctrine from which we shall never decline.
>
> That is our doctrine, That we Subjects owe such Natural, and just
> obedience unto our King, that no Power under any pretext soever,
> can either dispense with us, or free us thereof.[72]

It was the farthest the Irish Church had yet gone in its efforts to reconcile
the conflicting claims of Rome and the Crown and in reaffirming the
Stuarts undisputed right to the temporal loyalty of Irish subjects. A
similar reaffirmation was being accomplished simultaneously in the literary sphere. In 1666 the great antiquarian Dubhaltach Mac Fhirbhisigh
completed his mammoth 'Book of Genealogies', a definitive comprehensive collection of Irish genealogical material. In it the ancestral bonds

relating the Stuarts to the Kings of Ulster, Connaught, Leinster and Munster are set forth in detail; the collateral branches of their pedigree are traced back over centuries to the mythological ancestors of the Irish; their genealogy is updated to include contemporaneous descendants and concludes with 'so that he [Charles II] is their only King in the year 1666 in the three Kingdoms England, Scotland, Ireland'.[73]

To the niggling complaint that their gracious King had not restored to the Catholics of Ireland, as promised, their ancestral lands, there was a ready, convenient and satisfactory answer. Hugh Reilly explained that the King did indeed intend 'doing justice to the latter; but the craft and corruption of some grandees about him wrought upon him by degrees to give way . . . no, this plaine and palpable injustice cannot be called the effect of any policy in the King . . . but it was a form'd design of some of his ministers'.[74] Bishop French, writing from the Continent where he had been banished 'for religion and loyalty to my Prince', also insisted that Charles did intend 'the pardon and act of Indemnity as well for the Catholics of Ireland' but he was opposed specifically by Ormond, and prevented from implementing his benign intentions; the Irish themselves were not inculpable – 'in the ruins of our fortunes and country, our sinne is our unadvised trust in Ormond' – and, consequently, God's avenging hand was since lying heavily on the people.[75] God's anger was a two-edged sword, however, which would eventually be turned against those who were now temporarily in possession:

> Beare patiently your poverty, and you shall find poverty a great blessing. . . . Let this alone be some comfort to you, that you have but lost those things you could not long hould, nor shall the present possessors long enjoy them. Though they think their fortunes in that land surely settled; they are but pilgrims in the way as you are . . . and then they shall know and feel God's judgment for what they have done to you.[76]

The notion of Divine Providence was central to seventeenth-century Irish historicism.[77] It provided not only an all-pervasive literary conceit for secular and religious literati alike, but for the intelligentsia as a whole, and for the Irish in general, it seems, an acceptable satisfying explanation for Ireland's woes. To his own rhetorical question, 'Isn't it by chance that most of what happens – particularly evils – occur', the catechisist Gearnon replies 'No, but by the toleration of God, by virtue of Him not preventing them because of our sins'; their own sins, explains Carthún, and neither the strength nor the competence of the English, had caused the displacement of the Irish; there were few of the Gaeil or of the Old-English alike, explained Mac an Bhaird, who were not responsible for Ireland's wrong; not only their own sins, but those of their fathers, were being visited on a sinful people; a just God, taught Céitinn, could avenge their wrongs even to the third or fourth generation; it was salutary,

Gearnon concluded, for people 'to suffer their purgatory in this life'.[78]
The purgatory of the Irish had its biblical, historical and literary analogues
and they were all pressed into service: the Irish, according to Rothe,
were worse treated than the early Christians had been by either Romans
or Turks, or the Jews by the Emperor Hadrian; their cause of sorrow,
claimed Céitinn, was more doleful than that of the Israelites; their fate,
claimed Ó Gnímh, comparable to that of the people of Israel or of Troy;
the state of the country, wrote O Sullivan Beare, comparable to the
destruction of Troy; St Paul's prophecy had come to pass, concluded Ó
Maoil Chonaire; the persecution of the Irish under Cromwell, claimed
John Lynch, was worse than that inflicted by Nero on the Greeks, by
the Greeks on Troy, by the Moors on Spain, than that suffered by the
Israelites in bondage.[79] In Irish and Latin, in prose and verse, in secular
and religious writings, in sermons, tracts and creative literature alike, the
irrefutable palpable premise of all that was written and spoken on the
subject was brought home continuously to people: 'that they were a
despised people, and worse dealt with than any nation that hath been
heard or read of'.[80] But inherent in the powerful pervasive rhetoric of
Ireland's indescribable purgatory was its transience and finity.

The providential mode of thought was ultimately an optimistic one, for
no matter how incorrigible or sustained the purgatory, it was not destined
to last. The Irish themselves by means of repentance, and God by avenging the heineous sins of the English, would ultimately bring about salvation.[81] It is not surprising, then, that the literati found an exact parallel
for both their desolate tale of woe and their predictions of ultimate
salvation in the central literary metaphor of the period – the children of
Israel – and that it was invoked incessantly by them. The Flight of the
Earls in the beginning of the century, the transplantation to Connaught
in mid-century, James's exile at the end of the century were interpreted
and explained in the same biblical referential framework, but the notion
of *exile/exodus* was but one component of a literary conceit which
depended for its realization on the necessary complementary *return*.[82]
Parallel to the biblical analogue and both supplementing and sustaining
it was the irrefutable 'ancient' voice of autochthonous prophecy, proclaiming a similar messianic message.

Of the many mechanisms still available to seventeenth-century man, in
Ireland and throughout Europe, by which it was thought possible to gain
knowledge of the future (astrology, divination, prognostication, prophecy,
etc.) prophecy was distinctive in that it relied, for the most part, on a
literary genre which was attributed to some historical or mythological
personage and which relied for its prestige on its supposed antiquity.
Prophecy is the dominant and best-attested mode in Irish mantic literature
and its practitioners, or those to whom the prophecies are attributed,
always represent the sacerdotal class – *file*, 'poet'; *faídh*, 'prophet'; *draoi*,
'druid'; or *naomh*, 'saint' – the specialists in supernatural knowledge. The

'saint', albeit originally an accretion to the class, became in time the most prominent prophecy-author in the Irish tradition, and by the seventeenth-century it was almost exclusively to well-known venerable religious authorities – Colum Cille, Malachy, Ultan, Bearchán – that Irish political prophecies were ascribed.[83] Accordingly no conflict could be perceived or adduced between secular and religious sources of knowledge. In the context of seventeenth-century Ireland, the secular poets, who *composed* the prophecies, were invoking an infallible unquestionable source of authority in accrediting their compositions to their native saints. As one author pertinently related, 'the heroes believed that the holy prophet would not tell a lie'.[84]

In its main contours, but particularly in function, format and content, Irish political prophecy conforms to what would seem to be a universal pattern.[85] Revered historical authorities are invoked as authors who, by foreseeing present personages and their actions, legitimize them; ancient books are invoked as infallible sources; contemporaneous events are thus presented as being a continuation of the past. Inherent in the idea of prophecy is the assumption that the sages of the past were aware of present-day problems, thus an unbroken continuum between past and present is presupposed and an obvious link between them is established. Prophecies were not merely morale-boosters, although that was obviously one of their functions; rather did they provide a 'validating charter'[86] for people and actions, a sanction which brought contemporary aspirations into line with the pattern of the past. But as contemporary aspirations changed over time so did the prophetic message, its contents changing in response to the ever-shifting political and socio-cultural circumstances. During the Middle Ages the prophets foretold that the generic 'foreigners' would be banished from Ireland by him who was destined to be the rightful king; by the sixteenth century – as the English conquest of Ireland gathered momentum – it was 'the English' in particular who were to be banished; by the seventeenth century, when the conquest was complete and the Reformation had made its presence felt in Ireland, it was the 'followers of Luther and Calvin' and 'the English-speakers' for whom annihilation and ultimate defeat was being foretold. A parallel development, again in response to socio-political circumstances, can be traced in the environment and context in which the Irish Messiah is to arise. Throughout the Middle Ages he was perceived as residing in Ireland and was to be found, according to the poets, amongst the native aristocracy; towards the end of the sixteenth century he was identified specifically with O Neill and O Donnell as those two leaders waged war on the English invaders; in the seventeenth century, following the exodus from Ireland of the nobles, he was perceived to be abroad amongst the Irish émigrés, whence he would return one day to free Ireland.[87]

Poets did, from time to time, cry out despairingly, asking God if he had forsaken his people; if the prophecies were ever to be fulfilled?[88] But the non-fulfilment of the prophecy over time never did undermine its potency or lessen its credibility; it merely postponed its realization. A particular failure could always be admitted without undermining belief, since the essence of the prophetic message was that it would ultimately be fulfilled. The orthodox view is succinctly put by Tadhg Dall Ó hUiginn (d. 1591): 'Succour has been prophesied for Tara . . . it is destined for it that a man who will free its spells – it must needs come to pass – will arrive one day on the soil of Ireland.'[89] This central messianic theme of Irish political prophecy (a man . . . one day) was all-pervasive and pro-tean in its amenability to exegesis and application. To the poets of the 1680s, witnessing the accession of James II and the unprecendented reforms he implemented, it seemed indeed that, at last, the time had come. What 'prophets and saints in great numbers had prophesied' was now to be fulfilled, exulted Diarmaid Mac Cárthaigh; to his colleague, Ó Bruadair, it was evident that they now 'had a real king': 'the phoenix that rose from her ashes . . . James Stuart, the bright star of royalty, that hath risen under God to deliver us'.[90]

Ó Bruadair (*c.* 1625–98) is literary Ireland's royalist *par excellence*. The aristocratic ethic pervades his work as do the accompanying traditional values of clientship, patronage, hierarchy and deference. Most of his poetry, particularly his occasional verse, exudes the values and life-style of a settled, ordered, hierarchical society (which may reflect the comparative peace and prosperity of the period 1660–80), but some unspecified per-sonal disappointment intrudes, inducing both bitter gnawing introspection and haughty contempt for the great unwashed whom he perceives to be in the ascendant. On the acquittal in 1680 of his patron, on a false indictment, his poetry reverts to a joyous celebration of contemporary Irish affairs and for the next decade it constitutes a sustained literary realization of seventeenth-century Irish royalism. The 'purgatory of the men of Ireland' is minutely described by him and ascribed to 'the sins of the ancestors', by which 'power to kill, rob and persecute' was bestowed, by heaven on those 'who betrayed King Charles'.[91] Charles II was, accord-ing to Ó Bruadair 'my Prince', 'the Prince of the three Kingdoms', a 'prudent Prince who dearly loves his people' whom 'it were proper to love'; who because he upheld the law, the poet would make it known to the people of Ireland 'that in duty they are strictly bound to yield willing allegiance to him'.[92] The significance of the accession of James II to the Crown of the three Kingdoms was fully understood and appreciated by Ó Bruadair. James had not only an impeccable genealogy linking him with the Irish kings of yore, he was also a Catholic and unashamedly so. His policy and that of his Catholic deputy in Ireland – Richard Talbot – were bringing about unprecedented and revolutionary changes for the majority. In a poem entitled 'The Triumph of James II', Ó Bruadair addresses James as the 'Light of our Church, the stately majestic Prince . . . the first King of England who gave rank and dignity to Irishmen', and he welcomes him as 'the High-King who comes of the true blood of Corc, the renowned King of Cashel'; some of the changes brought about by James's policy are listed: 'your true clergy now live in peace, undishonoured . . . and Calvin's clerics no longer harangue Popery. . . . On the Bench now are seated the Dalys and Rices'; he concludes by cursing 'those perfidious persistent villains . . . who to King James are rebels and traitors'.[93] In a further poem on the same theme, significantly entitled 'The Triumph of Tadhg',[94] Ó Bruadair adds a rejoinder, pithily identifying the significance of the tumultous changes they were witnessing:

> We now have a real King over us who brings protection and joy to our priests and Tadhg, having sufferred insults and outrages, now has towns and fortresses under his command. The wheel [of fortune] has now taken a turn unforeseen. . . . O King of creation, who created sea and earth, preserve without fear or perversity the man who, with Thy help, has performed these wondrous deeds – James, son of Charles, from Scotland. A monarch of not ignoble genealogy, the darling of our clergy and a bulwark of help to us, a trueblooded Gael of Cashel's royal tree.[95]

For a few brief years all was right with Ó Bruadair's world and with that of the socio-cultural elite he represented. Catholicism was being openly practised, Catholics were being reappointed to positions of power, influence and state; the Irish language was again in public esteem and spoken openly on the Bench and in the army; Tadhg was coming into his own. Surveying the devastation that ensued and reflecting on the demise, in the aftermath of the Boyne, Aughrim and Limerick, he unerringly and unequivocally identifies the cause of 'the shipwreck':

> The Shipwreck of Ireland, composed by Dáibhidh Ó Bruadair on the misfortunes of Ireland in the year of the Lord 1691, viz., how the sins of her own children brought ruin and dispersion upon her in the month of October of that year: *Regnum in se divisum desolabitur.*[96]

His sentiments, analysis and attitude are exactly paralleled in the contemporary anonymous tract, *A Light to the Blind*:

> O people of Ireland, you were not, it seems, judged by heaven worthy of those blessings which you expected by undertaking this war, that is, to re-inthrone your King, and in sequel to establish your religion, your property and liberty. Your sins, your sins have been the barrier to that felicity.[97]

For both writers the sins in question were, naturally, those of the lower orders. Both of them too, in the midst of their despondency, could look forward to better times: to the return from abroad of his patron and Lord, in the case of Ó Bruadair; to the return and restoration of their rightful king in the other.[98] Both reflected the complementary and parallel sources of irrepressible hope which sustained Catholic Ireland in her purgatory. One source resided in the rightful king who ultimately, in spite of bad teachers, evil counsellors, and a puritanical bigoted Parliament, would by his grace and favour grant the Irish their civil and religious rights; the other source of hope was the Irish abroad, the descendants of O Neill, O Donnell, MacCarthy and O Sullivan who were destined to return one day and reclaim their patrimony. By the end of the seventeenth century those two sources had conjoined in the person of James II, who was both rightful king and leader of the Irish émigrés in St Germain. The welcome and reception extended to him by the Irish on his arrival in Ireland illustrate his standing and function, both in practical and ideological terms; among the Irish – to literate and illiterate alike – he was 'our true King'.[99] That standing, ironically enough, was not diminished, but rather enhanced, by his subsequent departure from Ireland and his return to St Germain. There, as leader of the Irish, James assumed the mantle of the archetypal ideal Irish king who was destined to return from exile and save his people.[100] By removing himself from the Irish scene, James merely cemented his position in Irish ideology. Abroad, he – and his descendants – could be identified with causes they never espoused; attributes they never possessed could be effortlessly applied to them. By grafting itself to, and subsuming, traditional ideology, Irish Jacobitism was able to survive over generations, and renew itself by the prophetic message of ultimate victory which was embedded in a notion at once mythical and relevant, traditional and contemporaneous: the image of the rightful king abroad whose inevitable return would bring about their deliverance and usher in an era of peace and prosperity.

NOTES

1 R. Flower, *The Irish Tradition*, Oxford, Clarendon Press, 1947, 166. A more recent illustration is T. J. Dunne, 'The Gaelic response to conquest and colonization: the evidence of the poetry', *Studia Hibernica* 20, (1980), 7–30. Dr Dunne's general conclusion, that 'the poets had no answers only rituals and memories' (op. cit., 30) is not borne out by the evidence; of the attributes he assigns to seventeenth-century Irish poetry ('It was highly pragmatic, deeply fatalistic, increasingly escapist and essentially apolitical' (op. cit., 11) only the first, 'highly pragmatic', applies. Unfortunately – for modern Irish historiography – R. F. Foster (*Modern Ireland 1600–1972*, London, 1989, 42) accepts unquestioningly Dunne's flawed and inadequate analysis.

2 T. Ó Donnchadha (ed.), *Leabhar Cloinne Aodha Buidhe*, Dublin, 1931, 203–10.

3 R. Mousnier, 'Trevor Roper's *General Crisis*', in T. Aston (ed.), *Crisis in Europe 1560–1660*, London, 1965, 97–104, esp. 103–4.

4 M. Kerney Walsh, *Destruction by Peace: Hugh O'Neill after Kinsale*, Armagh, 1986, 226.

5 P. A. Breatnach (ed.), 'Metamorphosis 1603: Dán le hEochaidh Ó hEodhasa', *Éigse*, 17 (1977), 169–80.

6 L. McKenna (ed.), *Aithdhioghluim dána*, London, 1939, 177.

7 For the functional characteristics of the ideal king in Irish ideology, see T. Ó Cathasaigh, *The Heroic Biography of Cormac mac Airt*, Dublin, 1977.

8 N. J. A. Williams (ed.), *Pairlement Chloinne Tomáis*, Dublin, 1981, 23.

9 L. McKenna (ed.), *Iomarbhágh na bhfileadh*, London, 1918, I, 138, II, 184.

10 For James's genealogy, see *Analecta Hibernica*, 3 (1931), 68–70; J. Lynch, *Cambrensis eversus*, St Malo, 1662, 248–51; R. O. Flaherty, *Ogygia, seu rerum Hibernicarum chronologia*, London, 1685, 499–700; Royal Irish Academy, Dublin, MSS C iv 1, C iv 2, 23 N 11. For a more detailed presentation of the argument being advanced here see B. Ó Buachalla, 'Na Stíobhartaigh agus an tAos Léinn: Cing Séamas', *Proceedings of the Royal Irish Academy*, 83 C, 1983, 81–134.

11 J. J. Silke, 'Hugh O'Neill, the Catholic question and the papacy', *Irish Ecclesiastical Record*, 54 (1965), 65–79; idem, 'Later relations between Primate Peter Lombard and Hugh O'Neill', *Irish Theological Quarterly*, 22 (1955), 15–30; idem, 'Primate Lombard and James I', *Irish Theological Quarterly*, 22 (1955), 124–50.

12 J. Bossy, 'The Counter-Reformation and the people of Catholic Ireland, 1596–1641', in T. D. Williams (ed.), *Historical Studies*, 8, (1971), 155–69, esp. 160; Ó Buachalla, 'Na Stíobhartaigh'.

13 B. Ó Cuív (ed.), 'A modern Irish devotional tract', *Celtica*, I (1950), 207–37, esp. 220; B. Ó hEodhasa, *An teagasg críosdaidhe*, Antwerp, 1611, ed. F. Mac Raghnaill, Dublin, 1976, 67.

14 A. Mac Aingil, *Scáthán shacramuinte na haithridhe*, Louvain, 1618, ed. C. Ó Maonaigh, Dublin, 1952, 96–7; F. Ó Maoil Chonaire, *Sgáthán an chrábhaidh*, Louvain 1616, ed. T. F. O'Rahilly, Dublin, 1955, 133.

15 Mac Aingil, *Scáthán shacramuinte na haithridhe*, 1666–7.

16 F. O'Brien 'Florence Conry, Archbishop of Tuam', *The Irish Rosary*, 31 (1927), 455; *Archivium Hibernicum*, 3, (1914), 303.

17 C. Ó Lochlainn (ed.), *Tobar fíorghlan Gaedhilge*, Dublin, 1939, 69; J. O'Donovan (ed.), *Annála ríoghachta Éireann*, Dublin, 1851, VI, 2362; O. J. Bergin (ed.), *Irish Bardic Poetry*, Dublin, 1970, 30; L. Mac Cionnaith (ed.), *Dioghluim dána*, Dublin, 1938, 190; L. McKenna (ed.), *Iomarbhágh na bhfileadh* II, London, 1918, 226; Mac Aingil, *Scáthán shacramuinte na haithridhe*, 97, 171, 183.

18 A. Clarke, 'The genesis of the Ulster rising of 1641', in P. Roebuck (ed.), *Plantation to Partition*, Belfast, 1981, 29–45, esp. 29.

19 The word *ríoghacht* (mod. *ríocht*) is a native formation based on *rí* 'king'; the earliest attested form for *nation* is *náision/naision*, (Mac Aingil, *Scáthán shacramuinte na haithridhe*, 242) which if it stands for *náisión* would be derived, like the variant *náisiún*, from French; if not a typographical error, *náision* is most probably derived from English.

20 *Archivium Hibernicum*, 3, (1914), 278; D. P. O'Sullevano Bearo, *Historiae Catholicae Iberniae compendium*, Lisbon, 1621, ed. M. Kelly, Dublin, 1850, VII, *Archivium Hibernicum*, 22 (1959), 146.

21 C. Mhág Craith (ed.), *Dán na mbráthar mionúr*, Dublin, 1967, 152; Bergin (ed.), *Irish Bardic Poetry*, 115; R. Ní Ógáin (ed.), *Duanaire Gaedhilge* III, Dublin, 1921, 13; T. Ó Raghallaigh (ed.), *Duanta Eoghain Ruaidh Mhic an Bhaird*, Galway, 1931, 170; Mac Aingil, *Scáthán shacramuinte na haithridhe*, 4.

22 G. Carew. 'A discourse of the present state of Ireland 1614', in *Calendar of Carew Manuscripts 1603–14*, London, 1873, 305–6.

23 C. P. Meehan, *The Fate and Fortunes of Hugh O'Neill, Earl of Tyrone, and Rory O Donel, Earl of Tyrconnel*, Dublin, 1886, 328.

24 Bergin (ed.), *Irish Bardic Poetry*, 25–7; B. Ó Buachalla, 'Cúlra agus Tábhacht an Dáin *A Leabhráin Ainmnighthear d'Aodh*', *Celtica*, 21 (1990), 402–16.

25 For other instances and further discussion, see Ó Buachalla, ibid., 413.

26 T. T. O'Donnell (ed.), *Selections from the Zoilomastix of Phillip O'Sullivan Beare*, Dublin, Irish Manuscripts Commission, 1960, 63.

27 A. Gwynn, 'An unpublished work of Phillip O'Sullivan Beare' *Analecta Hibernica*, 6 (1934), 1–11; esp. 9–10.

28 E. C. Mac Giolla Eáin (ed.), *Dánta amhráin is caointe Sheathrúin Céitinn*, Dublin, 1900, 63.

29 For a fuller discussion of *FFÉ* and its significance, see B. Ó Buachalla, '*Annála Rioghachta Éireann is Foras Feasa ar Érinn*: An Comhthéacs Comhaimseartha', *Studia Hibernica*, 22–3 (1985), 59–105; also idem, Foreword to 1987 reprint of D. Comyn and P. S. Dinneen (eds.), *Foras Feasa ar Éirinn*, I-IV, London, Irish Texts Society, 1902–14.

30 For this new sense of historical awareness see J. G. A. Pocock, *The Ancient Constitution and the Feudal Law*, Cambridge, 1957, 1–5; idem, 'The origins of study of the past: a comparative approach', *Comparative Studies in Society and History*, 4 (1961), 209–46; D. R. Kelley, *Foundations of modern Historical Scholarship*, New York, 1970; P. Burke, *The Renaissance Sense of the Past*, London, 1969.

31 Kelley, *Foundations*, 181.

32 ibid., 133.

33 Comyn and Dineen, (eds.) *Foras Feasa ar Éirinn*, I, 38, 76.

34 ibid., I, 4, 18, 32, 40, 42, 62, 56, 62, 74, 76.

35 See in particular D. B. Quinn, *The Elizabethans and the Irish*, New York, 1966; idem 'Ireland and sixteenth-century European expansion', in T. D. Williams (ed.) *Historical Studies*, 1, (1958), 20–32.

36 Comyn and Dineen, (eds.) *Foras Feasa ar Éirinn*, I, 2, 56–60, 78.

37 Dunne, 'The Gaelic response', 19; R. F. Foster, *Modern Ireland*, 43. For similar sentiments cf. note. 52 *infra*.

38 Comyn and Dineen, *Foras Feasa ar Éirinn*, I, 4, 206–8; II, 386.

39 The Browns were not decscended from the Normans, but had arrived from England in the second half of the sixteenth century. Being Catholics, however, they are included among the 'noble families' of Ireland by Keating and other contemporary writers. Cf. C. O'Rahilly (ed.) *Five Seventeenth-Century Political Poems*, Dublin, 1952, 77.

40 Comyn and Dineen, (eds.), *Foras Feasa ar Éirinn*, III, 345–68.

41 N. Canny, 'The formation of the Irish mind: religion, politics and Gaelic Irish literature 1580–1750', *Past and Present*, 95, (1982), 91–116, esp. 101. Professor Canny's claim that 'this approval was at least implied by the organizing principle which he adopted. . . . Keating argued that the conquest of Ireland by the clanna Mílidh (the Milesians or Gaelic Irish) had been the final one' is totally misleading and not consonant with the facts. The last conquest described by Keating is the Norman invasion, as I have illustrated above. (p. 19).

42 O. Ranum, *National Consciousness and Political Culture in Early Modern Europe*, Baltimore, 1975, 11.

43 'The Four Masters' is the popular name given to the compilers of the Annals and other related historiographical texts. The principal scribe among them was Micheál Ó Cléirigh. See B. Jennings, *Michael Ó Cléirigh and His Associates*, Dublin, 1936; P. Walsh, *The Four Masters and Their Work*, Dublin, 1944. J. O'Donovan (ed.) *Annála Ríoghachta Éireann*, I-VII, Dublin, 1851.

44 Ó Buachalla, '*Annála Ríoghachta Éireann*', 94–5.

45 Kelley, *Foundations*, 134–5.

46 P. Walsh (ed.), *Genealogiae regum et sanctorum*, Dublin, 1918, 8; idem, *Gleanings from Irish Manuscripts*, Dublin, 1918, 82.

47 Royal Irish Academy, MS C III 3, 3: Ó Buachalla, '*Annála Ríoghachta Éireann*' 89; Burke, *Renaissance Sense of the Past*, 98, 127–8; Kelley, *Foundations*, 131, 134.

48 Historical Manuscripts Commission, *Fourth Report*, 1874, 604.

49 W. Haller, *Foxe's Book of Martyrs and the Elect Nation*, London, 1963, 58–9, 108; Kelley, *Foundations*, 236; P. Walsh, *The Four Masters*.

50 Haller, *Foxe's Book of Martyrs*, 62; Kelley, *Foundations*, 181; Ó Buachalla, '*Annála Ríoghachta Éireann*', 74.

51 D. Knowles, *Great Historical Enterprises*, London, 1963.

52 J. F. Kenney, *The Sources for the Early History of Ireland*, New York, 1929, 37; Canny, 'Formation of the Irish mind', 102.

53 O'Donovan (ed.), *Annála*, VI, 2336.

54 ibid., VI, 2344, 2362,

55 ibid., V, 1778.

56 ibid., V, 1794–6.

57 ibid., VI, 2374.

58 The relevant Irish words are *iris/ires*, 'religion', 'the (true) faith', 'creed' and *athardha*, 'fatherland', 'patrimony', 'native land', (*Dictionary of the Irish Language*, Royal Irish Academy, Dublin). The same terminology and aims are applied to contemporary leaders of the O Donnells (O'Donovan (ed.)), *Annála*, VI, 2364; Paul Walsh (ed.), *Beatha Aodha Ruaidh Uí Dhomhnaill*, Dublin, 1948, 336).

59 R. A. S. McAlister (ed.), *Lebor Gabhála Érenn*, Dublin, 1938. See also R. M. Scowcroft, 'Leabhar Gabhála', *Ériu*, 38 (1987), 81–142; 39 (1988), 1–66.

60 Peter Walsh, *The History and Vindication of the Royal Formulary or Irish Remonstrance*, London, 1674, 736–44; S. Kavanagh (ed.), *Commentarius Rinuccinianus*, Dublin, 1932–49, V, 485–504; *Disputatio apologetica, de iure regni Hiberniae pro Catholicis Hibernis adversos haereticos Anglos*. Authore C. M. Hiberno, Francofurti, 1645.

61 C. O'Rahilly (ed.), *Five Seventeenth-Century Political Poems*, 95–9.

62 ibid., 22.

63 E. Ó Muirgheasa (ed.), *Céad de cheoltaibh Uladh*, Dublin, 1915, 23; M. Ní Cheallacháin (ed.), *Filíocht Phádraigín Haicéad*, Dublin, 1962, 48; H. Reily, *Ireland's Case Briefly Stated*, Louvain, 1695, 116.

64 R. Bagwell, *Ireland under the Stuarts*, London, 1963, II, 59.

65 J. C. McErlean (ed.), *Duanaire Dháibhidh Uí Bhruadair*, London, 1917, III, 12; Royal Irish Academy, MSS 23 C 8, 78; 23 G 24, 139; G. Murphy, 'Royalist Ireland', *Studies*, 24 (1935), 589–604, esp. 591; N. French, *The Bleeding Iphigenia*, Louvain, 1674, 13.

66 Lynch, *Cambrensis eversus*, 268.

67 McErlean (ed.), *Duanaire Dhábidh Uí Bhruadair*, II, 276.

68 T. Ó Fiaich, 'Edmund O'Reilly, Archbishop of Armagh, 1657–1669', in The Franciscan Fathers (eds), *Father Luke Wadding*, Killiney, 1957, 171–228, esp. 203.

69 Lynch, *Cambrensis eversus*, i.

70 Lynch, *Cambrensis eversus*, chs XXII–XXIII.

71 Peter Walsh, *History and Vindication*, 8. See P. Cosgrave, 'Peter Walsh and the Irish Remonstrance', unpublished, MA thesis, University College Dublin, 1965. I am grateful to my colleague, J. I. McGuire, for drawing my attention to this thesis.

72 Peter Walsh, *History and Vindication*, 685. See also J. Brennan, 'A Gallican interlude in Ireland', *Irish Theological Quarterly*, 24 (1951) 219–37, 283–309.

73 The 'Book of Genealogies' which is now in University College Dublin (MS 1411–957) was compiled mostly in 1650 and added to between then and 1666. I have quoted from the 'abridgement' written by Mac Firbhisigh in 1666 and now in the Royal Irish Academy, Dublin (MS 24 N 2, 162).
74 Reily, *Ireland's Case*, 72, 77, 78.
75 N. French, *The Unkinde Deserter of Loyall Men and True Friends*, Paris, 1676, 2, 421–2, 429–30.
76 French, *The Bleeding Iphigenia*, 5.
77 For a more detailed illustration, see Ó Buachalla, *Na Stíobhartaigh*, 107–12. For the general concept and its application, see C. Webster, *The Great Instauration*, London, 1975; P. Miller, *The New England Mind*, Cambridge, 1954.
78 A. Gearnon, *Parrthas an anma*, Louvain, 1645, ed. A. Ó Fachtna, Dublin 1953, 45; Mhág Craith (ed.), *Dán na mbráthar mionúr*, 254; Ó Raghallaigh (ed.), *Duanta Eoghain Ruaidh Mhic an Bhaird*, 212; O. Bergin (ed.), *Trí bior-ghaoithe an bháis*, Dublin, 1931, 168, Gearnon, *Parrthas an anma*, 45.
79 D. Rothe, *Analecta sacra 1616–1619*, Cologne, 1619, ed. P. F. Moran, Dublin, 1884, 35–9, 103, 187; Bergin (ed.), *Trí bior-ghaoithe*, 190; T. F. O'Rahilly (ed.), *Measgra dánta*, II, Dublin, 1927, 146; Ó Maoil Chonaire, *Sgáthán an chrábhaidh*, 118; D. P. O'Sullevano Bearo, *Historiae Catholicae Iberniae compendium*, 201–2; Lynch, *Cambrensis eversus*, 277–83.
80 *Calendar of State Papers of Ireland*, 1608–10, London, 503.
81 The call for repentance was a most potent weapon in the armory of the Post-Tridentine Church in Ireland, since it could be utilized, not only as a vehicle of social control and moral regeneration, but also of national rehabilitation. The notion that the English themselves, through their sins, would eventually wreak their own destruction, is found already in the work of Philip O'Sullivan Beare (d.c1635) and it became a common theme in later political poetry.
82 Ó Buachalla, 'Na Stíobhartaigh' 118; P. de Brún *et al.* (eds), *Nua-dhuanaire*, Dublin, 1971, I, 36; M. Kennedy, *A Chronological and Historical Dissertation of the Royal Family of the Stuarts . . .* Paris, 1705, 233–4.
83 B. Ó Buachalla, 'An Mheisiasacht agus an Aisling', in P. de Brún *et al.* (eds), *Folia Gadelica: Essays Presented to R. A. Breatnach*, Cork, 1983, 72–87, esp. 75–6.
84 Paul Walsh, *Beatha*, 178.
85 For some general accounts of prophecy in other cultures and literatures, see G. Holscher, *Die profeten*, Leipzig, 1914; M. Reeves, *The Influence of Prophecy in the Later Middle Ages*, Oxford, Clarendon Press, 1969; M. E. Griffiths, *Early Vaticination in Welsh with English Parallels*, Cardiff, 1937; R. Taylor, *The Political Prophecy in England*, New York, 1911; K. Thomas, *Religion and the Decline of Magic*, London, 1971.
86 Thomas, *Religion*, 503.
87 B. Ó Buachalla, 'Aodh Eanghach and the Irish King-Hero', in D. Ó Corráin *et al.*, (eds) *Sages, Saints and Storytellers*, Maynooth, 1989, 200–32.
88 C. O'Rahilly (ed.), *Five Seventeenth-Century Political Poems*, 9–10, 20, 27–8; Mhág Craith, (ed.), *Dá na mbráthar mionúr*, 255; Ó Buachalla, 'An Mheisiasacht', 84.
89 E. Knott (ed.), *The Bardic Poems of Tadhg Dall Ó hUiginn*, London, 1922, 2.
90 McErlean, (ed.), *Duanaire Dháibhidh Uí Bhruadair*, III, 78, 128.
91 ibid., III, 12,
92 ibid., II, 218, 272, 274, 276, 282.
93 ibid., III, 76.
94 *Tadhg* represents the archetypal Irishman.

95 McErlean (ed.), *Duanaire Dháibhidh Uí Bruadair*, III, 76.
96 ibid., III, 164.
97 J. T. Gilbert (ed.), *A Jacobite Narrative of the War in Ireland, 1688–1691*, Dublin, 1892, 66–7, 143. For the author and his work, see P. Kelly, ' "A light to the blind": the voice of the dispossessed elite in the generation after the defeat at Limerick', *Irish Historical Studies*, 24 (1985), 431–62.
98 McErlean, (ed.), *Duanaire Dháibhidh Uí Bruadair*, III, 225; Gilbert (ed.), *A Jacobite Narrative*, 38, 190.
99 T. Crofton Croker (ed.), *The Historical Songs of Ireland*, London, 1841, 22–9; Gilbert, (ed.), *A Jacobite Narrative*, 46; McErlean, (ed.), *Duanaire Dháibhidh Uí Bruadair*, III, 76. The phrase 'James our true King' is taken from a ballad said by Croker (*The Historical Songs of Ireland*, 28), to have been sung by 'oyster wenches, poultry and herb women' in Dublin on James's arrival there. It could be a later composition, but there is an uncanny parallel between the phrase and Ó Bruadair's *go bhfuil rí dáiríre againne* (McErlean, (ed.), *Duanaire Dháibhidh Uí Bruadair*, III, 128).
100 T. Ó Cathasaigh, *Heroic Biography of Cormac mac Airt*, 61; Ó Buachalla, 'Aodh Eanghach'.

2 Anglican political thought in the century after the Revolution of 1688

Robert Eccleshall

Historical interest in the ideas of the eighteenth-century Anglo-Irish ascendancy has been confined largely to the resentment expressed, a deal of it by Jonathan Swift, at England's disregard for Irish economic and political affairs. Recently historians have begun to explore other themes such as the colonial elite's preoccupation with their unfinished mission of civilizing the native poor by anglicizing them, though the constitutional theories fabricated in the century after the Glorious Revolution have been virtually ignored. Yet the literature dealing with such issues is far more extensive, as well as more persistent, than that articulating periodic outbursts of nationalist sentiment. Much of it is in the form of sermons, running into hundreds, delivered on political holy days in the Irish liturgical calendar and on various other occasions, and the focus of this chapter is the ideology of Irish Anglicans as revealed primarily though not exclusively through these printed addresses.[1]

The usual view, based largely on the utterances of colonial nationalists, is that the eighteenth-century ascendancy lacked original thinkers: 'Habit and cultural ties dictated a flow of ideas from English rather than native origins; they had absorbed completely the ideas of the English country Whigs and in particular their earliest prophet, John Locke.'[2] There is a grain of truth, but little more, in each of these propositions. In some respects the political ideas of Irish Anglicans were similar to those of their co-religionists across the water, particularly as many of the senior churchmen had been promoted from English benefices. There was the same persistent emphasis on the twin virtues of political obedience and religious conformity; the same gamut of theoretical devices vindicating the accession of William and Mary; the same flurry of ideological debate that divided Whigs and Tories in the turbulent years preceding the Hanoverian succession; the same assertion, repeated *ad nauseam* during the long Whig ascendancy of the eighteenth century, that the British Isles were uniquely fortunate in their possession of a parliamentary monarchy and a rational religion, each complementing the other by holding to a middle way between despotism and anarchy; and at the close of the century the same repudiation of the egalitarian doctrine of natural rights

by a vigorous defence of ordered hierarchy. To this extent the Anglo-
Irish intelligentsia of the period resemble an undistinguished cast, short
of star performers, playing to comparatively small audiences in an outpost
of English civilization, and using a script written by their co-religionists.

Unlike their English co-religionists, however, Irish Anglicans rarely
enjoyed the security normally associated with membership of a state
church. The Church of Ireland, miserably endowed, and confessed by
only about a tenth of the population, was more akin to a privileged sect
than a national church. And its members, though exuding the superiority
of a governing elite, were conscious of themselves as a minority within
a minority, threatened almost as much by the growing strength of Presbyterianism as by the Catholic majority. Few entirely discarded the siege
mentality fostered by events in the preceding century, particularly the
rebellion of 1641 and the occupation of Ireland from 1689 to 1690 by the
forces of James II, and there was often some disturbance or scare – of
Jacobite invasion, Catholic sedition, or Presbyterian fractiousness – to
remind Anglicans of their position as a numerically small group, albeit a
powerful one. Even during its most tranquil phase, from the collapse of
Jacobitism in the 1740s to the rise of a native Jacobinism in the 1790s,
the Anglican establishment never lost the sense of being a privileged but
precarious minority.

The peculiar situation of Irish Anglicans was reflected in their political
theology, a curious hybrid in which the confidence of Establishment
mingled with the insecurities more characteristic of a sect. As members
of a state church they were doctrinally comprehensive, acknowledging in
usual Anglican manner a tripartite balance of scripture, tradition and
intellect as the basis of sound religion: congregations were frequently told
to rejoice in their possession of 'an Apostolic Faith, a rational Worship,
and Primitive Disciplin'.[3] Like their co-religionists, too, they shaped their
political theology into a civil religion enjoining political loyalty and respect
for social hierarchy. As a defensive minority, however, Irish Anglicans
perceived themselves as being surrounded by an obdurate population,
which was generally ignorant, superstitious and indolent. Themes which
tended to surface in England during moments of crisis – the twinning of
Catholicism and Presbyterianism as being equally subversive of church
and state, for example – assumed in Ireland a monotonous quality. Others
were singularly Irish: the obsession with anglicizing the native population;
and the use made by conservative churchmen, when recalling the danger
to Protestant lives and estates before the Williamite victory in 1690, of
language that in England was associated with radical Whiggism. Irish
Anglicans had certainly not 'absorbed completely' the ideas of Locke,
since they were no more disposed than the English propertied classes to
concede that the 'body of the people' might refashion the constitution
when it suited them. But though they were unwilling to embrace an
unqualified doctrine of popular sovereignty, the Jacobite occupation of

Ireland made them less reluctant than English churchmen to characterize the Revolution in Lockean terms as a dissolution of government. Anglo-Irish political ideology was no mere imitation of that of the Church of England but a distinct and in some ways more intriguing mode of thought.

I

A principal theme in Irish Anglicanism was the inestimable value of English civilization. Their forebears, arriving in Ireland during the twelfth century, congregations were told, had expected to reside in a flourishing country inhabited by saints and scholars. Instead they found a barbarous people, remote from European culture, leading 'an unsettled and roving Life, in the Woods, Bogs and Mountains', and constantly squabbling among themselves.[4] As 'generous Conquerors' the English introduced learning and commerce,[5] and gradually displaced archaic customs by laws that secured property rights and enlarged civil liberties. So wild were the natives, however, that they were not subdued until the Elizabethan age. Before then they 'continued in a sort of State of Nature', according to a Whig bishop of Elphin, in which life was predatory, insecure and indigent.[6]

Churchmen spoke as one about the brutality of Ireland before colonization, and there is little in their utterances to substantiate the claim that in the first half of the eighteenth century the Anglo-Irish were swept by a 'wave of enthusiasm' for the Gaelic past.[7] Pre-Christian Ireland was depicted by John Richardson as one of the most backward countries in the world.[8] And Francis Hutchinson, a prelate whose *A Defence of the Antient Historians: With A particular Application of it to the History of Ireland and Great-Britain and other Nations* (1734) is cited as an example of Protestant respect for Irish civilization, made no mention of an earlier culture in his accession day sermon of 1721. Instead, he attributed the country's escape from vulgarity and disorder to successive endeavours by English government to 'abolish all Marks of Distinction either in *Habit*, *Language*, or *Manners*'.[9]

The one exception to this denigration of Celtic Ireland was acknowledgment of its freedom from papal dominion during the early centuries of Christianity. Roman Catholics, Hutchinson told the Lords on another occasion, were apostates from the apostolic purity of the primitive Church that had existed in Ireland and much of the rest of the world.[10] In his view the early Irish were in effect good Anglicans, and St Patrick, according to Rowland Davies, in a treatise whose historiography mirrored on a small scale the researches of James Ussher in the seventeenth century, was 'no *Papist*' but 'a true Professor of the *Catholick* Faith' now by law established.[11] From the twelfth century the religion of Ireland became defiled when its people were 'riveted down to the papal chair',[12] and began to believe in superstition and to practise idolatry. The point, of course, was that in Anglicanism the Irish nation had been restored to the true faith.

If the native Irish were to be reclaimed for the true Church, everyone agreed, they would be pacified, enlightened and imbued with a spirit of industry. But few underestimated the enormity of the task. In reflective moments Anglicans acknowledged the deficiencies of their Church as a missionary organization. Its deplorable condition during the turbulent seventeenth century; its doctrinal and liturgical sloppiness until the adoption in the 1630s of the articles and canons of the Church of England; the continuing sparsity of incumbents and the wretched state of many churches; the reluctance of English government adequately to finance evangelization; and divisions among the Protestant Churches: all were sometimes blamed for the incompleteness of the Reformation in Ireland. More often clergy attributed recusancy to the Roman Catholic mind being closed to rational persuasion. Here was a religion that sanctified ignorance, stealing 'the Key of Knowledge' from the laity by teaching them that 'all doubt or enquiry on their parts is a sinful curiosity'.[13] The philosopher George Berkeley, appointed bishop of Cloyne in 1734, was exceptional in absolving the Roman Church of responsibility for the idleness of the native poor.[14] Others were in no doubt that Catholicism consecrated indolence through the observance of numerous holy days, as well as by an indiscriminate distribution of charity to the shiftless.[15] Anglican insistence that Roman Catholicism induced 'civil Degeneracy' and 'religious Slavery' persisted throughout the century,[16] as did the allegation that this spiritual tyranny enjoined temporal disloyalty.

The Roman Church was said to cultivate sedition because its members were absolved by papal authority from allegiance to heretical princes. Anglican preachers, usually coy about displaying their scholarship, liberally cited authorities such as Suarez and Bellarmine to demonstrate that Roman Catholics were charged by various canons and decrees to assist in the destruction of Protestant religion and government. Occasionally they treated their congregations to a sustained analysis of the malignancy of Roman Catholicism as a political doctrine. In 1725 the younger Edward Synge, son of the Archbishop of Tuam, took the Commons through the arguments used to vindicate the Pope's coercive authority over princes. Interestingly, he compared the papal doctrine of ecclesiastical authority over temporal rulers with the Hobbesian theory of secular control of spiritual matters. Whereas the former justified the Church's interfering in the state as a means of expunging heresy, Erastianism sanctioned the sovereign's enforcement of religious dogma in the interests of political stability. Each was an illicit licence to absolutism.[17]

More frequently clergy reminded their congregations of 'the restless Ambitious and Persecuting Spirit of the Church of *Rome*' by bombarding them with instances of the massacres, conspiracies and rebellions it had excited.[18] Popish princes were said to be bound by a prior obligation to

extirpate heresy, whatever promises they might have made to their subjects, and the favourite examples given of their endeavours to convert
'by Force and Terror, by Fire and Faggot' were the murder of French
Huguenots and the sufferings of English Protestants during the reigns of
Mary and James II.[19] Among the litany of evidence of the seditious
conduct of Catholic subjects were conspiracies against Elizabeth and
Jacobite risings, as well as the Gunpowder Plot and the Irish rebellion
of 1641. Henry Maule's sermon of 23 October 1733, a detailed account
of the various tribulations of Protestants at the hands of papists, went
through several editions, each one enriched by the addition of a few
more historical titbits.[20]

Besides pandering to prejudice, these sermons were intended to encour-
age vigilance against the persistent threat of subversion. Thomas Leland,
whose ideologically hygienic *History of Ireland* appealed to few tastes,[21]
was exceptional in using an anniversary address to spread the blame for
the rebellion of 1641 to Protestants for treating the natives of Ireland as
racially inferior.[22] In Anglican demonology there was little space for this
kind of equivocation, and preachers generally made do with asserting the
inveterate untrustworthiness of Roman Catholics. Their affirmation of
loyalty to William must be 'only from the Teeth outward', John Travers
told the Commons, so long as their oaths of allegiance could be absolved
by the dispensing power of the Pope.[23]

The effect was to depict Protestants as a beleaguered minority surrounded by potential traitors. The 'Odds are vastly against us', a bishop
informed the Lords when stiffening their resolve against the threat of
Jacobite invasion: 'Let us then consider our selves encompassed with
Numbers much greater than our own, of Persons united in the same
Religion, the same Interest, and the same Principle to destroy our
Church, our Laws, and our Government.'[24] Even in calmer moments
clergy dwelt upon the danger to Protestants from an ecclesiastical despotism intent on world domination. 'It is true the *Pope* hath not of late set
his Foot upon the Necks of Princes', Hutchinson conceded in 1731, 'but
he is not afraid to place the Cross of Christ upon his own Slipper, and
make their Kissing that be the Token of their Subjection to his Jurisdiction.'[25] And there was periodically some fresh alert to revive their oratory.
Marmaduke Philips, preaching in the year of the Jacobite rising in Scotland, took issue with Protestants who wanted the liturgical calendar to
be purged of commemorations of deliverance from popery. Acknowledging that their intention was to reconcile Roman Catholics to the Anglican
ascendancy, he nevertheless begged

> leave to observe, that whilst the same wicked principles of *Popery* still
> subsist amongst us, and the same factious turbulent spirit of bringing
> anarchy and confusion upon us *by despising the powers that be*, and
> our present happy Constitution in Church and State, *by speaking evil*

incessantly *of dignities*, and, under the colour of liberty, running into the utmost degree of licentiousness, I think those lights as it were should be still hung out, those marks and signs still kept up, to shew posterity and the children yet unborn, the rocks and quicksands on which their forefathers so dangerously split.[26]

The Dean of Derry, speaking ten days before Philips, asked his congregation to contemplate the happiness of a free people, governed by laws to which they had consented in Parliament, accustomed to freedom of speech and other civil liberties, imbued with a spirit of civic virtue, and practising a 'decent, rational and manly' religion. Now, he told them, imagine yourselves at the disposal of an arbitrary ruler, without security of life and property, and 'reduced to a servile prostration at the confession-chair of an haughty priest'.[27] Such was the prospect should the nation be governed by a popish sovereign.

Hardly less subversive than Roman Catholicism, particularly in the view of High Churchmen, was Presbyterianism. Fears that the Kirk might eventually become the national church in Ireland, expressed among others by Swift,[28] were exacerbated by a wave of Scottish immigration at the turn of the century, as well as by pressures to abolish the sacramental test. A frequent Anglican allegation was that rival confessionists swam in the same doctrinal waters. This had been a common tactic in the seventeenth century. Presbyterian contractualism was dubbed the 'top-branch of Popery' by John Bramhall, the Laudian bishop of Derry and scourge of Hobbesian theory.[29] At the time of the Exclusion crisis the two doctrines were linked by Tories – as English royalists became known once their opponents began to call them by the name of Irish brigands – who accused Whigs of sharing with Catholic writers the notion that political authority had been conditionally delegated by a sovereign people. Restoration Irish churchmen, though largely immune from the hysteria of the Exclusion crisis, were not averse to drawing the same conclusions. In making princes servants of the people, said Richard Tenison in 1679, the followers of Geneva had refined the papal claim of an entitlement to depose heretical rulers.[30] Both doctrines cut the ties of allegiance by elevating ecclesiastical above civil authority. The rector of Abbeyleix put it succinctly: 'the Laws of God will not allow a Protestant of the Church of *England* to rebel: though both the Papist and Presbyterian can make the Scripture speak treason when they please.'[31] Post-Revolutionary churchmen vigorously pursued the same theme.

One ploy, sometimes used in sermons on the martyrdom of Charles I, was to allege that Calvinists had stolen their ideas directly from Catholic thinkers. According to St George Ashe, Bishop of Clogher, Jesuits had spread the seeds of rebellion in England during the 1640s by masquerading as radical sectaries.[32] His brother, the bibulous Dillon, also inclined to the conspiracy theory of the English civil wars. '*Milton* and *Goodwin* did but transcribe *Sanctarellus* and *Mariana*', he continued after denouncing Romish Quakers and Independent Jesuits, 'and the *Thirtieth* of January was but an Imitation of *the* Galican *Seventh* of May. . . . Thus *the Holy Brethren* (as they called themselves) tho' they *bitterly* disclaimed against *Popery*, yet licked up, we see, the worst of its Principles, and prosecuted its designs'.[33] Whereas Whig clergy were often even-handed in reminding their congregation that '*Popery* and *Presbytery*' claimed 'an Independance from all Temporal Power in the Exercise of their Ecclesiastical Jurisdiction,'[34] High Churchmen tended to dwell upon the anarchic implications of Calvinist theology. One of the most vociferous, the rabidly Tory vicar of Belfast, wrote several pamphlets in support of the Test Act. Presbyterians ought not to be trusted, said William Tisdall in his third tirade against them, because Bramhall among others had demonstrated that their doctrine robbed the crown of authority.[35] The two political theologies were connected in Anglican denunciations of sedition throughout the eighteenth century. After the repeal of the sacramental test in 1780, however, Presbyterians were accused of being potentially subversive not so much because of their disloyalty to the state, but on the ground that their antipathy to a national church could serve to dislodge the whole constitutional settlement. In *The Present State of the Church of Ireland*, written in defence of tithes at a time of agrarian unrest, Richard Woodward argued that Presbyterian 'principles do not, like those of the Roman Catholicks, tend to set up, but merely to pull down, an Ecclesiastical establishment'.[36] Given that Protestants constituted less than a quarter of the Irish population, according to Woodward, Anglican disestablishment would open the door to papal spiritual and temporal hegemony.

Everyone agreed that the Anglican Church and state would not have survived without divine assistance against their opponents, and sermons brimmed with instances of how God had maintained 'a Wall of Defence' around the Irish nation for five hundred turbulent years.[37] Colonization of Ireland, discovery of the Gunpowder Plot and of the rebellion of 1641, the curtailment of Mary's reign, the rout of the Armada, the Restoration, the Glorious Revolution – 'the Line of its mighty Progress . . . chalk't out by the Finger of the most high'[38] – the Hanoverian succession and the thwarting of the Pretender: all were evidence of the divine favours heaped upon the British Isles. By the end of the eighteenth century, illustrations of this 'perpetual superintendance of Divine Providence' amounted to a bulging catalogue.[39]

In sermons of this type some text from the Old Testament was usually elaborated, the message being that God's preservation of an Anglican Canaan in Ireland should be interpreted, no less than the deliverance of the Jews from the wilderness, as a token of the nation's special status. Alan Ford has suggested that the predominantly Calvinist theology of the Church of Ireland in the early seventeenth century – which was reinforced by the foundation in 1592 of Trinity College as an outpost of English Puritanism – provided a rationale for its inadequacies as a missionary organization. Anglicans were consoled by the belief that they were elected, chosen by the Lord, whereas Catholics were reprobate and therefore beyond redemption.[40] That may have been so in the early seventeenth century, though Ford's thesis has slipped perhaps a little too easily into the literature as one explanation of why the Reformation was not completed in Ireland. But there is little evidence – and certainly none from sermons – that post-Revolutionary Anglicans remained in a predestinarian straitjacket.

Rowland Davies, who tried as hard as anyone to expose the horrors of Roman Catholic doctrine, was accused by Dissenters in 1690 of being Arminian for preaching universal redemption during his exile in England.[41] And a preacher lavish in his description of Ireland as a modern Israel, guided by providence 'into the Covenant of Grace and Adoption', was Francis Higgins, soon to suffer a similar fate as Henry Sacheverell for his extravagantly high-flying political opinions.[42] Predestinarianism would have inhibited clergy from claiming, as so many of them did, that the Church of Ireland could become inclusive, confessionally as well as by statute, once Roman Catholics were persuaded of their errors. God had smiled upon his faithful servants for restoring the Irish Church to its primitive apostolic purity. And Catholics could enjoy the blessings of the reformed religion if they abandoned ignorance and superstition, and instead trod their own path to salvation by following the Anglican middle way of '*Reason*, and *Learning*, and *Grace*, and *Conscience*'.[43] Salvation was freely available to all who chose to walk in the light, not reserved for an elect few.

If Anglican theology was not Calvinist, it nevertheless exhibits the same anxiety which prompted the obsession of sixteenth- and early seventeenth-century churchmen, in England as well as Ireland,[44] with Jewish history. Preachers occasionally called upon Roman Catholics to acknowledge the persistent signs of providence by submitting to 'English Arms'.[45] But it was rare for them to conclude, as did the Bishop of Dromore in 1695, by entreating God to 'compleat his wonderful mercy to us, by the speedy conversion of the Corrigible, and the utter confusion of our implacable Enemies'.[46] Instead, they reminded the faithful that their entitlement to divine patronage could be easily forfeited. Hutchinson told his congregation that a nation's welfare depended partly upon the conduct of its members,[47] and everyone said that God expected returns for the blessings bestowed upon Ireland.

It was in this respect that the theme of a chosen people, stripped of Calvinist connotations, proved oratorically convenient. According to William Jephson, addressing the Lords a few months after William's entry into Dublin, the whole History of the Jewish Nation is little else but an account of how God Almighty raised or depressed, Blessed or Punished that Nation according to the various instances of obedience or disobedience, when they provok'd him to displeasure by the iniquities of their lives, he forsook and abandon'd them to themselves, when they repented of their Sins, and humbly return'd unto him again, he then *Saved them from the Adversaries hand, and deliver'd them from the hand of the Enemy; Psal.* 106:10. And that many times too, when their deliverance was beyond the power of second causes.[48]

When applied to Ireland the lessons of the Old Testament explained why the nation had been temporarily overwhelmed by the forces of darkness, as in the 1640s and during the Jacobite occupation. God's intention had been in part to allow the world to glimpse the odious political practice of Roman Catholicism, thereby exposing the hypocrisy of those of its adherents who pretended to eschew persecution. But His primary purpose was to chastise members of the true Church for their profanity and complacency. Most clergy said that rebellion was a judgement upon Protestants, a divine injunction to repent not so much of their treatment of the native Irish as of their own impiety and immorality. The Anglican deity intervened in human affairs not through the inexplicable performing of miracles, but by punishing sin and rewarding righteousness. Drawing upon Jewish history the elder Edward Synge, in the most impressive of the sermons about providence, explained that national deliverances 'may be look'd on as *Earnests* and *Engagements*, on GOD's Part, of what he will yet farther do for us and our Posterity, if by our Sins and Transgressions, we do not forfeit our Title to his Favour'.[49] God would continue to work out His purpose of redeeming the Irish nation, morally and politically, only if the recipients of divine assistance reciprocated with fidelity, virtue, and zealous regard for its civil and ecclesiastical polity. Otherwise, like the chosen people of old, they would again be engulfed by their enemies – and next time there might not be another reprieve.

This sense of being on probation, ever under the watchful eye of a sometimes wrathful deity, made urgent the mission of bringing all within the fold of the true Church. Conversion of the Irish was a test of fidelity and charity, a measure of the worthiness of Anglicans to retain their status as a 'favourite People';[50] it was also the only 'effectual way to remove all the Seeds of Rebellion, to root up all . . . Prejudices, and to cement us into one Interest'.[51] The problem was to penetrate the papish carapace of ignorance and irrationality. Some churchmen called upon Protestant landowners to lead the native poor into the light by their own example, which meant that they should become more pious and also act in a spirit of *noblesse oblige*.[52] And nearly everyone was optimistic about the capacity of Protestant schools to mould the minds of native youth before habits of mental and physical sloth had set in. Ironically, given the

Church of Ireland's abject record of evangelization, they were depicted as 'nurseries of the *Establish'd Religion'*,[53] possessing enormous potential to bring 'Multitudes into her Communion' by dispelling the gloom of error and superstition with the light of the gospel.[54] In them, too, eager young Irish minds would acquire habits of cleanliness, discover the difference between right and wrong, learn the principles of labour and industry as well as techniques of husbandary – might even be prompted to form a new 'Yeomanry'[55] – and in these ways become docile 'friends' of the ascendancy.[56]

If Anglicans enthused about schools as agencies of cultural cohesion, they were unsure about the appropriate medium of instruction. During the Restoration there had been a revival of interest in Gaelic,[57] and some churchmen still favoured translating the Bible and Prayer Book into the vernacular.[58] For John Richardson, a vigorous campaigner for the use of Irish, recusants were unlikely to be converted through a language inaccessible to many of them. The adoption by clergy of the native tongue was indispensable to the process of anglicization; and he justified translating the catechism, for example, on the ground that the Irish would thereby learn to be 'useful and orderly Members both in Church and State, by submitting themselves to every Ordinance of Man *for the Lord's Sake*, and by preserving the *Peace* and Unity of the Church, and the Quiet and Tranquillity of the Kingdom.'[59] For others, however, Gaelic was little better than gibberish, an aspect of the irrationality and barbarity of the native culture, and its encouragement would drive a deeper wedge between the enlightened elite and the backward majority. Nathanael Foy, who wanted the Irish to be gathered into villages and towns where children would be compelled to attend school, argued that promotion of their language could only 'retard' the Anglican mission.[60] Almost a century later Richard Woodward hoped that English would soon be the only language spoken in Ireland.[61]

The problem remained of how to deal with the lost sheep until they were persuaded to return to the fold of the true Church. Clergy were on the whole content to exhort Dissenters to join the Established Church as a means of strengthening the Protestant bulwark against popish subversion. Roman Catholics required sterner measures. In truculent mood after the Williamite victory, Anglicans called for firmness, arguing that it would be charitable to prevent Catholics from again suffering the miserable consequences of their rebellious predilections. 'They are no more to be govern'd without restraining Laws', said John Travers in 1698, 'than a School of unruly Boys without Rods and Ferula's.'[62] And though many came to acknowledge that the penal laws were ineffective in converting the natives, they spoke in unison about the need for constraints.

In doing so they managed to have their Protestant cake and eat it. There were lots of Whiggish statements about the violation of individual conscience being incompatible with the natural freedom of mankind. The

Roman Church tyrannized conscience through persecution, but religious conviction was properly a matter of inward persuasion rather than political coercion. If the Anglican state ought to respect the natural right to freedom of worship, it nevertheless had a responsibility to subdue those whose beliefs were politically dangerous. Such was the case with Roman Catholics because of their allegiance to a foreign power claiming authority to depose Protestant rulers. They had 'no Right to plead Liberty of Conscience in their Defence,' explained Trinity's Professor of Oratory and Modern History, 'they are punished, not as Hereticks, but as bad Subjects; not for their religious, but political evil Tenets'.[63] Neither could the civil magistrate be blamed, said the Archdeacon of Armagh, if he conferred economic and political favours upon loyal members of the national church. 'And this may be done without Persecution: Because, though Men have a Natural Right to Liberty and Protection, till they forfeit that Right by their evil Behaviour; yet not to Honours and Employments.'[64] In this way Anglicans clung to the principle of religious freedom while giving the state licence to do whatever was necessary for self-preservation. Government, in effect, could legitimately treat Roman Catholics as it pleased – short of killing, torturing or imprisoning them merely for professing their faith.

Historians searching for evidence of an irenic spirit within the eighteenth-century Church of Ireland usually settle on the younger Edward Synge's sermon of 23 October 1725, which caused a minor disturbance among Anglicans by suggesting that a degree of toleration might be extended to those Roman Catholics who renounced the offending doctrine of papal authority to depose heretical princes and absolve subjects of their oaths of allegiance.[65] Synge, who was familiar with John Locke's *Letter Concerning Toleration*,[66] argued that the apparatus of the state was inappropriate in matters of inward conviction. But if his sermon was 'the most vigorous statement of the case for toleration from an Irish churchman',[67] that is not saying much. The thrust of the sermon was a repudiation of the Roman doctrine that the care of souls was a matter for political control. Synge demonstrated, as Locke had done, that Catholics should be treated as enemies of their country, and therefore amenable to civil discipline, because of the political implications of their pernicious principles. Papists should be content with their treatment at the hands of the magistrate, said Synge, so long as they were neither encouraged nor prohibited from worshipping according to conscience. Similar words had been used by his father, the intellectually sharper of the two, who went on to say 'that to *tolerate a Religion*, and *not to persecute its Professors*, are two expressions exactly signifying the very same thing.'[68] Catholics could not accuse Protestants of religious intolerance, then, unless the latter resorted to the methods sanctioned by the canons and decrees of the Roman Church.

The younger Synge, like his co-religionists, also claimed that Catholics could not complain of an infringement of natural rights 'if places of Trust or Profit' were reserved for members of the state church. Again his father had already made the same point.[69] All this was standard Anglo-Irish political theology; it was hardly an instance of 'large-hearted toleration'.[70] What the utterances of the two Synges illustrate – albeit with more rigour than those of other Anglicans – is that the Protestant kernel of individual responsibilty for salvation could be comfortably accommodated within an authoritarian shell of unequal political rights and firm policing of those who adhered to religious principles potentially destructive of the post-Revolutionary settlement. In 1725 the younger Synge had advocated a policy of leniency to Roman Catholics who announced their loyalty to the state. In subsequent sermons, perhaps stung by earlier criticism, he made clear that the bulk of them had no intention of becoming politically quiescent. He was now as tough-minded as anyone in urging government to 'bear down all Opposition' upon those who appeared congenitally incapable of separating politics from religion.[71]

On religious toleration, as on so much else, the attitude of Irish Anglicans was the theological equivalent of the iron fist in the velvet glove. It is easy to ridicule their authoritarianism with a liberal face as the product of considerable self-deception: the blinkered mentality of colonial governors confident of their racial superiority and inclined to blame everyone except themselves for the failure of their Church to become inclusive, confessionally as well as in law, by taking refuge in a stereotype of the native Irish as degenerate, imprisoned by a barbaric culture and a repulsive faith that sanctioned ignorance, superstition, indolence, obduracy, rebellion, and spiritual and political despotism. From their own perspective, however, Anglicans were bearers of civilization and material progress, legitimately fearful of the Roman Church as a political organization, and prompted by Christian charity to strive to bring all within the fold of a religion that sanctified not dogmatism and blind obedience, but the sovereignty of individual consciousness guided by the light of scripture and the traditions of an apostolic church. Yet their labours were largely in vain. They were confronted not only by an intractable majority, sullenly reluctant to become rational beings, but also by a sizeable Presbyterian minority too committed to its own political agenda to be a reliable ally against the treacherous monolith of the Roman Church in Ireland. Little wonder that the arrogant gloss of Anglican thought could barely conceal a sense of bewildered unease.

II

Churchmen, though at odds about comparatively marginal issues such as the appropriate language for anglicizing the native culture, monotonously reaffirmed the benefits to Ireland of colonization, the role of providence in preserving English rule in less than propitious circumstances, the injunction upon Anglicans to remain worthy recipients of divine patronage, and the need for legislative vigilance against the perfidy of other confessionists. In explaining the grounds of obligation to the Williamite and Hanoverian monarchies, however, they were more varied.

It is true, as has been emphasized,[72] that Irish clergy did not participate in the reformulation of Anglican political thought during the eighteen months following James II's flight from England. From early 1689 English churchmen disengaged from the principle of indefeasible hereditary monarchy without embracing a general right of popular rebellion against tyranny. They did so by contending that James had abdicated, that Parliament had acted within the framework of the ancient constitution in filling the vacancy, that the Glorious Revolution was another instance of divine intervention in English affairs, that William was entitled to obedience as a just conqueror, that obedience was due to a *de facto* king, or that a circumscribed right of resistance was warranted in extreme circumstances. Irish Anglicans refrained from this initial exercise in casuistry because their country was in Jacobite hands until the summer of 1690. Those who became refugees in England were too preoccupied with material survival to assist the reshaping of Anglican ideology; while those who remained in Ireland could not publicly defend William's entitlement to the crown until his victory was certain. By this time they were able to draw upon a set of ideas prefabricated across the water.

In the century after the Revolution their constitutional arguments were nevertheless both more extensive and inventive than is usually acknowledged. For a start, they were expressed in far more sermons and pamphlets than the handful which historians have bothered to identify. Churchmen, secondly, had sound reasons for picking their way carefully through the ideological debate that had begun across the water: the process of dismantling those features of Restoration royalism that gave comfort to non-jurors required particular sensitivity in an Irish context to avoid licensing the sin of rebellion against a Protestant prince. They had, thirdly, to make sense of a series of events that had not been bloodless. In late 1688 England had not been plunged into the civil war envisaged by John Locke when, composing his *Two Treatises of Government* after the parliamentary failure of his Whig associates to prevent James succeeding to the throne, he wrote about the legitimacy of the 'body of the people' declaring a tyrannical government dissolved and transferring its functions to fresh officials. James's rapid departure following the arrival of William on English soil meant, as the various theories of the Revolution made plain, that he did not have to be forcibly removed by the kind of exercise of popular sovereignty contemplated by Locke at the time of the Exclusion crisis. In Ireland, however, the Revolution was a protracted affair involving, after 1685, the purging of Protestants from the army and civil administration; the exodus by early 1689 of all but a handful of senior Anglican clergy; the installation following

James's invasion in March 1689 of Roman Catholic priests in the chapter of Christ Church Cathedral; the violation of life and property; and the summoning of an overwhelmingly Catholic Parliament that declared Ireland a distinct kingdom, repealed the Restoration land settlement, and removed the disabilities on non-Anglicans – a process that in spite of William's entry into Dublin in July 1690 lingered on until the defeat of the Jacobites in late 1691. In subsequent years clergy reminded their congregations that the Anglican establishment in Ireland had been top-pled temporarily not only by the forces of the left – as it had been in England – during the Cromwellian period, but also by popish absolutism half a century later. And some of them, though generally reluctant to explore the radical implications of Lockean contractualism, were not averse to acknowledging that Ireland had experienced a breakdown of government during the Jacobite invasion.

One option was to side-step the question of allegiance to the new regime by alleging that the Revolution had occurred through divine inter-vention rather than human design. In post-Revolutionary England, though the assistance of the deity in destroying tyranny was frequently acknowledged, a full-blown doctrine of providence was comparatively rare, largely because of a reluctance to concede that short-term human triumphs necessarily bore the warrant of heavenly approval.[73] Some Irish churchmen were also aware of the difficulties in seeking to comprehend the activities of an inscrutable deity. In 1702 the Bishop of Down and Connor, having detected the hand of God in the Revolution and the defeat of the country's enemies at the onset of Anne's reign, nevertheless cautioned:

> I do not favour the making bold and unwarrantable Applications of GOD's Providence. Success is no certain argument to assert the Justice of a Cause: There is a depth in GOD's Ways, and Dispensations: And He sometimes Punisheth Men with Victories, as He Blesseth Them at other Times with Disappointments.[74]

Others were less cautious. As a privileged but precarious minority Angli-cans were receptive – as we have seen – to the idea of Ireland as a modern Israel, and William's victory was interpreted in a glut of sermons as a further sign of divine patronage.[75] In snatching Protestants from the clutches of popery and slavery, William was the latest instrument in the providential intervention in Irish affairs that had continued since the English conquest.

This argument served well enough for churchmen not versed in consti-tutional theory. After reminding the Commons that Ireland was a favoured nation, John Travers took a swipe at clergy, comparatively few in Ireland, who refused to take the oaths of allegiance to a king reigning 'by the special Deputation of the Almighty'.[76] Non-juring absolutism was inconsistent, according to Travers, with the principles of limited monarchy. ''Tis not my Province', he continued,

> to undertake the shewing how far the Regal Authority reaches; for without more caution than I am Master of, it may be stretch'd or clip'd, there would be as much danger in the one, as ungratefulness in the other; but the great Veracity and Moderation of our *Caesar* will stablish it's just boundaries, these, we may well trust, he will never Try to pass, knowing that to be the only means of making him the most potent Prince, and his Subjects the most happy People. So that we are now in the proper State of our Obedience; we need neither fear that we shall obey to the violation of Conscience, or that we shall have any just occasion to disobey.[77]

Knowledge of God's manifest intention to preserve Protestant liberties ought to suffice to stifle debate about either the grounds of obligation or the precise form of government.

Others, more sensitive than Travers to the charge that Williamites were apostates from divine-right principles, knew that consciences were not to be resolved merely by a presumption of heavenly beneficence. Throughout the seventeenth century Irish clergy had repudiated seditious doctrines, especially those of Rome and the Kirk, with the standard Anglican argument that subjects ought not in any circumstances to break their obligations to an anointed king. Rulers exercised indivisible sovereignty by divine commission, and therefore could be neither called to account by Parliament nor deposed by armed resistance. It was acknowledged that subjects were not required actively to assist an unrighteous sovereign whose edicts ran contrary to divine law. In such circumstances they were to be passively obedient by meekly submitting to whatever penalties the tyrant might inflict for refusing to comply with his commands. In counselling imprisonment or martyrdom in the face of arbitrary power, this doctrine of 'double obedience' certainly distinguished ungodly from godly rule.[78] What it did not sanction, as non-jurors were quick to emphasize, was abrogation of the oaths of allegiance to a living monarch – no matter how oppressive his regime.

One means of rescuing the doctrine of obedience was to allege that the Revolution had occurred because of James's abdication rather than any resistance to him, and that subjects were now obligated to the one whom God had sent to remedy the situation. This was John Vesey's theme when, addressing the first post-Revolutionary Irish Parliament, he announced that the empty throne had been filled with divine assistance. But Vesey, Tory Archbishop of Tuam, added an Irish gloss to the concept of vacancy. Preaching on a text from *Judges*, 'In those days there was no King in Israel; but every Man did that which was Right in his own Eyes', he argued that through a vacancy in the throne the Jews had experienced 'a Cessation of Civil Authority in general, and not of any particular Form of its Administration'.[79] This 'dissolution of civil Government' had plunged them into an anarchy in which everyone supposed they had a right to everything, and where in consequence there was insecurity of life and property, debauchery, disorder, civil war and exposure to foreign invasion, as well as endless ideological disputes because each imagined himself to be a competent judge in religious matters. Any people finding themselves in a similar chaotic condition were bound by interest and duty to apply the only remedy at their disposal, that of 'filling the Vacant Throne by a free Election, where they have Power so to do; or Peacable Submission to those, who have a Right without it'. Such had been the case in the recent past when, with England devoid of a king and Ireland overrun by enemies, William had providentially delivered those islands from the 'want of Civil Government'.

In England the argument that the events of 1688 had entailed a dissolution of government was confined to a few radical Whigs who sanctioned a right of popular revolution against tyranny.[80] But Vesey was no Lockean. As someone who subscribed to the doctrine of double obedience he had no wish to imply that the constitution could be suspended by a people resuming sovereignty in decreeing their government to be arbitrary.[81] The lawless situation he described was more akin to a Hobbesian state of nature: a *bellum omnium contra omnes* that required a disbanded people either immediately to reconstitute legal authority or, as Vesey believed was the case in the Revolution, to submit to the deliverer whom God had sent to protect them. In equating a vacant throne with the dissolution of government, Vesey was, in effect, depicting the hazardous condition of Irish Protestants during the Jacobite occupation, as close to annihilation then as they had been in 1641. He was also reminding a parliamentary congregation fearful of Catholic resurgency and the return of James that Ireland might again resemble a state of nature. A lapse into anarchy could be avoided only by the reform of Protestant morals coupled with an entrenchment of the Anglican establishment.

> The Mischief of this principle, of doing every one what is right in his own Eyes, shews the unreasonableness of those that contend for an Indefinite Liberty, either in Religious or Civil Matters under a Stated and Well-settl'd Government; for it is the first end of Law and Government to bound and limit such a Liberty. And if Men will not be confin'd by the Society in which they live, they Cancel the Obligations to which they are suppos'd to have consented, by entering into it; and so endeavour to Sap and Undermine the Foundation on which it stands; and consequently expose themselves and others to the same Inconviences and Insecurities they were in, when there was no Government. It is therefore the Interest of Government, and of those that are Protected by it, joyntly to oppose such a Principle as will destroy

both. And when a Government is so Supine and Careless as to suffer
Men to speak, Write, or Act, as they list, it is neither true to it self,
nor just to those that depend upon it; but seems to Conspire with the
Enemy to its own Destruction: For as, when there was *No King in
Israel*, every Man did what was *right in his own Eyes*; it is visible if
every man be allowed to do so, there cannot long be *a King in Israel.*[82]

Preservation of the Anglican interest in Ireland required the smack of
firm government.

The peculiar situation of Irish Protestants under Jacobite rule made it
feasible for Tory churchmen, reluctant to concede that resistance had
occurred, to allege that by his own behaviour James had released his
subjects from their oath of allegiance. By assaulting life, property and
the established religion, by disarming Protestants, by subjecting his crown
to a foreign power, and by repealing the oath in the Jacobite Parliament
of 1689, he had made it impossible, physically or morally, for his Irish
subjects to discharge their obligations to him. He had thereby '*Unking'd*
himself', according to Edward Wetenhall, Bishop of Cork, in a pamphlet
endorsing submission to William and Mary.

Irish Protestants, moreover, had not violated the doctrine of passive
obedience and non-resistance, because in declining to assist actively in
the destruction of their religion they had quietly submitted to imprisonment and other tribulations for following the dictates of conscience. As
to the charge that they were rebels by guilt of association with their
'*Brethren in England*', Wetenhall had two answers. The first was that the
doctrine of non-resistance could be disregarded by a nation, though not
by private persons, and that James's flight had left Parliament no option
but to make provision for the regulation of the state – though he was
unclear as to whether the English had actually engaged in rebellion in
securing William's accession. The second answer was that in accepting
William's protection both English and Irish Protestants had submitted to
the victor in a just war.

> God has now put us under the Power of the *Second William the
> Conqueror*, whom I must affirm . . . to have *a Right to our Allegiance
> by Conquest*; that which gave the King of *England* the first (and still
> avowed) Title to *Ireland*. I do averr us in *Ireland conquered*, and with
> my Heart bless God for it. For besides our being thereby *delivered
> (intirely* and *finally* I hope) *from Popery*, we are delivered also . . .
> from *all Scruple*, which would stick in us touching the Will of God as
> to our Subjection to our new King: For we cannot doubt but that we
> *ought to be subject to them, whom God hath set over us*. And when
> by his Providence, he so plainly *pulls down one*, and *sets up another*,
> we *cannot doubt*, who it is whom he has set over us.

It was a neat argument. If Wetenhall wobbled on the question of whether the English had engaged in rebellion, he was clear that Irish Protestants had been assigned 'a *passive Lot*' in 'the whole Revolution'. They were responsible neither for the cessation of allegiance to James nor for their rescue from tyranny by a foreign sovereign – 'the *Prince of Orange* was no Subject, and therefore could not *be a rebel*' – providentially guided to wield the sword in 'a most just' cause. And in submitting to their deliverer they were in conformity with traditional Christian doctrine.[83]

The claim that William's entitlement to the throne derived from a valid conquest was fashionable for a while in England, where the argument was often reinforced by reference to the theory of Hugo Grotius, in *De Jure Belli ac Pacis*, of a *jus gentium*.[84] What gave the theory appeal was its capacity to confer legitimacy upon William's invasion without any suggestion that the Revolution entailed an exercise in popular rights. Its utility for Irish churchmen is evident in a martyrdom sermon of 1707 by Samuel Synge who, like Wetenhall, gave the argument a local twist. Synge was concerned to repudiate the allegation that the Church was inconsistent in justifying the Revolution while condemning the murder of Charles I. The burden of his case was that Parliament waged war on Charles, an ill-advised king but no tyrant, even though he had sought to redress grievances; whereas James, having declined to make amends through Parliament, fled the country after encroaching upon life, property and religion. Here, unlike Wetenhall, Synge was clear that in filling the vacant throne Parliament had not resorted to resistance. James's desertion left the English people 'by the Law of self preservation, at liberty to take the best and speediest Course they could think of, to save themselves from utter ruin and destruction'.

This still left the problem of William's legitimacy to the crown. Synge's solution, citing Grotius, was to invoke the concept of a just war. The cause was undeniably just because of James's tyranny; though an oppressed people could not resort to arms in their defence, it was lawful for a neighbouring sovereign to wage war on their account; William was such a sovereign; he had, moreover, a hereditary entitlement to the English crown that was jeopardized by the 'supposititious *Prince of Wales*'; he had resorted to war in pursuit of that right only after the failure of peaceful methods; and the English, by accepting William's protection, had 'preserved the Succession in the Royal Family' by placing 'Her who had the next Right, together with Her Husband, who, under God, had been their Deliverer in the Throne'.[85] Synge, contrary to Wetenhall, did not claim that England had been subdued in the manner of the Norman conquest. Military invasion by a neighbouring sovereign had instigated James's flight, but in filling the vacant throne Parliament had expressed the consent of the nation. It was James, not the English, who had been conquered. Turning to Ireland, Synge did not trouble, as Wetenhall had, to examine the status of Protestants there during the Jacobite occupation. He simply argued that their allegiance to James had ceased in 1688, because the kingdom of Ireland was inseparably united by law to the English crown.

This begged the question of what Irish Protestants should have done during the eighteen months of their subjection to a king to whom no allegiance was owed. Synge was distant enough from the Revolution not to provide, as Wetenhall had in its aftermath, an elaborate justification of their behaviour prior to the Williamite victory. By this time clergy were turning from such considerations to participate in a slanging match among themselves. The year in which Synge preached marked the onset within Ireland of a fierce controversy similar to the ideological turmoil – vividly described by Swift during an extended visit to England[86] – embroiling the mother Church. This period, which ended with the accession of George I in 1714, was the only time in the century following the Revolution that Irish churchmen frequently used the occasion of a sermon as an opportunity to insult one another.

Whigs, portraying themselves as custodians of the Revolution and of the principle of toleration for Dissenters, accused Tories of endangering the Hanoverian succession by accommodating papists and Jacobites. Tories retorted by smearing their opponents as irreligious republicans who disgraced the Church of Ireland by transforming the events of 1688 into a theory of permanent revolution: fifth columnists within the state Church who aroused popular discontent by frightening 'Men almost out of their Wits' with the prospect of Jacobite invasion and Catholic resurgency, even though 'there are not above two *Papists* to one *Protestant*' in Ireland, 'and *those* despicably poor and unarm'd'.[87] In the course of this Whig-baiting, High Flyers retreated to an ideological position little different from that of Restoration royalism.

A major complaint against Whigs was that they had been prompted by resentment, particularly during their exclusion from government after 1710, to 'explode *Divine Right* both in Church and State'.[88] On the pretext of defending the Revolutionary settlement they had discarded the doctrine of non-resistance to become heirs of mid- seventeenth-century populism. By alleging that rulers were trustees of 'the Giddy unthinking Populace',[89] 'acting by a precarious Commission from Them, which can be granted no otherwise than during Pleasure',[90] Whigs had issued a licence for popular rebellion. But if members of the Established Church propagated such subversive ideas, then 'might not the *Papists* say, *Unless the late Laws against* Popery *be Repealed we will Rebell, as we have heretofore done*. And might not the *Dissenters* likewise alledge, that *unless the* Sacramental Test *be Abolish'd*, they will Resist as they have *formerly threatened us*'?[91] In supposing that government hinged upon a bargain struck between ruler and people, moreover, Whigs had entered a moral vacuum in which subjects might cancel oaths of allegiance from self-interest and the sovereign would be tempted to assume arbitrary powers as a safeguard against the whims of the governed. The truth was that rulers derived their authority not from some conditional delegation in a fictional state of nature, but directly from God, and subjects were therefore bound by biblical injunction to obey the powers that be not merely 'for fear of the *Axes of Leviathan*, but *also* for *Conscience sake*'.[92]

In all this there was little consideration of the events of two decades earlier. High Churchmen, enraged that Whigs had raised the banner of Revolution principles, were on the defensive in explaining how one monarch had been displaced by another. They were certainly disinclined to equate, in the manner of Vesey, a vacancy in the throne with a dissolution of government. John Winder was unusual among Tories in making more than a passing reference to the Revolution. James's departure had been occasioned by '*absolute and inevitable Necessity*', he conceded, but Whigs had foolishly derived political maxims of universal validity from this isolated event.

> When a Man's House has been on Fire, the people have pull'd down the next Neighbours, and have us'd irregular and uncommon Methods to prevent a general Destruction; but it does not from thence follow, that my Neighbour's House must be blown up every time the Mob cries, Fire: If so, 'tis but saying the Word to the *Rabble*, who love to have it so, for the sake of Plunder in the Hurry, and the Work may soon be done. If the *Populace* is once apprised of its Power and Liberty this way, they may destroy Houses at Pleasure, and tell you *they are all on Fire*, when there is none to be found but in their own Heads, and in the hot Brains of those who set them on.[93]

Swift, Winder's friend and his predecessor as prebendary of Kilroot, argued in similar vein.[94] Other Tories, reluctant to depict the Revolution as an exercise, however exceptional, in resistance, fell back on the official explanation of a '*voluntary Desertion of the Throne*'.[95]

This was George Berkeley's explanation when, soon after the Hanoverian succession, he advised Tories not to break their allegiance to George I in favour of the Pretender. Belief in the sanctity of oaths was consistent with support of the Revolution because 'when any person, by forfeiture or abdication, loseth dominion, he is no longer sovereign . . . [and] the allegiance ceaseth to be due to him, and the oath of course to bind. In the judgement of most men this was the case at the Revolution.'[96] Three years earlier he had preached three sermons at Trinity College on the sin of rebellion, which gave rise at the time to the spurious allegation that he espoused the Jacobite cause. Modern scholarship, manifestly ignorant of the ideological context in which the homilies were delivered, has perpetuated this mistaken judgement.[97] In fact, the sermons were an eloquent exposition of the conventional doctrine of double obedience. When they were collected into *Passive Obedience*, Berkeley made plain in the preface that he was disturbed by the current fashion of propagating Revolution principles. He acknowledged that 'the general good of a nation may require an alteration of government, either in its form, or in the hands which administer it',[98] but denied that the bounds of political obligation were properly a matter for private judgement. What distressed him was the use being made by Whigs of contractual arguments to represent rulers as trustees of the people, 'deputies' who could be dispatched willy-nilly on the presumption of a natural right of every individual to resist arbitrary power. *Passive Obedience* was a characteristic expression of Irish Toryism, and there is not a shred of evidence that Berkeley was a Jacobite in 1712.

What its publication does illustrate, however, is the extent to which ideological divisions had hardened by this time. Three years earlier, in correspondence with Sir John Percival, Berkeley had taken to task William Higden, an apostate non-juror, for claiming that allegiance was due to a *de facto* ruler. In making possession of the crown the sole ground of political obligation, according to Berkeley, Higden appeared to disallow resistance against the sovereign, thereby casting doubt on the validity of the Revolution. As an antidote to Higden he advised Percival to consult Locke's second *Treatise*.[99] Berkeley's surprising choice of reading indicates his readiness in 1709 to admit, albeit privately, the legitimacy of the community cashiering its governors for their misdemeanours. Three years later, with Whigs occupying the high ground of contractualism and Revolution principles, he preferred with other Tories to emphasize the doctrine of non-resistance to higher powers. His rapid ideological journey was not unique. In 1708 Swift was in unusually Lockean mood when he wrote that James's departure had left 'the Body of the People' free 'to choose whatever Form of Government they pleased, by themselves, or their Representatives'.[100] Within a couple of years he too was busily condemning high-flying Whigs for championing resistance.

By embracing the idea of James's abdication High Churchmen were able to attach the pre-Revolutionary concepts of divine right, non-resistance and hereditary succession to Anne and the Hanoverian monarchy, thereby repudiating the charge of being closet Jacobites. The remaining link in the chain between Toryism and Restoration royalism was provided by the concept of indivisible regal sovereignty. This was done by refuting the proposition, as Restoration writers had been careful to do, that the monarch exercised a co-ordinate authority in conjunction with the other estates of the realm through Parliament.[101] If God's vicegerent was 'unaccountable' as well as 'irresistible', however, there was little ideological space left for explaining by what authority Parliament had invited William to fill the throne – regardless of how it had been emptied. The problem was that this theory of royal absolutism brought some clergy perilously close to Jacobitism, however much they might affirm their loyalty to the existing regime by railing against papists and non-jurors. Once George I was installed on the throne and Whigs were entrenched in office, in consequence, the Toryism of Irish churchmen crumbled as quickly as that of their English co-religionists. Some of its assumptions were now absorbed into the varieties of Whiggism.

The first Whiggish vindication of the Revolution had been provided in 1691 by William King, future Archbishop of Dublin, whose *The State of the Protestants of Ireland Under the late King James's Government* so graphically described their plight that it became a principal source for preachers dwelling upon political themes.[102] In his riposte to the book Charles Leslie, the non-juring Irish polemicist, gleefully demonstrated that King had subscribed to the doctrine of double obedience before the Revolution.[103] He did not discard the doctrine when, as Dean of St Patrick's Cathedral, he was imprisoned twice for leading the remnant of senior clergy remaining in Jacobite Ireland. In what in effect was a manifesto for the dissolution of the state church under a popish prince, the unpublished 'Principles of Church Government' of 1689,[104] King posed the question of what ought to be done if the ruler meddled with the *potestas ordinis*, those spiritual and priestly prerogatives bestowed by Christ upon the Church through apostolic succession. What if, for instance, he refused to nominate bishops or to permit priests to preach the true faith – as was the case in Ireland? King's answer was that the Christian community could inflict spiritual penalties upon a heretical prince, even to the extent of excommunication, and in the last resort might voluntarily disestablish itself. As to temporal matters, however, subjects were bound to submit to the edicts of an ungodly ruler. Members of the Church were obliged to obey the episcopate, moreover, if a decision was taken on grounds of expediency to accept a temporary civil encroachment upon priestly functions. The welfare of church and state would be better served

> by leaving the legislative power entirely to our governors in both societies, than by suffering private persons to oppose their laws however unjust (especially since every man may secure his conscience by a passive obedience). . . . Furthermore Government being the only means appointed by God for the determining disputes & differences in this world . . . they therefore that take the way of opposition to government, to secure themselves from a fancyed or feared inconvenience, doe it either because they believe Gods providence will not or cannot secure them, and hence rebellion in the state, & schism in the church are effects of infidelity.[105]

Returning to the theme of divine intervention in a thanksgiving sermon of 1690, King claimed that the recent deliverance from tyranny had been due exclusively to 'the *over-ruling Providence* of God. 'Twas manifestly God, rather than the people, set our King and Queen on the Throne. The People Obstructed it as much as they could, by their Divisions; the Nobles Opposed it.'[106] Even by the standards of the day this was a brutal denial of the efficacy of human agency in shaping the course of political events. When he came to write *The State of the Protestants of Ireland*, however, King had a different message to relay.

Much of his argument was a hotch-potch of Grotian ideas. *Jus gentium* was used to demonstrate that allegiance could be transferred to a neighbouring prince who had conquered the tryant. But he also cited Grotius in arguing both that an arbitrary ruler could be deemed to have abdicated – regardless of whether he had voluntarily vacated the throne – and that in extreme necessity the doctrine of non-resistance was suspended. When explaining why Irish Protestants were justified in submitting to William, King turned to another authority.

> 'Tis Property that makes Government necessary; and the immediate End of Government is to preserve Property; where therefore a Government, instead of preserving, intirely ruins the Property of a Subject, that Government dissolves it self. Now this was the State of the Protestants in *Ireland*.[107]

This was pure Locke, though the source was unacknowledged. King's retort to the allegation that subjects were incompetent to determine when a government had forfeited their allegiance also resembled that given in the final chapter, 'Of the Dissolution of Government', of the second *Treatise*:

> I know 'tis commonly objected, *Who shall be Judge*? And for this Reason alone some conclude it can never be lawful to make any opposition against a Governor, or to side with a Deliverer that comes only to rescue miserable Subjects; but I answer, there are some Cases so plain, that they need no Judge at all: Every Man must be left to judge for himself; and for his Integrity he must be answerable to God and his own Conscience. Matters of Fact are often of this Nature, and I take this to be one of them; for either the People must be left to judge of the Designs of their Governor by what they see and feel from him, or else they must be obliged to a blind and absolute Submission, without employing their Understanding in the Case.[108]

Before James's defeat King had used the doctrine of double obedience to warn against an anarchy of private judgement in public affairs: people were to refrain from infidelity by meekly submitting to tyranny, confident that the supreme judge would eventually remedy their plight. Here, by contrast, he was allowing individual conscience discretion to decide at what point allegiance ceased and resistance became legitimate.

The right of people to judge that a ruler had declared war upon them, their appeal to heaven in exercising conscience in such circumstances, the resulting dissolution of government and the reversion of authority to the community: these were the ingredients of a radical Whiggism that in England led to demands for a refashioning of the constitution to secure popular rights. King was probably unaware that he had strayed into such dangerous ideological territory. His intention was to explain the grounds of obligation to a deliverer who had restored the Anglican establishment in Ireland, not to advocate a programme of radical reform. There is some truth in Leslie's allegation that King was a constitutional gadabout, staggering from one principle to another in an effort to vindicate his apostasy from the doctrine of passive obedience.[109]

His naïveté as a political theorist, however, does not fully explain King's recourse to Lockean principles. The Jacobite occupation made it plausible to argue that Ireland, unlike England, had suffered a breakdown of government, leaving people free to exercise their conscience in submitting to a righteous prince. Lockean theory fitted the Irish case not as a pretext for future political radicalism – as some Whigs intended it should in England – but as an explanation of the escape of Protestants from the state of war into which they had already been plunged.

The first explicit use of the *Two Treatises*, in Ireland or England, was that made in 1698 by William Molyneux, in his famous *The Case of Ireland's being bound by Acts of Parliament in England, stated*, to assert the natural right of the Irish people, by which he meant the colonial elite, to legislative independence. Otherwise there was little Anglo-Irish thought of a recognizably Whig character until the turbulent years before the Hanoverian succession. There was then an upsurge of Whiggism which, unlike Irish Toryism, persisted through the century.

Political power was ultimately of divine origin, Whig churchmen typically argued, but specific forms of government had been left to human discretion; civil society originated from an agreement among individuals to make 'a Cession of their natural Rights' for the common safety;[110] government hinged upon a '*Mutual Contract, Express or Tacit, between Prince and People, under the reciprocal Obligations of Protection and Allegiance*';[111] rulers fulfilled their part of the bargain by governing in accordance with the laws and other conditions determined at the inception of the political community; when natural rights were violated by arbitrary power 'the True Ends of Government are so little answer'd, that 'tis really worse to live under it than in a State of Nature';[112] an unrighteous prince forfeited his entitlement to obedience because subjects were '*under no Obligations from the Laws of God, of Reason, or of Nature to suffer themselves Born Free, to be tamely inslav'd by the insolence of* Tirannical Power'.[113] Much effort was expended demonstrating that the scriptural injunction to obey the higher powers applied to lawful authority. Only the political arrangements chosen by each community were divinely sanctioned, and allegiance was therefore conditional upon rulers respecting the people's 'Original and Fundamental Agreement'.[114] One suggestion was that the right of disobedience did not become legitimate until the collapse of the Roman empire. Primitive Christians had been obliged to submit to despotism, according to Anthony Lowcay, because heathen princes exercised unbridled authority. In establishing Christian polity, however, God decreed that rulership should be constitutionally limited for the common welfare, and He had not left people without a remedy against overweening power.[115]

There was plenty here to confirm the Tory stereotype of their opponents as rabble-rousers besotted with Revolution principles. But the Whig bark was worse than its bite. Although Whigs acknowledged a right to resist arbitrary power, few characterized the Revolution as the deposition of a king by the sovereign people. They tended instead to opt for conventional explanations, arguing that William had been providentially sent to occupy a throne vacated by voluntary desertion. Their intention, certainly in an Irish context, was to establish the illegitimacy of Jacobite claims to the crown, not to issue a licence for popular revolt. The blast of Whig political theory was therefore directed upon the proposition that kings were entitled to unlimited passive obedience by virtue of an indefeasible divine right, transmitted in lineal succession from the familial dominion bestowed upon Adam and Noah. Patriarchal absolutism was a recipe for slavery, Whigs retorted, and 'bare Anointing' did not confer legitimacy upon an hereditary monarch who broke his coronation oath by violating those constitutional safeguards erected by the community at its foundation.[116]

After the Hanoverian succession Whigs even managed to recast divine right in their own mould. God smiled upon the British political system because it was more consistent than most with 'the *Original Freedom* wherein he created Man; every *Englishman* having a Representative present, at the making of those Laws which he is afterwards to obey'.[117] George's rulership conformed with the laws of nature and scripture because the 'mix'd Legislature' had acted constitutionally in setting a righteous Protestant prince on the throne to protect civil and religious liberties,[118] and to him was owed 'a double Duty of Obedience':[119] everyone was bound by a '*conscientious Subjection*',[120] not merely by fear of the 'Axes of *Leviathan*'.[121] This was precisely the language of pre-Hanoverian Tories. The implication was that the injunction to obey the powers that be had been transgressed by those who encouraged people to despise their oaths of allegiance to a lawful prince. It was Jacobites, intent on imposing a Roman Catholic authoritarianism in church and state, who were guilty of the sin of rebellion.

Sometimes ideas with a ferociously radical potential were pressed into service on behalf of the Hanoverian regime. For Rowland Davies, preaching a martyrdom sermon in 1715, British government was the people's '*Creature*', and since God sanctioned the form they had agreed upon in the '*National Compact*' subjects were bound conscientiously to submit only to laws made by their consent in Parliament. This was close to Whig orthodoxy, notwithstanding the colourful language. In a startling account of the Revolution, however, he said that James's departure had left 'the People destitute of any *Sovereign Power*; so that they were evidently in a *State of Nature*, and under the *Necessity* of setting the Crown upon another Head, for the Conservation of their Peace and Safety'. Even Locke had not characterized the state of war following a dissolution of government as a reversion to the state of nature. No more than the Tory Vesey, however, did Davies wish to suggest that subjects could refashion their constitution at will, still less that they were freed from oaths of allegiance at the drop of a hat. Indeed, his rather confused explanation of the Revolution exonerated

> all the Actors in it from the Censure of *Rebellion*, since it was no *Resistance of the Royal Power, but an Assertion of the Peoples Right* . . . by *Necessity imposed upon them*: And therefore their Proceedings were not only consonant to the *Law of Nature*, but the very *Municipal Constitution of the Kingdom.*

His point was that an entitlement to repair the damage done by arbitrary power could never serve as a pretext for resisting legitimate authority. The heinous crime of rebellion was 'abundantly more Irrational', he concluded, when committed on behalf of a '*Stranger*' whose insistence upon an indefeasible hereditary right to the crown ran contrary to divine and natural laws, as well as the terms of the British constitution.[122]

Another preacher prone to florid utterances was Joseph Story who, unusually for an Irish churchman, had been educated in Edinburgh. In 1739, the year before his consecration to the see of Killaloe, he treated the Commons to a Lockean gloss on Richard Hooker's *Of the Laws of Ecclesiastical Polity*, the sixteenth-century classic of Anglican political thought, declaring that people had put themselves into civil society by consenting to escape the 'Inconvenience' of their 'naturally free and equal' condition.[123] Two years earlier, in another sermon on the anniversary of the Gunpowder Plot, he had said that James was repelled by 'open War' for invading the natural rights of his 'free-born Subjects'. His purpose in both sermons, however, was to urge loyalty to the present regime. People were bound by the doctrine of double obedience to submit to laws that, having been made by their consent in Parliament, guaranteed civil and religious liberties. Armed with this constitutional theory Story was able to use blunderbuss tactics against everyone who threatened to disturb the Hanoverian state and church: Jacobites, of course, but also deists and free-thinkers who had fallen under the spell of fashionable opinions brought to Ireland from 'beyond the *Alps*' by 'unsettled travelling Youths'.[124]

By now most Whigs were more circumspect than Story in using contractual theory. They extolled the British political system as 'a just Ballance between the three Constituent parts of the Legislative Power',[125] but made little effort to demonstrate the correspondence of this mixed polity to the original freedom of mankind. And there was not much mention of an immutable ancient constitution requiring reparation whenever breached by arbitrary power. History had more or less begun at the Revolution when, as the younger Edward Synge put it, the 'Foundation' of the present 'well temper'd *Distribution of Power*' had been laid.[126] This insistence that British government was nicely poised between the extremes of absolutism and populism served to remind Anglicans of what they stood to lose should Ireland again be overwhelmed by popish tyranny. As the century unfolded, however, sanitized Whig constitutionalism was trotted out to condemn every manifestation of civil unrest. Hugh Hamilton, preaching at the time of the Oakboy disturbances, declared that law-breaking was inexcusable within 'this beautiful System of Government, which has been raised and improved by the wisdom of ages, and is now envied and admired by all nations.'[127] Unconditional obedience was due to the king-in-parliament, a form of sovereignty so impeccable as to invalidate any exercise of popular rights.

What finally persuaded churchmen to disentangle their political thought from the language of contractualism was the crisis of the 1790s. Until then they accommodated the notion of the original freedom of mankind by extolling the balanced constitution as a bulwark of inalienable rights. But the doctrine of natural rights, with its assumption of fundamental human equality, was not the safest ideological landscape for those intent on justifying the privileges of a colonial elite. From 1791 the pitfalls of that terrain became visible when dissident Protestants and Catholics began to explore the radical potential of contractual theory, initially to demand an extension of the franchise and other reforms, but eventually to call upon French assistance to rid Ireland of colonial rule. Anglicans responded by distancing themselves from a doctrine that had served well enough as a defence of their establishment against popish tyranny, but was now being used by United Irishmen to assert that the people were 'the supreme sovereign.'[128]

One ploy was to rescue Locke from the clutches of radicals by repudiating a democratic reading of the *Two Treatises of Government*.[129] In a fervently bourgeois – though not entirely inaccurate – interpretation of Locke, Lawrence Parsons suggested that inequalities arose within the state of nature because of the different uses which individuals made of their basic rights. A correct understanding of Locke's account of the origins of civil society revealed that government had been established by an agreement of the industrious to protect their possessions from 'the idle and improvident', not by the consent of the people at large.[130] The poor had forfeited political rights through their own indolence or that of their ancestors, and it was absurd to suppose that power should now be detached from property. Thomas Elrington, having argued that there was no need to reprint Locke's first essay on government because hardly anyone now believed in passive obedience to absolute hereditary monarchy, claimed that he had edited the second *Treatise* in response to the use made of Lockean principles to declare the divine right of the people.

Locke's mode of expression was careless, according to Elrington, but he certainly meant to restrict 'the people' to men of property, since only they were capable of exercising sound political judgement.[131] A misreading of Locke, he explained more fully in *Thoughts on the Principles of Civil Government*, led to the silly conclusion that Irish non-freeholders and Roman Catholics ought to be enfranchised.

Elrington also claimed that speculation about the terms of an original contract was of little assistance in determining the proper extent of political rights. The transition from a state of nature to civil society had occurred 'by insensible degrees' too remote in time for adequate research,[132] and among the theories based upon fanciful conjecture about the beginning of human history was that of patriarchal absolutism. Others made the same point. The original equality of mankind was a philosophical construct, said William Hamilton, and those who set sail on the 'boundless ocean of metaphyiscal adventure' in search of raw human nature were apt to lose sight of the landmarks of experience and tradition, including that 'extensive train of unequal rights which reason teaches and history demonstrates'.[133] Political institutions had not emerged full-fledged from some formal contract, but were gradually refined by the intricate processes of civilization. And the British constitution, a 'beautiful edifice' elaborately constructed by the wisdom of ages,[134] ought not to be demolished by militant republicans equipped with a simplistic doctrine of abstract rights.

A few preachers continued to acknowledge that government had been established by 'free born' individuals to protect their inalienable rights. They did so not to alert their congregations to the dangers of arbitrary power, but to commend the founders of the British constitution for blending the 'choicest merits' of diverse political forms into the best system of government in the world.[135] Its perfection was secured by a distribution of power in proportion to the ownership of property.

> Divided powers, of different classes, in a community, check and balance each other; and are the surest, perhaps the only effectual, means to prevent arbitrary sway, in one tyrant, or a multitude. Among the variety of opportunities, talents, and inducements, to be serviceable in social life, which a diversity of ranks and fortunes produces, we may particularly notice the leisure for acquiring information, cultivated faculties, and early habits and sentiments of liberality; qualifications highly necessary for conducting the great interests of a community.[136]

The concept of the balanced constitution had become primarily a justification of social hierarchy. In this way the minutiae of constitutional argument that had once engaged the attention of Anglicans was displaced by an uncomplicated vindication of the inequalities of rank and property. As a political theory it was less equivocal than that fabricated since 1690 from Revolution principles, and therefore perhaps was a more comfortable ideology for Ireland's privileged but precarious minority.

NOTES

1 In the Irish liturgical calendar there were four political holy days, three of which – 30 January (commemorating the martyrdom of Charles I), 29 May (celebrating the restoration of Charles II), and 5 November (recalling the Gunpowder Plot) – were shared with the Church of England, and the fourth – the anniversary of the failure on 23 October 1641 of Catholic rebels to seize control of the Irish government – was singularly Irish. On these dates the Irish Commons gathered in St Andrew's Church to listen to one of their chaplains, and the Lords assembled in Christ Church Cathedral to be addressed, usually – though not invariably – by a bishop. These state sermons were regularly printed, as were those given before the Incorporated Society for Promoting English Protestant Schools in Ireland. Also published, though more intermittently, were some assize sermons as well as sundry other thanksgiving addresses marking events such as victory in war, the quelling of the latest Jacobite rising and the anniversary of the accession of a particular monarch. Sometimes sermons were printed at the initiative of the preacher, fired by the urgency of his message or anxious to rebuff critics. One churchman, lamenting the Jacobite tendencies of some of his co-religionists, justified printing his sermon of 23 October with the claim that

> since the Pulpit and the Press are our peculiar Weapons, I take it to be our Duty to make use of both, if by any Means we might contribute to the publick Peace and Tranquillity. And therefore what I have spoken to a small Congregation from one, I now deliver to the Publick from the other.
>
> Richard Davies, *Loyalty to King George. In a sermon preach'd on the three and twentieth day of October, 1715*, Dublin, 1715, A3-A4)

There has been little historical interest in these addresses apart from a few studies of those delivered on 23 October: Joseph Leichty, 'Irish evangelicalism, Trinity College Dublin, and the Mission of the Church of Ireland at the end of the eighteenth century', unpublished Ph.D. thesis, St Patrick's College, Maynooth, 1987, 194–208; T. C. Barnard, 'The uses of 23 October and Irish Protestant celebrations', *English Historical Review*, CVI (1991), 889–920, which also deals in part with the Gunpowder Plot sermons. The author kindly allowed me to read this excellent article in typescript, as well as pointing me in some fruitful directions. Research for the chapter was based upon collections in various parts of Ireland including Trinity College, the Royal Irish Academy, Marsh's Library, the National Library of Ireland, Belfast Linen Hall Library – where much of the material is uncatalogued – and the diocesan libraries of Armagh (technically a public library), Cashel and Derry. I am indebted to the staff at these libraries for their help, and also to Gordon Wheeler and Chris Shorley of Queen's University for their advice.

2 Marianne Elliott, *Partners in Revolution: The United Irishmen and France*, New Haven and London, Yale University Press, 1982, 10.

3 Francis [Hutchinson], *A sermon preached in Christ's-Church, Dublin, on the first of August, 1721. Being the anniversary of His Majesty's happy accession to the throne*, Dublin, 1721, 21.

4 Henry [Maule], *God's goodness visible in our deliverance from popery: with*

some fit methods to prevent the further growth of it in Ireland. In a sermon preached at Christ-Church, Dublin, &c. on the twenty-third day of October, 1733, 6th edn, Dublin, 1746, 37.

5 Edward [Smyth], *A sermon preach'd in Christ-Church, Dublin, on Saturday the 23rd of October, 1703*, Dublin, 1703, 10.

6 Robert [Howard], *A sermon Preach'd in Christ-Church, Dublin, before The Incorporated Society for promoting English Protestant Schools in Ireland*, Dublin, 1738, 17.

7 Jacqueline R. Hill, 'Popery and Protestantism, civil and religious liberty: the disputed lessons of Irish history 1690–1812', *Past and Present*, 118 (1988), 102.

8 John Richardson, *The true interest of the Irish nation: in a sermon preached in the church of Belturet, on Sunday the 23d of October, 1715*, Dublin, 1715, 13–19.

9 Hutchinson, *A sermon preached in Christ's-Church, Dublin, on the first of August, 1721*, 18.

10 Francis [Hutchinson], *A sermon preached in Christ-Church, Dublin, on Friday, November 5th. 1731*, Dublin, 1731.

11 Rowland Davies, *The Truly Catholick and Old Religion, shewing that the Establish'd Church in Ireland, is more truly a Member of the Catholick, than the Church of Rome. And that All the Antient Christians, especially in Great-Britain and Ireland, were of her communion'*, Dublin, 1716, 69.

12 John [Garnet], *A sermon preached at Christ-Church, Dublin. On the 28th of March, 1756. Before the Incorporated Society, for promoting English Protestant Schools in Ireland*, Dublin, 1756, 14.

13 Benjamin Bacon, *A sermon preach'd at St. Andrew's, Dublin, before the Honourable House of Commons, on Sunday the twenty-third of October, 1743*, Dublin, 1743, 15; Richardson, *The true interest*, 31; Nicholas [Forster], *A sermon preach'd in the parish-church of St. Audeon, Dublin, December 1st. 1717. Being the first Sunday in Advent, at the anniversary meeting of the children educated in the charity-schools in the city of Dublin*, Dublin, 1717, 15.

14 *The Works of George Berkeley Bishop of Cloyne*, ed. A. A. Luce and T. E. Jessop, London and New York, Nelson, 1953, VI, 231.

15 Thomas [Rundle], *A sermon preach'd in Christ-Church, Dublin, on the 25th day of March 1736. Before the Incorporated Society, for promoting English Protestant Schools in Ireland*, Dublin, 1736, 20; Michael [Cox], *A sermon preached at Christ-Church, Dublin, on the 20th day of March, 1747. Before the Incorporated Society, for promoting English Protestant Schools in Ireland*, Dublin, 1748, 12; Richard Woodward, *A sermon preached at Christ-Church, Dublin, on the 13th of May, 1764, before the Incorporated Society, for promoting English Protestant Schools in Ireland*, Dublin, 1764, 4.

16 James [Trail], *A sermon preached at Christ-Church, Dublin, on the 7th of February, 1779. Before the Incorporated Society in Dublin, for promoting English Protestant Schools in Ireland*, Dublin, 1779, 16–17.

17 Edward Synge, *The case of toleration consider'd with respect both to religion and civil government, in a sermon preach'd in St. Andrew's, Dublin, before the Honourable House of Commons; on Saturday, the 23d of October, 1725*, Dublin, 1726.

18 Edward [Smyth], *A sermon preached before Their Excellencies the Lords Justices at Christ-Church, Dublin, on the 3d of December, 1702. Being the general thanksgiving for the signal successes vouchsafed to Her Majesties forces both by sea and land: as also to those of her allies*, Dublin, 1703, 4.

19 William Hamilton, *A sermon preach'd before the Honourable House of Com-*

mons, at St. Andrew's Church, Dublin, On Friday the fifth of November, 1725, Dublin, 1725, 7.

20 Maule, *God's goodness visible*.

21 Joseph Liechty, 'Testing the depth of Catholic/Protestant conflict: the case of Thomas Leland's "History of Ireland", 1773', *Archivium Hibernicum*, XLII (1987), 13–28.

22 Thomas Leland, 'Sermon XXVIII On the anniversary of the Irish Rebellion. Preached in Christ's Church, Dublin, October 23, 1771', in *Sermons on Various Subjects*, Dublin, 1787, III, 7.

23 John Travers, *A sermon preached in St. Andrew's Church Dublin. Before the Honourable the House of Commons the twenty-third of October, 1698*, Dublin, 1698, 15.

24 Nicholas [Forster], *Unanimity in the present time of danger recommended. In a sermon preach'd before their Excellencies the Lords Justices of Ireland, at Christ's Church, Dublin, on Sunday, Feb, 5th, 1715/16*, Belfast, 1715–16, 12.

25 Hutchinson, *A sermon preached . . . on Friday, November 5th. 1731*, 40.

26 Marmaduke Philips, *Sermon preached at St. Andrew's, Dublin, before the Honourable House of Commons on Wednesday the 23d of October, 1745*, Dublin, 1745, 4.

27 Arthur Smyth, *A sermon preached at Londonderry, October the 13th*, 1745. *On occasion of the rebellion in Scotland*, Dublin, 1745, 14–16.

28 'A letter from a member of the House of Commons in Ireland to a member of the House of Commons in England, concerning the Sacramental Test' (1709), in *The Prose Works of Jonathan Swift*, ed. Herbert Davis, Oxford, Basil Blackwell, 1939, II, 109–35.

29 'A fair warning to take heed of the Scottish discipline; as being of all others most injurious to the civil magistrate, most oppressive to the subject, most pernicious to both' (1649), in *The Works of the Most Reverend Father in God, John Bramhall, D.D.*, ed. John Henry Parker, Oxford, Library of Anglo-Catholic Theology, 1852, III, 272.

30 Richard Tenison, *A sermon preached at the primary visitation of the Most Reverend Father in God Michael Lord Arch-Bishop of Armagh, Primate and Metropolitan of all Ireland, and Lord High Chancellor of the same. Held at Drogheda, August 20. 1679*, Dublin, 1679.

31 Jo[hn] Vesey, *A sermon preached at Clonmell, on Sunday the sixteenth of September, 1683. At the assizes held for the County Palatine of Tipperary*, Dublin, 1683, 22; see also the sermon by another John Vesey, Archbishop of Tuam, *A sermon preached at Windsor before his Majesty, the second Sunday after Easter, 1684*, London, 1684.

32 St. George [Ashe], *A sermon preach'd at Christ's Church, January 30th, 1715/16. Before Their Excellencies the Lords Justice and the House of Lords*, Dublin, 1716, 12.

33 Dillon Ashe, *A sermon preach'd before the Honourable House of Commons, at St. Andrew's Church, Dublin, January the 31st. 1703/4*, Dublin, 1704, 11–12.

34 Timothy [Godwin], *A sermon preach'd before their Excellencies the Lords Justices of Ireland, at Christ's Church, Dublin, on Sunday February the 26th, 1715/16*, Dublin 1716, 25.

35 William Tisdall, *A Seasonable Enquiry into that Most Dangerous Political Principle of the Kirk in Power. Viz. That the Right of Dominion in the Prince, and the Duty of Allegiance in his Presbyterian Subject, Are Founded upon The Prince's being a Subject of what they call, Christ's Kingdom of Presbytery: or, upon His Professing and Maintaining the Presbyterian Religion*, Dublin, 1713, 5.

36 Richard Woodward, *The Present State of the Church of Ireland: Containing a Description of it's Precarious Situation; and the consequent Danger to the Public. Recommended to the serious Consideration of the Friends of The Protestant Interest. To Which Are Subjoined, Some Reflections on the Impracticability of a proper Commutation for Tithes; And A General Account of the Origin and Progress of the Insurrection in Munster*, 7th edn, London, 1787, 14.

37 Hutchinson, *A sermon preached . . . on Friday, November 5th. 1731*, 28.

38 John Travers, *A sermon preached in St. Andrew's-Church, Dublin; before the Honourable the House of Commons the 8th day of October, 1695. The day appointed by the Lord Deputy and Council for a solemn thanksgiving, for the preservation of our Gracious King William, and the good success of his, and his Allies forces this last campaign*, Dublin, 1695, 3.

39 Richard Graves, *A sermon on the deliverance of this kingdom from the invasion lately attempted by the French, preached in the chapel of Trinity College, Dublin, on the 1st of January, 1797; and in St. Peter's on the 8th of January; and preached in the same church on January 15th, at the request of the parishioners in vestry assembled*, Dublin, 1797, 5.

40 Alan Ford, *The Protestant Reformation in Ireland, 1590–1641*, Frankfurt am Main, Verlag Peter Land, 1985, ch. 8.

41 *Journal of the Very Rev. Rowland Davies, LL.D. Dean of Ross, (And Afterwards Dean of Cork,) From March 8, 1688–9, to September 29, 1690*, ed. Richard Caulfield, London, Camden Society, 1857, 68.

42 Francis Higgins, *A sermon preach'd before Their Excellencies the Lords Justices, at Christ-Church, Dublin; on Tuesday the 28th of August, being the day appointed for a solemn thanksgiving to Almighty God, for the late glorious success in forcing the enemies lines in the Spanish Netherlands, by the arms of Her Majesty, and her allies, under the command of the Duke of Marlborough*, Dublin, 1705, 7.

43 Davies, *The Truly Catholick and Old Religion* , 74.

44 Carol Z. Weiner, 'The beleagured isle: a study of Elizabethan and Early Jacobean anti-Catholicism', *Past and Present*, 51 (1971), 27–62.

45 Benj[amin] Pratt, *A sermon preach'd before the Honourable House of Commons, at St. Andrew's Church, Dublin, October the 23d. 1703*, Dublin, 1703, 23.

46 Tobias [Pullen], *A sermon preached in Christ Church before His Excellency the Lord Deputy and the Parliament, on the fifth day of November, 1695*, Dublin, 1695, 19.

47 Hutchinson, *A sermon preached . . . on the first of August, 1721*, 6.

48 Michael Jephson, *A sermon preached at St. Patrick's Church Dublin, on the 23th of October. 1690*, Dublin, 1690, 9.

49 Edward Synge, *Thankfulness to Almighty God for his more antient and later mercies and deliverances vouchsafed to the British and Protestants within the kingdom of Ireland, recommended and press'd, in a sermon before the Honourable House of Commons, October the 23d, 1711*, 3rd edn, London, 1744, 22–3.

50 Smyth, *A sermon preached . . . on the 3d of December, 1702*, 24.

51 Smyth, *A sermon preached . . . on Saturday the 23rd of October, 1703*, 23.

52 e.g. Bacon, *A sermon preach'd . . . the twenty-third of October, 1743*, 20.

53 Philips, *Sermon preached . . . the 23d of October, 1745*, 19.

54 Forster, *A sermon preach'd . . . December 1st 1717*, 16.

55 Rundle, *A sermon preach'd . . . the 25th day of March 1736*, 23.

56 Patrick Delany, *A sermon preach'd before the society corresponding with the*

Incorporated Society in Dublin, for promoting English Protestant Working Schools in Ireland, London, 1744, 18.

57 T. C. Barnard, 'Protestants and the Irish language, *c*. 1675–1725', *Journal of Ecclesiastical History* (forthcoming).

58 e.g. St. George [Ashe], *A sermon preached to the Protestants of Ireland now in London, at the parish-church of St. Clement Dane. October 23, 1712*, 2nd edn, London, 1713, 21; William Hamilton, *A sermon preach'd . . . the fifth of November, 1725*, 21.

59 [John Richardson], *A Proposal for the Conversion of the Popish Natives of Ireland, to the Establish'd Religion; With the Reasons upon which it is Grounded: And an Answer to the Objections made to it*, Dublin, 1711, 29.

60 Nathanael [Foy], *A sermon preached in Christ's*=Church, Dublin; on the 23d. of October, 1698, Dublin, 1698, 30.

61 Woodward, *The Present State of the Church of Ireland*, 73–4; see also Maule, 'God's goodness visible', 36.

62 Travers, *A sermon preached . . . the twenty third of October, 1698*, 14.

63 John Lawson, 'A sermon preached in St. Andrew's, Dublin. Before the Honourable House of Commons: on Tuesday, the 23d of October, 1753', Dublin, 1753, 13.

64 Hamilton, *A sermon preach'd . . . on Friday the fifth of November, 1725*, 18.

65 Synge, *The case of toleration*, 36.

66 Edward Synge, *A vindication of a sermon preach'd before the Honourable House of Commons of Ireland. On Saturday the 23d of October, 1725. In which the question concerning toleration, particularly of popery under certain conditions and limitations is farther consider'd, and the mistakes and weak reasonings about it are laid open. In answer to the Rev^d. Mr. Radcliffe's Letter*, Dublin, 1726, 34.

67 Caroline Robbins, *The Eighteenth-Century Commonwealthman: Studies in the Transmission, Development and Circumstance of English Liberal Thought from the Restoration of Charles II until the War with the Thirteen Colonies*, Cambridge, Mass., Harvard University Press, 1959, 165.

68 Edward [Synge], *A sermon against persecution on account of religion: preached before His Grace Charles Duke of Grafton, Lord Lieutenant: and the R^t Hon$^{ble.}$ the House of Lords of Ireland; in Christ's-Church, Dublin: on Monday, October, the 23d. 1721*, Dublin, 1721, 17.

69 ibid., 8; Synge, *The happiness of a nation, or people. In a sermon preached at Christ's-Church, Dublin, before the Government and House of Lords, May 29th. 1716*, Dublin, 1716, 30.

70 R. R. Hartford, *Edward Synge (1691–1762) Fellow and Bishop: A Memorial Discourse Delivered in the Chapel of Trinity College on Trinity Monday, the 2nd June, 1947*, Dublin University Press, Dublin, 1947, 17.

71 Edward [Synge], *A sermon preach'd at Christ-Church, Dublin. On Saturday, the 23d. of October, 1731*, Dublin, 1731, 19; Edward [Synge], *A sermon preach'd in Christ-Church, Dublin, before His Grace William, Duke of Devonshire, Lord Lieutenant: and the Lords Spiritual and Temporal of Ireland: on Saturday, November 5, 1737*, Dublin, 1737, 22.

72 J. I. McGuire, 'The Church of Ireland and the "Glorious Revolution" of 1688', in A. Cosgrave and D. McCartney (eds), *Studies in Irish History Presented to R. Dudley Edwards*, Dublin, University College, 1979, 137–49.

73 J. P. Kenyon, *Revolution Principles: The Politics of Party 1689–1720*, Cambridge, Cambridge University Press, 1977, 24–6.

74 Smyth, *A sermon preached . . . on the 3d of December, 1702*, 11.

75 e.g. John Finglas, *A sermon preached in the Cathedrall Church of St. Patrick's Dublin, on the 5th of November 1690*; Jephson, *A sermon preached . . . on*

the 23th of October. 1690; Richard [Tenison], *A sermon preached at Christ's-Church, Dublin On Sunday, November 13. 1692. Before His Excellency the Lord Lieutenant of Ireland*, Dublin, 1692; Edward Walkington, *A sermon preached Octob. 23. 1692. In St. Andrews Church, Dublin; before the House of Commons*, Dublin, 1692.

76 Travers, *A sermon preached . . . the 8th day of October, 1695*, 11.

77 ibid., 12.

78 The expression was used by Edward Wetenhall, 'True religion and loyalty inseparable. The nature of both opened, and their connexion proved. In a sermon preached at Bandon, in the County of Cork, in the heat of Monmouths rebellion; and afterwards elsewhere', in *Hexapla Jacobae. A Specimen of Loyalty towards His present Majesty James the II. Of Great Britain, France and Ireland King, &c in Six Pieces*, Dublin, 1686, 16.

79 John [Vesey], *A sermon preached before His Excellency the Ld. Lieutenant and the two Houses of Parliament, in Christ's-Church, Dublin; when they first met there together: on Sunday, October 16. 1692*, London, 1692, 6.

80 Mark Goldie, 'The roots of True Whiggism 1688–94', *History of Political Thought*, I (1980), 195–236.

81 Vesey, *A sermon preached . . . the second Sunday after Easter, 1684*, 18.

82 Vesey, *A sermon preached . . . on Sunday, October 16. 1692*, 14–15.

83 [Edward Wetenhall], *The case of the Irish Protestants: in relation to recognising, or swearing allegiance to, and praying for King William and Queen Mary stated and resolved*, London, 1691, 6, 14, 22, 25.

84 Mark Goldie, 'Edmund Bohun and *Jus Gentium* in the Revolution Debate, 1689–1693', *Historical Journal*, 20 (1977), 569–86.

85 S[amuel] Synge, *The case of King Charles the First and King James the Second, stated and compar'd; in a sermon. Preach'd at Christ-Church, Dublin. Jan. the 30th. 1706/7*, Dublin, 1707, 26, 28.

86 'The sentiments of a Church-of-England man, with respect to religion and government' (1708), in *The Prose Works of Jonathan Swift*, ed. Herbert Davis, Oxford, Basil Blackwell, 1939, II, 1–25.

87 [John Winder], *A postscript in vindication of Mr. Winder's Sermon*, Dublin, 1714, 4.

88 Joseph Trapp, *A sermon preach'd at Christ-Church, Dublin, before Their Excellencies the Lords Justices of Ireland on Tuesday May the 29th; being the anniversary of the happy restoration*, Dublin, 1711, 14.

89 Jonathan Wilson, *A sermon preach'd at Christ-Church, Dublin, before Their Excellencies the Lords Justices of Ireland; on Friday May the 29th, 1713*, Dublin, 1713, 20.

90 [Joseph Trapp], *The character and principles of the present set of Whigs*, Dublin, 1714, 5.

91 Stephen Radcliff, *A sermon preached at the assizes held at Naas, for the County of Kildare, April the 6th, 1714*, Dublin, 1714, 13–14.

92 E[dward] Mathews, *The divine original of civil government: a sermon preached at the assizes held at Carrickfergus, for the County of Antrim, the 17th of July, 1713*, Dublin, 1714, 18.

93 John Winder, *The mischief of schism and faction to church and state. In a sermon preach'd at St. Mary's Church, Dublin. May the 30th, 1714. And at the request of many loyal gentlemen, preach'd at St. Michael's 20th of June following*, Dublin, 1714, 13–14.

94 Jonathan Swift, 'The publick spirit of the Whigs', in *Political Tracts 1713–1719*, ed. Herbert Davis and Irvin Ehrenpreis, Oxford, Basil Blackwell, 1953, 45.

95 Mathews, *The divine original of civil government*, 29.

96 *The Works of George Berkeley Bishop of Cloyne*, ed. A. A. Luce and T. E. Jessop, London and New York, Nelson, 1953, VI, 56–7.
97 David Berman, 'The Jacobitism of Berkeley's *Passive Obedience*', *Journal of the History of Ideas*, 47 (1986), 309–19.
98 *The Works of George Berkeley*, VI, 27.
99 ibid., VIII, 22–3.
100 'The sentiments of a Church-of-England man, with respect to religion and government', in *The Prose Works of Jonathan Swift*, II, 20–1.
101 Matt[hew] French, *Of submission to the supreme and subordinate magistrates. A sermon preach'd at the assizes held at Carrickfergus for the County of Antrim, the 23d of April, 1712*, Dublin, 1712, 4–5.
102 Synge, *Thankfulness to Almighty God . . . October the 23d, 1711*, 23–5; William Hamilton, *The dangers of popery, and blessings arising from the late revolution, consider'd in a sermon preached in the Cathedral Church of Armagh. November, 5th. MDCCXXII*, Dublin, 1723, 15–18.
103 [Charles Leslie], *An Answer to a Book, Intituled, The State of the Protestants Under the Late King James's Government*, London, 1692, 113–15.
104 Andrew Carpenter, 'William King and the threats to the Church of Ireland during the reign of James II', *Irish Historical Studies*, 18 (1972–3), 22–8.
105 Trinity College, Dublin: MS F.I.22, fol. 264^v. Cited from the transcript in Andrew P. Isdell-Carpenter, 'Archbishop King and Dean Swift', unpublished PhD thesis, University College, Dublin, 1970, 495.
106 William King, *A sermon, preached at St. Patrick's Church, Dublin, on the 16th. of November, 1690. Being the day of thanksgiving for the preservation of His Majesties person, his good success in our deliverance, and his safe and happy return into England*, London, 1691, 23.
107 William King, *The State of the Protestants of Ireland under the late King James's government. In which their Carriage towards him is justified, and the absolute Necessity of their endeavouring to be freed from his Government, and of submitting to their present Majesties is demonstrated*, Dublin, 1730, 110.
108 ibid., 14. Compare with John Locke, *Two Treatises of Government*, ed. Peter Laslett, Cambridge, Cambridge University Press, 1967, II, sections 240–1, pp. 444–5:

> Here, 'tis like, the common Question will be made, *Who shall be Judge* whether the Prince or Legislative act contrary to their Trust? . . . To this I reply, *The People shall be Judge*; for who shall be *Judge* whether his Trustee or Deputy acts well . . . but he who deputes him? . . . But farther, this Question, (*Who shall be Judge*?) cannot mean, that there is no Judge at all. For where there is no Judicature on Earth, to decide Controversies amongst Men, *God* in Heaven is *Judge*: He alone, 'tis true, is Judge of the Right. But *every Man* is *Judge* for himself, as in all other Cases, so in this, whether another hath put himself into a State of War with him, and whether he should appeal to the Supreme Judge, as *Jephta* did.

109 Leslie, *An Answer to a Book*, 6–7.
110 David Burches, *The case of obedience to humane laws stated. In a sermon preached at the Cathedral and metropolitan church of St. Patrick's, Armagh. On Saturday August, 1st, 1724. Being the anniversary day of his Majesty King George's happy accession to the throne. Wherein the principal objection of the disaffected against our present legal establishment is occasionally consider'd*, Dublin, 1715, 6.
111 Synge, *A sermon preach'd . . . the 23d. of October, 1731'*, 6.

112 Edward Synge, 'A sermon preach'd in Christ's-Church, Dublin, before his Excellency the Lord Carteret; on Thursday, Nov. 5. 1724, Dublin, 1724, 9.

113 [William] Stoughton, A sermon preach'd before the state in Christ-Church, on Monday the 31st of January, 1708/9, Dublin 1709, 'The Dedication'.

114 Theo[philus] Bolton, A sermon preach'd in Christ's Church, Dublin, upon the thirtieth of January 1716/17. Before his Excellency Henry Earl of Galway, being the day of the martyrdom of King Charles I, Dublin, 1717, 9.

115 Anthony Lowcay, Obedience to the supreme power. A sermon preach'd on the occasion of the intended invasion, by the Pretender, Dublin, 1715, 8–9.

116 Stoughton, A sermon preach'd . . . on Monday the 31st of January 1708/9, 16.

117 Jonathan Smedley, A sermon upon the original freedom of mankind, preach'd to the Protestants of Ireland, residing now in London, on the anniversary, appointed by Act of Parliament, in that Kingdom, in commemoration of the deliverance from a general massacree, begun by Irish Papists, on the 23ᵈ of October, 1641; in the parish-church of St. James's Westminster, London, 1715, 33.

118 Jonathan Smedley, A Rational and Historical Account of the Principles which gave Birth to the Late Rebellion. And of the Present Controversies of the English Clergy, Dublin, 1718, 32.

119 Lowcay, Obedience to the supreme power, 12.

120 Synge, The Happiness of a Nation, 26.

121 Burches, The case of obedience to humane laws, 8.

122 Rowland Davies, A sermon preach'd in the cathedral church of Cork, on the 30th of January, 1715, Dublin, 1715, 7, 11–12, 14.

123 Joseph Story, A sermon preached at St. Andrew's-Church, Dublin, on Monday, November 5th. 1739, Dublin, 1739, 7.

124 Joseph Story, A sermon preach'd before the Honourable House of Commons, at St. Andrew's church, on the fifth of November 1737, Dublin, 1737, 22, 25.

125 Robert [Clayton], A sermon preached at Christ-Church, Dublin, on the thirtieth of January 1731/2. Before His Grace Lionel Duke of Dorset, Lord Lieutenant of Ireland, Dublin, 1731, 13.

126 Synge, A sermon preach'd . . . November 5, 1737, 20–1.

127 Hugh Hamilton, On the duty of obedience to the laws and of submission to magistrates. A sermon occasioned by the late disturbances in the north of Ireland, preached before the Judges of Assize in the cathedral church of Armagh, on Sunday, April 12, 1772, Dublin, 1772, 17.

128 Graves, A sermon on the deliverance of this kingdom, 29.

129 See Patrick Kelly, 'Perceptions of Locke in eighteenth-century Ireland', Proceedings of the Royal Irish Academy, 89, C 2, 1989, 30–2; R. B. McDowell, Irish Public Opinion 1750–1800, London, Faber & Faber, 1944, ch. IX.

130 [Sir Lawrence Parsons], Thoughts on Liberty and Equality, Dublin, 1793, 5.

131 John Locke, An Essay Concerning the Original Extent and End of Civil Government, ed. Thomas Elrington, 2nd edn, Dublin, 1798, 'Avertisement'.

132 S. N. [Thomas Elrington], Thoughts on the Principles of Civil Government, and their Foundation in the Law of Nature, Dublin, 1793, 1.

133 William Hamilton, Letters on the Principles of the French Democracy, and their Application and Influence on the Constitution and Happiness of Britain and Ireland, Dublin, 1792, I, 11, 13.

134 Thomas Thompson, A sermon preached in the parish church of Castlebar, on Tuesday the 16th of January, 1798, being the day appointed by His Excellency the Lord Lieutenant for a general thanksgiving to Almighty God, for the many signal and important victories which His divine providence hath

vouchsafed to His Majesty's fleets in the course of the present war, Dublin, 1798, 8.

135 James Widman Sterling, *A sermon preached in the parish church of Moat, County of Westmeath, Friday, the 12th of July, 1799*, Athlone, 1799, 8–9.

136 Gabriel Stokes, *Love of our country, distinguished from false pretences; a sermon preached in the cathedral of Waterford, January 15th, 1797, being the first Sunday after it was ascertained that the invading fleet had entirely quit the coast*, Dublin, 1797, 10.

3 The school of virtue

Francis Hutcheson, Irish Presbyterians and the Scottish Enlightenment

Ian McBride

One by-product of the current interest of scholars in the United Irish movement has been a greater awareness of the role of Ulster Presbyterianism in the evolution of Irish republican ideology. In addition to obvious borrowings from America and France, the radicals of the 1790s were conversant with older languages of opposition which can be traced back to the neglected decades of the early eighteenth century. In her pioneering work on the subject, Marianne Elliott has highlighted the importance of Presbyterians as transmitters of the cluster of ideas commonly described as 'real Whiggism', 'civic humanism' or 'classical republicanism'. Stressing Wolfe Tone's ideological debt to the northern Presbyterians, and especially to Dr William Drennan, she suggests that the training of the Dissenting clergy at the Scottish universities, and the theories of religious toleration elaborated by 'new light' ministers, go some way to explain the emergence of the United Irish programme in Belfast.[1] These findings are echoed in a recent survey of the 1790s by Roy Foster, who notes 'not only the percussion of events in Ireland from the early 1790s, but also the Presbyterian tradition of libertarian republicanism that long antedated 1775 or 1789'.[2]

A key figure in this tradition was Francis Hutcheson, master of a Dissenting academy in Dublin during the 1720s and professor of moral philosophy at Glasgow University from 1730 until his death in 1746. Hutcheson has been hailed as the prophet of all manner of ideas from the philosophical revolutions of Adam Smith and David Hume to the political theory of Jefferson's Declaration of Independence. Historians of the political and social thought of eighteenth-century Scotland have called for a proper investigation of his intellectual background, while their colleagues in the history of philosophy are beginning to make more room for his writings. It seems likely that we shall also hear more of Hutcheson's disciples in colonial America, as the debate on the ideological origins of the American Revolution continues. By way of contrast, Irish historians have so far shown little interest in Hutcheson's career: in his own country the prophet remains unacknowledged.

More generally, we are trailing behind in the search for the origins of late eighteenth-century radicalism. The relationship between Protestant Dissent and English radicalism has long been taken for granted, and recent research has witnessed renewed interest in the religious basis of the political and social ideologies of eighteenth-century Britain.[3] At the same time, Professor J. G. A. Pocock and his followers have shown how political debate in the eighteenth century was permeated with the language of classical republicanism or (as Pocock prefers) civic humanism.[4] This work offers an obvious vantage-point for Irish historians, yet it is fair to say that few have been tempted by the view. The result is an increasingly detailed map of eighteenth-century political ideas in which Ireland constitutes an embarrassing void.

The essential framework for the study of Irish intellectual history during this period is the eighteenth-century British empire, and this was especially so for Presbyterians, who inhabited a transatlantic subculture stretching from Scotland to Ulster to the American colonies. At the centre of this intellectual world rested the Scottish universities, then at the height of their international fame. Excluded from Trinity College Dublin until 1793, Irish Presbyterians looked to Glasgow and, to a lesser extent, Edinburgh for their training in the arts, medicine and divinity. These students, described as 'Scoto-Hiberni' in the matriculation records, not only sustained the intellectual life of Presbyterian Ulster, but as Scots-Irish emigrants to North America they became the chief exporters of enlightenment to the colonies.[5] In many ways the English Dissenting community belongs here too: its much-acclaimed academies were staffed by Scottish-trained masters, many of whom had received financial assistance from funds like the Dr Williams Trust.[6]

It is with the intellectual links between the Presbyterians of Scotland and Ireland that this chapter will be primarily concerned. To some extent the story is one of a spill-over of Scottish thought, but I hope to show that Ulster Presbyterians were not only beneficiaries of the Scottish Enlightenment but also participants in it. The story begins with a curious Scots-Irish dialogue which took place between Presbyterians in Dublin and Glasgow in the 1720s. It entails a definition of the Scottish Enlightenment as a campaign for cultural reform, equipped with a vigorous ideological component which was supplied by the academic discipline of moral philosophy. Characterized in this way, Hutcheson's centrality to the culture of eighteenth-century Scotland will become evident. Finally, I want to look for echoes of the political and social thought of enlightened Scotland in the radicalism of the later eighteenth century. It is hardly necessary to remark that Irish Presbyterianism was a diverse religious tradition which contained a wide spectrum of theological and political opinions. The Scots-Irish traffic of ideas examined in this chapter constitutes only one strand of Presbyterian political thought; nevertheless it is an essential part of the ideological background against which the radicalism of the later eighteenth century should be measured.

I

The territory of the Scottish Enlightenment remains a fiercely contested one despite the dozens of monographs and essay collections which have been devoted to the subject over the last twenty years. One crucial faultline has opened on the question of the importance of the Act of Union and the impact of English culture on the eighteenth-century Scottish renaissance. Occasionally patriotic sensitivities can be discerned; a renaissance, after all, implies a preceding dark age. Other debates, not unrelated, focus on the chronology of the Enlightenment in Scotland, and the relative weight which should be accorded to civic humanism on the one hand, and to continental natural law theories on the other. Problems of a different sort arise from the multifarious interests of the Scottish philosophers which seem to defy comprehensive treatment. The task of providing a conceptual framework for the study of the subject has been further hampered by the steady stream of articles contributed by specialists from a wide range of disciplines.

On the most basic level, the Scottish Enlightenment is an episode in intellectual history, 'that efflorescence of intellectual vitality' after 1745 which brings to mind a succession of internationally recognized thinkers: David Hume, Adam Smith, Adam Ferguson, William Robertson, John Millar, Thomas Reid, Dugald Stewart.[7] Their collective aim was to place the study of the moral, social and economic activities of humankind on a new empirical footing; to create a 'science of man'.[8] For the purposes of this essay, however, the Scottish Enlightenment will be viewed as a broader cultural and social phenomenon. Its luminaries sought not only to analyse the causes and implications of economic progress, but to set standards of taste and instil the values which befitted a modern commercial society. Their attempts to clarify, defend and delineate the pursuit of virtue cannot be divorced from their practical task of preparing citizens for public life and legislators for government. They claimed for themselves, and were accorded, a prominent social role. The Enlightenment was a self-conscious enterprise, an ideological battle; it was about power, patronage, and social networks. The view put forward here, as those familiar with Scottish historiography will recognize, is indebted to the historical research on civic humanism pioneered by J. G. A. Pocock and carried into Scottish territory by Nicholas Phillipson.

Civic humanism is the name given by historians to certain ways of thinking and talking about politics and society which were derived from the city-states of ancient Greece and Rome.[9] Its original sources included the political philosophy of Aristotle and Polybius, the historical writings of Tacitus and Sallust, and Ciceronian moralism. At the centre of this configuration of ideas lies the classical opposition of virtue and corruption. Man is viewed as an inherently political animal; it is only by participation in the public life of the *polis* or republic that he can be fulfilled. Virtue was accordingly bound up with the practice of citizenship. It demanded the sacrifice of private interest to the common good, it offered the individual a share in his own government through participation in civil and military affairs, and it was dependent upon the preservation of a state of equality within the citizenry. Full membership of the republic was limited to that part of the male population which was 'independent', that is, in possession of sufficient property to guarantee freedom from another's influence. But the citizen, although naturally sociable, was also subject to selfish passions which prompted him to place his own interests before the general welfare of the community. The history of Greece and Rome, and more recently of European states, contained terrible warnings of how once virtuous nations had become corrupted by wealth and blindly stumbled into slavery. In political terms this meant that all states were prone to degeneration. Britons, it was believed, were uniquely fortunate in having escaped this cycle by establishing a mixed constitution which balanced the three pure forms of monarchy, aristocracy and democracy, and thus conformed to the republican theories of the ancient world. But the maintenance of this balance called for the constant renewal of public spirit and eternal vigilance against corruption in the state.

The odyssey of civic humanism from the Florentine renaissance to revolutionary America and beyond was first charted by Pocock in a series of articles which culminated in his *The Machiavellian Moment* (1975). The civic tradition found its classic English formulation in James Harrington's *Oceana* (1656), a defence of the English commonwealth and the key text in the Pocockian canon. Following the restoration of the monarchy, English republicanism was forced underground, but Harrington's admirers were able to rescue the central tenets of his work, albeit in modified form; divested of its anti-monarchical elements and allied to the ancient constitution, the language of classical republicanism was made fit for public consumption. Foremost among these neo-Harringtonians, often labelled commonwealthmen by their opponents, were Robert, Viscount Molesworth, the free-thinker John Toland, and the journalists Trenchard and Gordon. In the late 1690s, and again in the 1720s, commonwealth or true Whig ideas supplied the language of political dissidence, exposing corruption in the guise of standing armies, public credit, and patronage, the three pillars of the 'Whig oligarchy' constructed as part of William III's continental war effort, and perfected in the reign of Sir Robert Walpole. It is worth adding that much of the real Whig offensive was directed not at parliamentary corruption but at the spectre of 'priestcraft', that is the influence of the Church in politics and its grip on education.[10] As the political climate cooled, the rhetoric of the commonwealthmen gave way to the milder opposition of the 'Country persuasion', but the 1760s yielded something of an Indian summer as radicals like Thomas Hollis, Francis Blackburne and Richard Baron resuscitated the commonwealth canon in their efforts to defend the cause of the American colonists in England.

It was soon realized that the language of civic humanism offered a promising context for the re-evaluation of the Enlightenment in eighteenth-century Scotland. 'North Britain' had produced its own fleeting 'Machiavellian moment' in the speeches and writings of Andrew Fletcher of Saltoun, the outstanding opponent of the Anglo-Scottish Union. Identifying his country's backward economy and corrupt political culture with its dependence on the English Crown, Fletcher argued that liberty could be preserved only by curtailing the influence of the court, reasserting the independence of the Scottish Parliament, and establishing a citizens' militia. A reinvigorated gentry would then be able to stimulate commerce and to implement a programme of agricultural improvement. It was not until after the Union, however, that a peculiar variant of the civic tradition took hold north of the border, and then only by a surprisingly circuitous route. It owed much less to Fletcher, with his hostility to cultural refinement, than to Anthony Ashley Cooper, the third Earl of Shaftesbury.[11]

Nicholas Phillipson has sought to explain the Scottish Enlightenment as an attempt to provide an updated version of civic humanism which would enable the Scots to describe and understand their position after the Union of 1707. Deprived of its parliament by the absorption of Scotland into the United Kingdom, the rump of the governing classes found itself bereft of any public role or collective identity. Simultaneously, the Union heightened awareness of the relative economic backwardness which persisted north of the border. A solution for this identity crisis was discovered in the emerging ideology of improvement, in projects for the modernization of the Scottish economy and the refinement of Scottish manners. The theoretical foundations and, what is more remarkable, the institutional framework, for the provincial elite's new role were furnished by a generation of intellectuals who began to emerge in the early decades of the century, first in polite societies like the Rankenians and the Easy Club, and later in the universities. This partnership of improving landlords and intellectuals secured a wide social constituency for the enlightenment in Scotland, and dictated its central theme, the relationship between virtue and commerce.[12] As the ideology of improvement was vindicated by an upturn in the economy the Scots began to analyse the social and cultural implications of economic change; they suggested historical models for the development of civilization; and above all they sought to reconcile the pursuit of virtue with the reality of commercial society.

In this process the language of civic virtue was re-interpreted for a more urban, commercial audience. The Scots drew heavily on the polite Ciceronian manners which had been popularized by Addison's *Spectator*, but whose philosophical origins can be traced back to Shaftesbury's cultural essays, *Characteristicks of Men, Manners, Times, Opinions*, first published in 1711. Fletcher's patriotism was tempered by Shaftesbury's politeness as the sociability of clubs and coffee-houses took the place of participation in the political process. Scottish intellectuals were thus able to exploit tensions in the civic humanist heritage which had always manifested itself as a programme for cultural reform as well as a political creed.[13] This is not to say, however, that the republican dimension was completely repressed. The classical conception of the armed citizen would later be evoked in the militia campaigns of the Seven Years' War and the American War of Independence.[14]

Phillipson's work has been complemented by Richard Sher's collective profile of the 'Moderate *literati*' who propagated the gospel of enlightenment from the pulpits of the kirk, and in the classrooms of Scotland's four universities.[15] Theologically they were Moderates, their sermons suffused with practical morality rather than sectarian doctrine. In politics they were impeccable Whigs, loyal to the Hanoverian monarchy and the constitution as confirmed in 1688, with just a tinge of classical republicanism. Opposed to American independence and parliamentary reform, they nevertheless revealed their patriotic colours when Scottish interests were at stake, and demonstrated their commitment to religious toleration by supporting concessions to Roman Catholics. On a range of issues they clashed with the orthodox 'popular party' over their use of polite literature as a vehicle for the inculcation of moral virtues.

Such a brief summary can do little justice to the sophistication which Phillipson, Sher, and many other historians have brought to our understanding of eighteenth-century Scotland. For present purposes, however, it will be sufficient to underline two points. The first is the remarkable prestige and authority which the Scottish men of letters enjoyed as a reward for their services in the legitimation of a new social and political order. The Scottish brand of Enlightenment, in contrast to its French counterpart, was institutionalized in the Established Church and in the universities from its inception. These conditions were conspicuously lacking in Ireland, where Dissenters were excluded from the institutions of the Anglican ascendancy. Denied the patronage of the aristocracy, the Ulster Presbyterian intelligentsia found its natural allies among the mercantile elites of Belfast and its hinterland who smarted under the commercial restrictions imposed by Britain.

Secondly, it should be stressed that the discipline of moral philosophy was the core of the Scottish curriculum, the definitive component in enlightened thinking. Bound up with theology and politics, ranging over economics and sociology, it lay at the heart of the political and cultural ethos of the 'Moderate *literati*'. Threaded throughout the diverse enquiries of Hutcheson, Smith, Ferguson, Reid and Stewart, is a unifying theme – the pursuit of virtue – which gave eighteenth-century Scottish culture its distinctive character. The reflections of the Scottish *philosophes* themselves, always conscious of their participation in the enterprise of enlightenment, justify the adoption of this interpretative framework. Looking back over the eighteenth century, the moral philosopher Dugald Stewart described a renaissance, not just in the field of metaphysics, but in literary taste and political culture too. Significantly he dated this cultural awakening from Hutcheson's arrival at Glasgow: it was the Irish professor's investigations which 'contributed powerfully, in our northern seats of learning, to introduce a taste for more liberal and elegant pursuits than could have been expected so soon to succeed the intolerance, bigotry, and barbarism of the preceding century.'[16]

II

Until recent years Francis Hutcheson was known primarily as the architect of 'moral sense' theory, the belief in an internal sense of perception which directs the individual towards that course of action which will promote the common good.[17] The moral sense was lifted from the writings of the Earl of Shaftesbury and employed by Hutcheson in his attacks on the egoism of Hobbes and Mandeville. Where their theories reduced morality to a rational calculation of self-interest, Hutcheson argued that human behaviour was governed not by reason but by a moral faculty; where they stressed self-love he countered with the principle of 'benevolence', a concern for the welfare of mankind. The moral sense won few adherents, however, and in the late eighteenth century it would be regarded as a disastrous blind alley in the early history of 'the Scottish philosophy'. Hutcheson's part in the genesis of the Scottish Enlightenment derived more from his success as the purveyor of a uniquely persuasive model of civic virtue. Indeed the memoirs and correspondence of his pupils and friends capture Hutcheson's achievements as a didactic moralist in a way that a reading of his treatises and textbooks cannot.

Born in 1694, the son of an Armagh clergyman, Francis Hutcheson received his early education at James MacAlpin's 'philosophy school' in Killyleagh, County Down, before matriculating at Glasgow in 1710.[18] Two of Hutcheson's Scottish professors stand out as innovators. Gershom Carmichael, the college's first professor of moral philosophy, has been credited with the introduction of the natural law tradition into that subject. His edition of Pufendorf's *De Officio Hominis et Civis* was enhanced by his own copious notes, which Hutcheson maintained were of more value than the original text.[19] Many of the modifications in Carmichael's commentary pointed in the direction of Locke, and it has been suggested that his lectures provide the first use of the *Two Treatises* in the curriculum of a British university.[20] More controversial was the divinity professor, John Simson, whose reputation for heterodoxy led to two notorious heresy trials and eventually to his suspension. Completing his divinity studies in 1717, Hutcheson soon returned to Ireland, and after a brief spell as a probationer in the Presbyterian Church he accepted an invitation from the Dublin Dissenters to open an academy in the metropolis. Here he quickly made a name for himself with two ethical treatises, *An Inquiry Concerning the Original of our Ideas of Beauty and Virtue* (1725) and *An Essay on the Nature and Conduct of the Passions and Affections* (1728). In 1729 he returned to Glasgow to fill the moral philosophy chair left vacant by the death of his old professor, Carmichael.

As an Irish Presbyterian, Hutcheson's early experience differed widely from that of his Scottish colleagues. To begin with, the Glorious Revolution had enabled Presbyterianism to supplant episcopacy as the national church in Scotland; by contrast the Anglican Church of Ireland had survived the Revolution intact and was strengthened in 1704 by the passage of a sacramental test designed to exclude Protestant Dissenters from public office. Presbyterians were also subject to a series of minor legal restrictions which prevented them from maintaining their own schools and from marrying in their own churches. By 1719, when a Toleration Act granted Dissenters some legal protection, these religious grievances had combined with severe economic hardship to produce the first great exodus of Ulster Presbyterians to the American colonies. Proof of the insecure position of Protestant Dissent is furnished by Hutcheson's own career: the Killyleagh school was denounced by High-Churchmen, and Hutcheson himself was twice prosecuted in the Archbishop's court for teaching at the Dublin academy.[21]

In its theological make-up too there were signs that Irish Presbyterianism was beginning to diverge from the Calvinist doctrines of the parent church. The precarious existence of the Irish congregations in the seventeenth century meant that the ecclesiastical structure was not properly organized until the 1690s, and subscription to the Westminster Confession of Faith, the formal creed of the Church of Scotland, was not made compulsory until 1705. This may be one reason why a non-subscribing party crystallized in the Synod of Ulster long before the Confession was called into question in the Scottish General Assembly. At any rate, the issue of subscription was debated at successive meetings of the Synod and in numerous pamphlets in the 1720s as a number of ministers, led by Samuel Haliday of Belfast, chose to defy the 1705 rule.

The non-subscribers took their stand on the right of private judgement, arguing that the imposition of creeds and confessions usurped Christ's sovereignty over the Church, and entailed the adulteration of the word of God with human sentiments. To the majority of ministers, however, it seemed that these objections merely disguised the drift of the non-subscribers towards the heresies of Arminianism and Arianism. Such suspicions were apparently confirmed by the activities of the Belfast Society, which had met since 1705 to discuss theological questions. The sermons of these 'new light' ministers broke with orthodox Calvinism by stressing a capacity for moral improvement through human reasoning rather than the intercessory work of Christ. Although Hutcheson studiously avoided controversy, there can be no doubt where his sympathies lay. Throughout his life he remained a close friend of leading non-subscribers like Samuel Haliday and James Kirkpatrick of Belfast, John Abernethy of Antrim, Michael Bruce of Holywood and Thomas Drennan, his assistant at the Dublin academy. Hutcheson's 'new light' reputation would get him into trouble at Glasgow where he was tried for heresy in 1738, and posthumously denounced as a propagator of heterodoxy in John Witherspoon's biting satire *Ecclesiastical Characteristics*.[22] While more research is needed into the religious dimensions of Whig and real Whig ideologies, it seems clear that the non-subscribers' elevation of individual conscience, and their growing confidence in human perfectibility, paved the way for the reception of classical republican ideas in 'new light' circles.

The political debates of the period, in Ireland as in England, turned on the meaning of the Glorious Revolution. Almost certainly there were large sections of the Presbyterian laity who rejected the 1688 settlement, adhering to the seventeenth-century Solemn League and Covenant: in future years Ulster would provide fertile ground for Seceding and Covenanting missionaries. However, leading Presbyterian spokesmen quickly adjusted to their position as Dissenters and drew on the vocabulary of Whig constitutionalism to articulate a new understanding of their relationship with church and state. This new identity, which remained unchanged until the late eighteenth century, was forged in reaction to the crude attempts of High Church propagandists to depict the Presbyterians as the heirs of the Puritan regicides. The splenetic vicar of Belfast, William Tisdall, reported that Presbyterian toasts coupled William III with Cromwell in order to 'put the *Late Revolution* upon the same foot with the *Former Rebellion* . . . and to dispose the People toward such *Revolution Principles*, as overturn'd the *Constitution* and brought the *Best of Princes* to the Block'.[23] In a series of ill-tempered polemics he asserted that the Presbyterian Synod of Ulster claimed direct jurisdiction over the civil magistrate, that ministers could absolve their communicants from their allegiance to the king, and that their covenants and catechisms bound them to extirpate both episcopacy and monarchy.[24] Presbyterian rejoinders concentrated on the historical evidence mustered by Tisdall to implicate their ancestors in the upheavals of the seventeenth century, but the Dissenters were forced also to define their stance on the more abstract issues raised by the Revolution.

James Kirkpatrick led the way with *An Historical Essay on the Loyalty of Presbyterians* (1713), a cumbersome survey of Presbyterian trials and tribulations in the three kingdoms. Dismissing the High Church theories of non-resistance and passive obedience, he was uninhibited in his defence of the 'doctrine of resistance', citing the classic statements of English Whiggism in his support: Hoadly's famous 1705 sermon on Romans 13:1, Burnet's *An Enquiry into the Measures of Submission to the Supreme*

Authority (1688) and the speeches from the Sacheverell trial.[25] 'True Christian Loyalty', submitted Kirkpatrick, consisted in obedience to the monarch as required by the 'Laws of God, Nature and Nations, the Original Contract *between the Prince and the People, and* the just *Laws of the State*'.[26] His colleague John McBride defined 'Presbyterian loyalty' as '*a strict Bond, between the King and his Subjects: mutually obliging each to other; the King to Protection and Just Government; the Subjects to pay Tribute and Obedience*'.[27] Marking the accession of George I in 1714, John Abernethy triumphantly rattled through the history of the kings of Israel, discrediting divine right theory and concluding that 'the *Consent of the People is the only Just Foundation of Government*'.[28]

Although firm in their support for Revolution principles, Presbyterian apologists took care not to step beyond the boundaries of mainstream Whiggism. The whole thrust of their propaganda effort was designed to disassociate themselves from the charge of regicide and to vindicate their interregnum record. The Synod of Ulster insisted that no 'Anti-monarchical Principle' was taught to the Dissenting students at Killyleagh.[29] A handful of Irishmen were less circumspect in their treatment of the turbulent events of the previous century. The infamous John Toland, who had studied at both Edinburgh and Glasgow, reprinted the republican works of Harrington, Milton and Sydney. To those who branded him a commonwealthman, he replied

> Now if a Commonwealth be a Government of Laws enacted for the common Good of all the People, not without their own consent or Approbation; and that they are not wholly excluded, as in absolute Monarchy . . . Then it is undeniably manifest that the English Government is already a Commonwealth, the most free and best constituted in all the world.[30]

Of much more significance for the Irish political scene was the retirement of Toland's sometime friend and patron, Robert, Viscount Molesworth, to his Dublin home in 1722. Following an abortive diplomatic career the Viscount had carved out his own niche in the commonwealth canon with his requiem for Danish liberty, *An Account of Denmark, as it was in the year 1692* (1694). Lamenting the decline of parliamentary institutions throughout Europe, Molesworth fulminated against the priests whose stranglehold on education allowed them to tranquillize the people with the principles of passive obedience. The only remedy was the replacement of the priesthood with philosophers who would instruct citizens in the classical virtue of Brutus and Cato.[31] In his influential declaration of faith, *The Principles of a Real Whig* (1711), Molesworth defended Britain's mixed constitution and did not hesitate to classify it as a commonwealth,

For where in the very *frame* of the *constitution*, the good of the *whole* is taken care of by the *whole* (as it is in our case), the having a *king* or *queen* at the head of it alters not the case.[32]

It is not known how Hutcheson first met the Viscount, yet it seems certain that it was via this route he encountered the republican theories of Harrington, and found an answer to the self-centred philosophy of Hobbes and Mandeville in the writings of Molesworth's mentor, the Earl of Shaftesbury. In 1725, the same year in which his *Inquiry* was published, Hutcheson attacked Mandeville's *Fable of the Bees* in the pages of the *Dublin Weekly Journal*, edited by James Arbuckle, another Ulster Presbyterian and a Glasgow graduate, who had recently settled in the capital. Arbuckle's editorials, later collected together as *The Letters of Hibernicus*, were published at the instigation of Molesworth.[33] Although he followed Molesworth and Swift in his support of Irish manufactures, Arbuckle's primary objective was to correct the vices and improve the tastes of the Irish elite.[34] He was impatient with those who were 'always talking in the *Dialect* of *statesmen* or examining the principles of a *Leviathan* or an *Oceana*', and proposed instead to further the cause of liberty and virtue by a reformation of Irish manners.[35] *The Letters of Hibernicus* hints at that mixture of Shaftesburian philosophy and Addisonian politeness which was to become so popular with the Scottish Moderates.

What scanty evidence there is suggests that a reconstruction of Hutcheson's intellectual and social milieu in Dublin, although a painstaking task, would be extremely rewarding. Manuscript sources for Irish Presbyterianism at this time are disappointingly thin; of Hutcheson's partner in the Dublin academy, Thomas Drennan, we know virtually nothing, while the biographical details of the poet and essayist James Arbuckle are tantalizingly obscure. The same is true of William Bruce, one of the most prominent figures in the Dublin Dissenting community, a cousin of Hutcheson and undoubtedly his closest friend in Ireland. It is possible that Bruce spent some time at the philosophy school in Killyleagh, where his father was minister, before his college education in Glasgow. Unlike his two brothers he chose not to follow his father into the Church, but moved instead to Dublin where Hutcheson encouraged him to enter into partnership with the bookseller John Smith, also an Ulster Presbyterian. Given what we know of Hutcheson's relations with other printers like the Foulis brothers in Glasgow and the English republican Richard Baron, there can be little doubt that Hutcheson had some say in his cousin's business. Throughout his Glasgow years Hutcheson continued to correspond with Bruce, who circulated the manuscript of *A System of Moral Philosophy* among the professor's Irish colleagues and contributed many comments himself.[36] As a firm 'new light' man and a convinced patriot Bruce wrote pamphlets calling for the repeal of the Test Act, and defending the Irish linen interest and the privileges of the Dublin Parliament against the encroachments of the British government.[37] Smith and Bruce, who specialized in philosophical and theological works, published Arbuckle's essays and Hutcheson's treatises as well as editions of Shaftesbury and Harrington.[38] Together with Hutcheson, they helped introduce the language of civic virtue, now cured of its Deist associations, to the Presbyterian intelligentsia.

III

Unfortunately all too little is known about the Molesworth circle, but it is possible to fill in some of the gaps by turning to the other end of the Dublin–Glasgow axis, to an odd dispute in which some future members of the Dublin circle would take part. The *casus belli* was the infringement by the principal of the Glasgow students' electoral rights. According to the original statutes of the university, the right of choosing the rector – the college magistrate – fell to the *comitia*, that is, the masters and students assembled. But in the unsettled state following the Revolution the principal and the professors had taken it upon themselves to appoint the rector, a practice which continued until 1716. In that year the principal, John Stirling, who ran the university with the assistance of John Simson, his nephew by marriage, had alienated a number of the professors by his dictatorial and irregular management of the faculty business. Seven disaffected masters decided to challenge the principal by convening a meeting of *comitia* and encouraging the students to elect a rector. The principal succeeded in having a Royal Commission appointed which came down on his side, but the dispute dragged on for a decade, the students protesting yearly, until another Royal Commission resolved the matter in their favour in 1726.[39]

The friction in the university was exacerbated by a number of minor confrontations between the students and the college authorities. In the first place the ringleaders, many of whom were *Scoto-Hiberni*, were closely associated with a college society, the Trinamphorian Club, which met once a week, 'with no other Design in the World than to discourse upon Matters of Learning for their Mutual Improvement'.[40] Although questions of religion and politics were excluded from discussion, Simson, whose own slippery theological stance proved so controversial, branded the members as 'a set of Latitudinarians, Free-thinkers, Non-subscribers, and Bangorians, and in a word, Enemies to the Jurisdictions, Powers and Divine Authority of the Clergy'.[41] The principal attempted to ban all such meetings by an 'Act to suppress immorality' but could not obtain the compliance of the faculty.[42] Secondly, a group of students clashed with the authorities on that traditional bugbear of Calvinist divines, the theatre. James Arbuckle was among a company of Trinamphorians who were censured for their performances of Addison's *Cato* and Rowe's *Tamerlane* in 1720, two Whiggish plays which according to Arbuckle were designed 'to raise in their Minds the most beautiful Sentiments of Liberty and

Virtue'.[43] Finally, as Simson's allegations suggest, there was a theological dimension to these quarrels: Arbuckle had caused something of a stir in Glasgow by boldly defending Haliday and Kirkpatrick – the Belfast 'new light' ministers – fuelling fears that the contagion of non-subscription was spreading to the student clubs.[44]

Arbuckle was saved from expulsion by the intervention of Carmichael, but John Smith, the future bookseller, was not so lucky. Smith had helped to draw up a petition to Parliament presenting the students' case, and had solicited the aid of Viscount Molesworth, who was currently standing for re-election to the British House of Commons. When a false rumour of Molesworth's victory reached Glasgow, the Irish students celebrated with a bonfire just outside the college, and Smith foolishly ended up in a scuffle with Carmichael. The faculty ordered his expulsion, five masters dissenting.[45] In a replay of this incident, William Robertson was sent packing in March 1725, after he and a band of Irish students had broken into the rector's house to protest at the method of his election. By now it should come as no surprise to learn that Robertson made his way to Dublin to seek the advice of the Molesworth circle.[46] Once more the Trinamphorians were involved: in January the orthodox clergyman and diarist Robert Wodrow had gloomily recorded the revival of the club and noted the spread of heretical doctrines among the Irish members.[47]

The influence of Molesworth shows clearly in the classical republican rhetoric employed by the students, who according to the college rector had been corrupted by 'foolish notions put into their Heads by unthinking and selfish Men, concerning Matters of Government and publick Affairs'.[48] Disenchanted with the scholastic university curriculum, Arbuckle and a few others had been pursuing an alternative syllabus suggested by the Viscount. Recommended reading included Harrington, Toland and Shaftesbury, as well as Molesworth's own pamphlets.[49] Accordingly, Arbuckle's perception of the Glasgow dispute was hardening; where he once saw the electoral rights as 'a kind of feather in our caps', he now spoke of a battle between liberty and arbitrary power.[50] An account of Smith's expulsion, published in 1722, was phrased in similar terms: the author noted 'the happy resemblance between the academic and national constitutions, both founded on the generous old *Gothic* rule, governing all by all'.[51] Another of Molesworth's correspondents hailed the Glasgow troubles as an example of a 'revival of ancient virtue and the love of true liberty' which was sweeping through Britain. Inevitably these events passed into university mythology, and in later decades Glasgow students would learn of the heroic 'contest between aristocracy and democracy' which had taken place in the 1720s.[52]

As a direct result of the campaigns of the rebellious *Scoto-Hiberni* the college was reorganized by a Royal Visitation in 1726, but the significance of this bizarre episode does not end there. In the course of the dissensions a party took shape in the faculty which sympathized with the students and advocated the sort of liberal educational reforms associated with Shaftesbury. Naturally they were eager to recruit like-minded fellows. It was the leader of this faction, Alexander Dunlop, the professor of Greek, who secured the election of Hutcheson to the moral philosophy chair in 1729, after a bitter contest with the principal.[53] The partisans of enlightenment were greatly strengthened by the accession of the Irish philosopher who, according to one student, took control of all university affairs in conjunction with Dunlop.[54] The exertions of this enlightened caucus culminated in the election of William Leechman to the divinity chair in 1743, carried by the rector's casting vote to 'the furious indignation of our zealots'.[55] This victory marked a decisive shift in the balance of power within the faculty: Leechman, whose election Hutcheson predicted would 'put a new face on theology in Scotland' would later become principal of the college.[56]

IV

When Hutcheson took up his chair in 1730 the battle for Moderate values was just beginning, and a good deal of circumspection was in order. The suspicious Robert Wodrow noted with approval that Hutcheson started off by teaching Carmichael's edition of Pufendorf, and chose for his inaugural lecture 'a very safe generall subject'.[57] Yet Pufendorf (and Locke) smacked too much of Hobbes for Hutcheson's liking, hence his complaint that philosophers had reduced morality to a mask for self-interest, overlooking the classical virtues.[58] When Hutcheson published a short textbook for the use of his students he therefore signalled his intention to break with the prevalent framework. In addition to the natural law theories of Grotius, Pufendorf and Locke, he recommended the civic humanism of Cicero and the ancients, Shaftesbury and Harrington.[59]

Hutcheson's picture of humankind in its natural state was designed as a refutation of Hobbes's war of all against all. Before civil society, he contends, humans were joined by natural bonds of goodwill, and their conduct towards each other subject to the regulations prescribed by the moral sense.[60] The law of nature, to which Hutcheson devoted so much space, was nothing more than the formal expression of these rules. Since natural rights belong to all the state of nature is also a state of equality.[61] But our benevolent disposition is not always sufficient to overcome our selfish passions, and the consequent disagreements make necessary the institution of civil society. It follows that all political authority must be founded on the consent of the people. Here Hutcheson adopts the threefold social contract of Pufendorf: the population constitutes itself as a political community, agrees to a form of government, and promises obedience to the law.[62] The specific details of the contract are not important, however; what matters is that civil power is held in trust for the promotion of the public good, for as Hutcheson reiterates 'the general happiness is the supreme end of all political union'.[63]

In the *System* Hutcheson champions the rights of women, servants and slaves, animals, colonies and conquered nations, arguing that all authority must be exercised for the benefit of the governed. 'Mankind have generally been a great deal too tame and tractable,' he laments, 'hence so many wretched forms of power have always enslaved nine-tenths of the nations of the world, where they have the fullest rights to make all efforts for a change.'[64] He consistently defends the right of an oppressed people to rebel against the sovereign. Furthermore, if a nation finds that the constitution it has chosen is dangerous, it has the right to revoke the powers granted to the government and remodel the political system as it sees fit.[65] The doctrine of resistance, argued Hutcheson, was less likely to produce sedition and rebellion than unbounded licence to vicious rulers. A bad polity may lead to harsh oppression whereas in the state of nature,

> where the manners of a neighbourhood are not yet corrupted by ease, wealth, and luxury, there might be much happiness, and simplicity, and innocence of manners, much zeal for mutual defence, and for preserving justice toward each other, and even some considerable improvements in arts.[66]

Turning to the constitutional machinery of the state Hutcheson identifies himself as a classical republican, acknowledging his debt to Harrington. Considering the pros and cons of the simple forms of government – monarchy, aristocracy and democracy – Hutcheson, like any good Whig, counselled a mixture of all three, but his ideal polity was a far cry from the King, Lords, and Commons of the British constitution. The largest share of legislative power should be committed to a popular assembly, consisting of deputies elected by ballot. The distribution of representatives should reflect the wealth and size of population in each district.[67] Since a wide diffusion of property was considered necessary to underpin a democratic constitution, Hutcheson's hypothetical republic, like Oceana, required the enactment of an agrarian law to prevent a monopoly of wealth.[68] A senate, with powers of deliberating and initiating legislation, was also to be elected by the people from distinguished individuals. A system of rotation would entail the retirement of a third or a quarter of the senators every one or two years.[69] Finally, to maintain the balance between the two assemblies, a 'monarchick or dictatorial power' was suggested, either a hereditary family or a council elected by the senate.[70] On religious matters, needless to say, Hutcheson supported a wide measure of toleration.[71]

V

The extent and nature of Hutcheson's influence on eighteenth-century political and social thought differed as it was carried through the various provinces of the Anglo-Saxon world. In Scotland, some distant echoes of Hutcheson's brand of classical republicanism can be found in the 'principles of Government' expounded by John Millar, the Glasgow professor of civil law from 1761 until 1801. A staunch Whig, Millar was accused in 1784 of propagating republican doctrines and was obliged to tone down his lectures accordingly.[72] The Ulster radical Steel Dickson, who had heard the unedited version, drew the lesson that 'rational republicanism' had never had a fair trial.[73] He would recall Millar's classes during the American war: 'Having paid considerable attention to jurisprudence, in the course of my studies, and read Locke, Montesquieu, Pufendorf, &c. &c. my mind instantly revolted against the mad crusade.'[74]

With the possible exception of Millar, none of Hutcheson's successors was to match the radicalism of the *System*. But all of them, to a greater or lesser degree, followed his lead in the schooling of polite and public-spirited citizens who might play a beneficial role in the community. The preoccupation of Scottish moral philosophers with the inculcation of civic virtue can be traced to the didactic moralism of Hutcheson's teaching. At a period when lectures were generally dictated in Latin from the pulpit, Hutcheson was renowned for his dynamic, hortatory, classroom style. Even students who were unconvinced by the moral sense theory, like Alexander Carlyle, raved about the professor's teaching:

> He was a good-looking man of an engaging countenance. He delivered his lectures without notes, walking backwards and forwards in the arena of his room. As his elocution was good, and his voice and manner pleasing, he raised the attention of his hearers at all times; and when the subject led him to explain and enforce the moral virtues and duties, he displayed a fervent and persuasive eloquence which was irresistible.[75]

Another of Hutcheson's disciples recalled how he 'lectured, to appearance, *extempore*, and walked up and down the classroom, and spoke with an animation of countenance, voice, and gesture, which instantly went to the heart'.[76]

Tributes of this sort abound in the biographies and reminiscences of Hutcheson's pupils and should be taken seriously as an indication of his success in introducing this activist, didactic strain into the culture of enlightened Scotland. Inevitably, the professor-preacher was a tough act to follow. Thomas Craigie, Hutcheson's short-lived successor, made valiant but unconvincing efforts to imitate him. Adam Smith, who was elected to the chair in 1752, was initially given a hard time by the disciples of his 'never-to-be-forgotten' teacher. After a brief stab at Hutcheson's 'ease and animation' he gave up and settled for reading his lectures from his desk.[77] Much more typical of the Scottish moral philosophers, however, was Adam Ferguson, who consciously modelled his lectures on Hutchesonian moralism.[78]

The pedagogical activities of Hutcheson and his emulators formed an integral part of moral philosophy, as they conceived of it. Given the role they accorded to rhetoric in shaping the human personality, it was natural that they should direct all their energies towards presenting the beauty of virtue to their youthful scholars. The Hutchesonian ideal of the moral philosopher ruled out David Hume, whose sceptical analysis of human nature had exposed the moral sense as an artificial creation of custom and convention. Hume's well-known reply to Hutcheson's accusation that his work lacked 'a certain warmth in the cause of virtue' brings out well the difference between the two men: 'There are different ways of examining the mind as well as the body', he argued, 'One may consider it either as an anatomist or as a painter; either to discover its most secret springs and principles or to describe the grace and beauty of its actions.'[79] That Hutcheson's enquiries into the human constitution had broken new ground Hume always acknowledged, but the failure of the Glasgow professor to push his enquiries to their logical conclusion exasperated him. The full consequences of Hume's poor performance in 'the cause of virtue' became apparent when he announced his candidacy for the Edinburgh chair of moral philosophy in 1744. With naïve surprise he found Hutcheson, who had refused the position himself, foremost among his opponents: 'What can be the meaning of this conduct in that celebrated and benevolent moralist, I cannot imagine.'[80] Ironically neither Hume nor Smith fit into the mainstream of the Scottish Enlightenment; at best they stand with one foot in and one foot out.

A large percentage of the students who listened to the prelections of Hutcheson and his emulators were of course *Scoto-Hiberni*. Thomas Reid, complaining to a friend of the 'great number of stupid Irish teagues who attend classes for two or three years to qualify them for teaching schools', reckoned that 'near a third' of the four or five hundred students at Glasgow came from Ireland, a figure which is confirmed by the university records.[81] These Scottish-trained schoolmasters, ministers and physicians formed an important part of the communications network of the Enlightenment, not only in Ulster but also in colonial America. In the last quarter of the eighteenth century a handful of academies were founded by Ulster Presbyterian ministers, the most notable of which were situated in Belfast and Strabane.[82] In his opening address to the Strabane academy, where the curriculum was naturally modelled on Glasgow university, the Rev. William Crawford discoursed on the importance of enlightening the mind, refining the taste, and cultivating the moral sense.[83] There can be little doubt that as in the Presbytery of Antrim, which trained its own candidates for the ministry, divinity scholars were examined on Hutcheson's works.[84]

Despite ambitious beginnings, the Ulster academies would never be anything more than grammar schools. Nevertheless, these seminaries had much in common with the more successful American ventures outlined in Benjamin Franklin's *Proposals Relating to the Education of Youth in Pennsylvania* (1749) and William Smith's *A General Idea of the College of Mirania* (1753), both of which were Scottish in inspiration. Smith's blueprint for a New York college envisaged 'one great school of virtue' where students would study Hutcheson in conjunction with Pufendorf and Locke.[85] The same authorities were recommended to students at the College of New Jersey (later Princeton) where John Witherspoon was elected president in 1768. In spite of his well-publicized objections to Hutcheson's 'new light' theology, Witherspoon's lectures closely followed the *System*, especially where they touched on natural rights, the contractual basis of government, and the right of resistance.[86] Smith and Witherspoon were both Scots, but many of the Presbyterian academies which offered higher education courses in the western and southern settlements were staffed by Ulster Presbyterian emigrants.[87] The most dedicated of Hutcheson's American disciples was Francis Alison, a Presbyterian settler from Donegal educated at Edinburgh and probably Glasgow, who established the New London Academy in Pennsylvania, and in the 1750s became Vice-Provost and professor of logic and moral philosophy at the College of Philadelphia.[88] Alison consulted his mentor for advice concerning the curriculum and books to be used in the New London Academy, and it has been demonstrated that his moral philosophy lectures were taken almost verbatim from Hutcheson's *Short Introduction*.[89]

The fundamental question remains: who practised what Hutcheson and his fellow moralists preached? One answer has been suggested by a profile of Francis Alison's pupils, who included five future signatories of the Declaration of Independence, and fifteen members of the Continental Congress between 1776 and 1783.[90] In Ireland, where Presbyterians were excluded from public life until the repeal of the Test Act in 1780, only a handful of Dissenters were able to dent the monopoly of political power exercised by the Protestant Ascendancy, usually at the price of occasional conformity. It may be significant that the best known of these MPs was Sir John Blackwood, who had completed an MA thesis on civil government under the direction of Hutcheson at Glasgow. A copy of this treatise was preserved at Blackwood's Ballyleidy estate and was said to merit 'the attention of every legislator, and of every man who wishes to know the principles of civil government'.[91] Despite the restrictions imposed by the sacramental test, however, distinctive Presbyterian attitudes to church and state were sustained by political sermons, some of which were published. Gilbert Kennedy's *The Wicked Ruler*, preached on the occasion of the 1745 Jacobite rebellion, cited Locke's *Second Treatise* on the equality of mankind, but his discussion of man's natural benevolence and the formation of civil society, his defence of religious toleration, his insistence that even the state of nature is preferable to arbitrary rule, and the language he uses to assert the right of resistance, all tell us more about the impact of Hutcheson's lectures on the Dissenting clergy.[92] It is therefore no surprise that when the Money Bill dispute of the 1750s offered an unusual opportunity for extra-parliamentary activity, we should find Kennedy and other friends of Hutcheson like the Rev. Thomas Drennan, Dr Alexander Haliday and William Bruce active in the Patriot Clubs of Antrim and Down.[93]

In the light of the continuing research on eighteenth-century concepts of citizenship it seems incredible that the Irish Volunteer movement, which finally gave a voice to the Ulster Presbyterians, has received so little attention from historians. It seems likely that future scholars will turn away from the dubious achievements of 1782 to study popular politicization, especially in Ulster, and the importance of the Volunteer associations as a means of affirming civic identity. As companies from all over the northern province congregated for sham fights, reviews and conventions, the political sermons of the Dissenting clergy reached a wider audience than ever before. The ideal of the citizen-in-arms, enshrined in the first resolution of the Dungannon Convention and in the constitutions of many Volunteer associations, was elaborated in sermons by William Steel Dickson, William Crawford, James Crombie and others. These ministers, educated at Glasgow while the Scottish militia debates were in full swing, compared the moral corruption of the British empire, as evidenced by the American war, with the degeneration of the classical republics, and maintained that the public spirit of the Volunteers was the only means of preserving liberty.[94] For the young radical William Drennan, the Volunteers not only protected the country from invasion and maintained domestic peace, but promoted religious liberality, consolidated national feeling, preserved the liberties of the people, and circulated republican virtue through the ranks of Irish society.[95] As A.T.Q. Stewart has shown, it was Drennan's Determination to recapture the momentum of the early Volunteer movement which led him to propose a 'benevolent conspiracy' for the attainment of Hutcheson's famous principle 'the greatest happiness of the greatest number', a scheme which later evolved into the Society of United Irishmen.[96]

There is an impressive continuity here – both genealogical and ideological – between Hutcheson's circle of friends and the leading Belfast reformers of the revolutionary era.[97] The most outstanding example is Dr Alexander Haliday, the son of Hutcheson's friend Samuel, and the moving spirit behind the Northern Whig club, the voice of moderate reformers established in 1790. According to the club's declaration, drawn up by Haliday, government is an original compact between the governors and the governed, instituted for the good of the whole community; that in a limited monarchy, or, more properly speaking (respect being had to the constitution of these realms), a regal commonwealth, the majority is in the people; and though the person on the throne is superior to any individual, he is but the servant of the nation.[98]

The 'Volunteer Earl', Lord Charlemont, found the phrase 'regal commonwealth' difficult to swallow, but it was merely vintage Whiggism for Haliday, who had been 'nurtured under the philosophy of Hutcheson' and had belonged to the Patriot Club of County Antrim in the 1750s.[99] Turning to the more radical end of the Presbyterian spectrum, William Drennan attributed his ardent patriotism to the influence of his father, another close friend of Hutcheson, and confessed his debt to the early non-subscribing ministers.[100] Finally, the Rev. William Bruce, whose early radicalism was to cool so dramatically in the 1790s, was descended from the Dublin publisher of the same name.[101] Of course one must be wary of reading too much into these connections. In the late eighteenth century new questions were pushed to the fore by events in America and France as natural rights theories and republican ideas were redefined and clarified to meet new situations. Thus one of Hutcheson's treatises found its way into the library of the United Irishman William Tennent, from which other members of the Belfast society borrowed books; but the list, made in 1818, contained many other names: enlightened Scots like Blair, Beattie, Turnbull and Reid, as well as Locke, Delolme, Paley and Voltaire.[102] Presumably Tennent had also possessed copies of Paine and Godwin before his reincarnation as a respectable Belfast merchant and banker.

VI

Any final assessment of Hutcheson's contribution to the political and social ideologies of Britain, Ireland and America must take into consideration the distinction, made at the beginning of this chapter, between the Scottish Enlightenment as a school of philosophy on the one hand and as an attempt to reform Hanoverian political culture on the other. When this distinction is borne in mind, it becomes clear that Francis Hutcheson's teachings point in two contrary directions. The epistemology – his insistence that our knowledge of good and evil comes from our powers of perception rather than our rational understanding of the law of nature – leads to scepticism. The verdict of later philosophers was that Hutcheson had let in Hume by the back door, and to a large extent the Common Sense school of Reid and Stewart was an attempt to repair the damage. At this point it should be recalled that Hutcheson seems to have grown dissatisfied with his own work towards the end of his life. *A System of Moral Philosophy*, begun in the late 1730s, was still incomplete when he died over fifteen years later. He complained to Thomas Drennan that he 'had pretty much dropped the thoughts of some great Designs I had once sketched out. In running over my papers I am quite dissatisfied with Method Style Matter & some Reasonings.'[103] It is tempting to suggest that Hutcheson, who had met Hume in the winter of 1739–40, realized that the younger man had undermined his attempts to provide a scientific basis for his mixture of Christian theology and classical morality.

This mattered little to Hutcheson's pupils and associates who announced the publication of *A System of Moral Philosophy* in 1755. For them the significance of Hutcheson's teaching lay not in the intricacies of the moral sense, but in his reconciliation of the kingdom of God with the republic of virtue. In Ireland subscriptions were collected by Hutcheson's old comrades William Bruce and Dr Haliday.[104] The list included a new generation of non-subscribing ministers whose sermons steered clear of Calvinist doctrine and aimed instead to imitate the civic moralism of their teacher. At Glasgow William Leechman supplied an introduction extolling Hutcheson's 'rational enthusiasm for the interests of learning, liberty, religion and virtue'.[105] Robert Foulis, the university printer and another of the professor's protégés, described the book simply as 'a capital work for promoting the cause of virtue, accompanied with just notions of government and Liberty'.[106] Ironically it is this unsophisticated reading of his treatises and textbooks which, for the historian of political ideas at least, must serve as Hutcheson's epitaph.

NOTES

I am indebted to Dr Nicholas Phillipson of the University of Edinburgh, and to Dr David Hayton of the History of Parliament, London, for many helpful comments on an earlier draft of this chapter.

1 Marianne Elliott, *Partners in Revolution: The United Irishmen and France*, New Haven and London, Yale University Press, 1982, xiii, 20, 27–9; idem, *Wolfe Tone: Prophet of Irish Independence*, New Haven and London, Yale University Press, 1989, 103–4, 116–7; idem, *Watchmen in Sion: The Protestant Idea of Liberty*, Derry, Field Day Theatre Company, 1985, esp. 6–12.

2 R. F. Foster, *Modern Ireland 1600–1972*, London, Allen Lane, 1988, 265.

3 J. C. D. Clark, *English Society 1688–1832: Ideology, Social Structure and Political Practice During the Ancien Regime*, Cambridge, Cambridge University Press, 1985, ch. 5; Martin Fitzpatrick, 'Toleration and truth', *Enlightenment and Dissent*, 1 (1982), 3–31; Mark Philp, 'Rational religion and political radicalism', ibid., 4 (1985), 35–46; James E. Bradley, *Religion, Revolution and Radicalism: Nonconformity in Eighteenth-Century Politics and Society*, Cambridge, Cambridge University Press, 1990; Russell E. Richey, 'The origins of British radicalism: the changing rationale for dissent', *Eighteenth-Century Studies*, 7 (1973–4), 179–92.

4 J. G. A. Pocock, *Virtue, Commerce, and History: Essays on Political Thought and History, Chiefly in the Eighteenth Century*, Cambridge, Cambridge University Press, 1985, esp. chs 2, 11.

5 Douglas Sloan, *The Scottish Enlightenment and the American College Ideal*, New York, Teachers College Press, Columbia University, 1971, ch. 2.

6 For the English Dissenting academies see H. McLachlan, *English Education Under the Test Acts*, Manchester, Manchester University Press, 1931.

7 Hugh Trevor-Roper, 'The Scottish Enlightenment', *Studies on Voltaire and the Eighteenth Century*, 58 (1967), 1637.

8 For the most part the 'science of man' was restricted to the study of the male personality, but some of the Scottish philosophers also examined the changing role of women in society, a subject which has so far received little notice.

9 The term originates with Pocock. John Robertson prefers 'civic tradition' in his 'The Scottish Enlightenment at the end of the civic tradition', in Istvan Hont and Michael Ignatieff (eds), *Wealth and Virtue: The Shaping of Political Economy in the Scottish Enlightenment*, Cambridge, Cambridge University Press, 1983, 139. 'Civic humanism' can be a misleading term; I have retained it here merely as an explanatory device.

10 This neglected dimension is the subject of Mark Goldie's 'The civil religion of James Harrington', in Anthony Pagden (ed.), *The Languages of Political Theory in Early-Modern Europe*, Cambridge, Cambridge University Press, 1987, 197–222.

11 Lawrence Klein contrasts Fletcher with Shaftesbury in 'Liberty, manners and politeness in early eighteenth-century England', *Historical Journal*, XXXIII, 3 (1989), esp. 585.

12 Phillipson's thesis has been expanded and refined in a series of essays: 'Culture and society in the eighteenth-century province: the case of Edinburgh and the Scottish Enlightenment', in Lawrence Stone (ed.), *The University in Society*, 2 vols, Princeton, Princeton University Press, 1975, II, 407–48; 'The Scottish Enlightenment', in Roy Porter and Mikulas Teich (eds), *The Enlightenment in National Context*, Cambridge, Cambridge University Press, 1981, 19–40; 'Politics, politeness and the Anglicization of early eighteenth-century Scottish culture', in Roger A. Mason (ed.), *Scotland and England 1286–1815*, Edinburgh, John Donald, 1987, 226–46.

13 Robertson, 'The Scottish Enlightenment at the end of the civic tradition', 141.

14 The ideological aspects of the militia question are explored in John Robertson, *The Scottish Enlightenment and the Militia Issue*, Edinburgh, John Donald, 1985.

15 Richard B. Sher, *Church and University in the Scottish Enlightenment: The Moderate Literati of Edinburgh*, Princeton, Princeton University Press, 1985.

16 William Hamilton (ed.), *The Collected Works of Dugald Stewart*, 11 vols, Edinburgh, 1854–60, I, 428, 429n.

17 See W. T. Blackstone, *Francis Hutcheson and Contemporary Ethical Theory*, Athens, Ga., University of Georgia Press, 1965; the articles by K. Winkler and D. F. Norton in *Journal of the History of Philosophy*, 23 (1985); T. D. Campbell 'Francis Hutcheson: "Father" of the Scottish Enlightenment', in R. H. Campbell and Andrew S. Skinner (eds), *Origins and Nature of the Scottish Enlightenment*, Edinburgh, John Donald, 1982, 167–185 looks at the relationship between Hutcheson's epistemology and his political thought.

18 The standard biography is W. R. Scott, *Francis Hutcheson: His Life, Teaching and Position in the History of Philosophy*, London, Cambridge University Press, 1900.

19 Francis Hutcheson, *A Short Introduction to Moral Philosophy*, Glasgow, 1747, i.

20 John Dunn, 'The politics of Locke in England and America in the eighteenth

century', in J. W. Yolton (ed.), *John Locke: Problems and Perspectives*, Cambridge, Cambridge University Press, 1969, 45–80; Carmichael's treatment of natural law is discussed in James Moore and Michael Silverthorne, 'Natural sociability and natural rights in the moral philosophy of Gershom Carmichael', in V. Hope (ed.), *Philosophers of the Scottish Enlightenment*, Edinburgh, Edinburgh University Press, 1984, 1–12.

21 [William Tisdall] *The Conduct of the Dissenters of Ireland*, Dublin, 1712, 55; Francis Hutcheson, *A System of Moral Philosophy*, 2 vols, Glasgow, 1755, viii.

22 John Witherspoon, *Ecclesiastical Characteristics . . . Wherein is Shewn a Plain and Easy Way of Attaining to the Character of a Moderate Man, as at Present in Repute in the Church of Scotland*, Glasgow, 1753, 25, 27. Hutcheson had previously been attacked in *Shaftesbury's Ghost Conjur'd: or, a Letter to Mr Francis Hutcheson Professor of Moral Philosophy in the University of Glasgow*, [Glasgow] 1738.

23 William Tisdall, *The Nature and Tendency of Popular Phrases*, Dublin, [1714?], 7.

24 In addition to the two pamphlets already cited, see [Tisdall] *A Sample of Treu-Bleu Presbyterian-Loyalty*, Dublin, 1709.

25 [James Kirkpatrick] *An Historical Essay Upon the Loyalty of Presbyterians*, [Belfast?], 1713, 4–6; the English background is discussed in J. P. Kenyon, *Revolution Principles: The Politics of Party, 1689–1720*, Cambridge, Cambridge University Press, 1977, chs 7–8.

26 [Kirkpatrick] *Historical Essay*, 21.

27 [John McBride] *A Sample of Jet-Black Prelatic Calumny, in Answer to a Pamphlet, Called Treu-Blue Presbyterian Loyalty*, Glasgow, 1713, 8.

28 John Abernethy, *The People's Choice, the Lord's Anointed: A Thanksgiving Sermon for his Most Excellent Majesty King George his Happy Accession to the Throne, his Arrival and Coronation*, Belfast, 1714, 9.

29 [Kirkpatrick], *Historical Essay*, 505.

30 John Toland (ed.), *The Oceana and Other Works of James Harrington*, London, 1737, viii.

31 See the preface to his *An Account of Denmark as it was in the Year 1692*, London, 1694.

32 Robert Molesworth, *The Principles of a Real Whig, Contained in a Preface to the Famous Hotman's Franco-Gallia*, London, 1711, reprinted by the London Association, London, 1775, 7. Further information on Molesworth can be found in Caroline Robbins, *The Eighteenth-Century Commonwealthman: Studies in the Transmission, Development and Circumstances of English Liberal Thought from the Restoration of Charles II until the War with the Thirteen Colonies*, Cambridge, Mass., Harvard University Press, 1959.

33 *A Collection of Letters and Essays on Several Subjects, Lately Published in the Dublin Journal*, 2 vols, London, 1729, I, v.

34 *A Collection of Letters*, I, 324–5. Irish issues are dealt with ibid., I, 259–60, 297–306; Hutcheson's attacks on Hobbes and Mandeville can be found ibid., I, 77–107, 370–407.

35 ibid., I, 5.

36 Public Record Office of Northern Ireland (hereafter PRONI), T.3060/5, 8, Hutcheson to Drennan, 17 April 1738, 15 June 1741; National Library of Scotland (hereafter NLS), MS 9252, Dunlop papers, ff. 106, 125, Hutcheson to Bruce, 9 February 1737, 15 May 1738.

37 Bruce assisted John Abernethy with *Scarce and Valuable Tracts and Sermons*, London, 1751. Dr Williams's Library, London, contains a copy of this collection which belonged to the commonwealthman Thomas Hollis. A manuscript

note from the editor, Richard Baron, explains that the publication was suggested by Hutcheson while Baron was a student at Glasgow.

38 M. Pollard, *Dublin's Trade in Books*, Oxford, Clarendon Press, 1989, 198–203.

39 Details of this quarrel are taken from *A Short Account of the Late Treatment of the Students of the University of G-----w*, Dublin, 1722, probably written by John Smith. For the background see James Coutts, *A History of the University of Glasgow*, Glasgow, James MacLehose, 1909, 197–204; David Murray, *Memories of the Old College of Glasgow*, Jackson, Wylie & Co., Glasgow, 1927, 489–90, 326–7; Peter Jones, 'The Scottish professoriate and the polite academy' in Hont and Ignatieff (eds), *Wealth and Virtue*, 89–117; and, above all, M. A. Stewart, 'John Smith and the Molesworth circle', in *Eighteenth-Century Ireland*, II, 1987, 89–102.

40 *Short Account*, 20.

41 ibid., 20–1.

42 ibid., 22–3; see also NLS, pamphlet 1.7, no. 53.

43 *Short Account*, 16. Arbuckle's prologue to *Cato* was published in *The Edinburgh Miscellany: Consisting of Original Poems, Translations, etc*, Edinburgh, 1720, 79–81.

44 NLS, pamphlet, 1.7, nos. 48–51.

45 *Short Account*, 27–39.

46 Robert Wodrow, *Analecta: or, Materials for a History of Remarkable Providences: mostly relating to Scotch Ministers and Christians*, edited by Matthew Leishman for the Maitland Club, 4 vols, Glasgow, 1842–3, III, 184–5, 248.

47 ibid., III, 178–9, 183.

48 *Short Account*, 33.

49 See the letters from James Arbuckle, George Turnbull and William Wishart to Molesworth in Historical Manuscripts Commission, 55, *Report on Manuscripts in Various Collections*, VIII (1913), 343–4, 347–9, 351–2, 352–5, 360–1, 366–7.

50 Arbuckle to Molesworth, 31 October 1722, ibid., 351.

51 *Short Account*, 5.

52 William Wishart to [Molesworth], 13 October 1722, *Report on Manuscripts*, 347; Samuel Kenrick to John Kenrick, 3 May 1808, in W. Byng Kenrick, *Chronicles of a Non-Conformist Family: the Kenricks of Wynne Hall, Exeter and Birmingham*, Birmingham, Cornish Brothers, 1932, 149.

53 Wodrow, *Analecta*, IV, 99. Wodrow states that Dunlop had married Hutcheson's aunt.

54 John Hill Burton (ed.), *The Autobiography of Dr Alexander Carlyle of Inveresk*, London, William Blackwood & Sons, 1910, 78.

55 PRONI, T.3060/16, Francis Hutcheson to Thomas Drennan, 20 February, 1743/4; Coutts, *History*, 237.

56 PRONI, T.3060/11, 16, Hutcheson to Drennan, 31 May 1742, 20 February 1743/4; see also Hutcheson to William Mure, 23 November 1743, *Selections from the Family Papers Preserved at Caldwell*, 3 vols, edited by William Mure for the Maitland Club, Glasgow, 1853–4, part 2, vol. I, 53–5.

57 Wodrow, *Analecta*, IV, 185–7.

58 [Arbuckle], A Collection of Letters, vol. 1, 78.

59 Hutcheson, *Short Introduction*, ii–iv.

60 Hutcheson, *System*, I, Book I, 24–5.

61 ibid., I, Book II, 299.

62 ibid., II, Book III, 212–27.

63 ibid., II, Book III, 226, 272.

64 ibid., II, Book III, 280.

65 ibid., II, Book III, 270–7.
66 ibid., II, Book III, 218.
67 ibid., II, Book III, 260.
68 ibid., II, Book III, 259.
69 ibid., II, Book III, 261–2.
70 ibid., II, Book III, 263.
71 ibid., II, Book III, 310–13.
72 William C. Lehmann, *John Millar of Glasgow 1735–1801*, Cambridge, Cambridge University Press, 1960, 71–2.
73 W. S. Dickson, *A Narrative of the Confinement and Exile of William Steel Dickson*, Dublin, 1812, 4–5.
74 ibid., 7.
75 *Autobiography of Dr Alexander Carlyle*, 78.
76 James Wodrow (ed.), *Sermons by William Leechman, D. D., Late Principal of the College of Glasgow to which is Prefixed Some Account of the Author's Life, and of his Lectures*, 2 vols, London, 1789, I, 28.
77 Dr Williams's Library, London (hereafter DWL), MS 24.157, no. 263, James Wodrow to Samuel Kenrick, 5 July 1808; see also DWL, MS 24.157, no. 16, Wodrow to Kenrick, 21 January 1752.
78 See Richard B. Sher, 'Professors of virtue: the social history of the Edinburgh moral philosophy chair in the eighteenth century', in M. A. Stewart (ed.), *Studies in the Philosophy of the Scottish Enlightenment*, Oxford, Clarendon Press, 1990, 94–9, 118–20.
79 Hume to Hutcheson, 17 September 1739, J. Y. T. Grieg (ed.), *The Letters of David Hume*, 2 vols, Oxford, Clarendon Press, 1932, I, 32.
80 Hume to William Mure, 4 August 1744, *Letters of David Hume*, I, 58.
81 Reid to Andrew Skene, 14 November 1764, in William Hamilton (ed.), *The Works of Thomas Reid, D. D., Now Fully Collected, with Selections from his Unpublished Letters*, 2nd edn, Edinburgh, 1849, 40–3; W. Innes Addison, *A Roll of Graduates of the University of Glasgow, 1727 to 1897*, Glasgow, 1898.
82 For a general history of the Irish Dissenting academies see David Kennedy, 'The Ulster academies and the teaching of science (1785–1825)' in *Irish Ecclesiastical Record*, 5th ser., 63, (January–June 1944), 25–38, and Herbert McLachlan, 'The Irish academies', in idem, *Essays and Addresses*, Manchester, Manchester University Press, 1950, 167–77.
83 William Crawford, *Regulations of the Strabane Academy. And an Address to the Students in General, on Opening that Seminary, Delivered on Monday, November the 7th, 1785*, Strabane, 1785, 11–19.
84 PRONI, T.1053/1, Records of the Presbytery of Antrim, II, 61.
85 'A General Idea of the College of Mirania', first published in 1753, reprinted in *The Works of William Smith, D. D., Late Provost of the College and Academy of Philadelphia*, 2 vols, Philadelphia, 1803, I, 226, 184; see also 'Account of the college, academy, and charitable school of Philadelphia', ibid., I, 239.
86 Thomas P. Miller, 'Witherspoon, Blair and the rhetoric of civic humanism' in Richard B. Sher and Jeffrey R. Smitten (eds), *Scotland and America in the Age of Enlightenment*, Edinburgh, Edinburgh University Press, 1990, 105–8.
87 Sloan, *Scottish Enlightenment*, esp. chs 2 and 3.
88 Further information on Alison can be found in Elizabeth A. Ingersoll, 'Francis Alison: American *philosophe* 1705–1779', unpublished PhD thesis, University of Delaware, 1974.

89 PRONI, T.3060/21, Hutcheson to Drennan, 16 April 1746; David Fate Norton, 'Francis Hutcheson in America' in *SVEC*, 154 (1976), 1553–5.

90 Norton, 'Francis Hutcheson in America', 1567–8. Gary Wills finds some echoes of Hutcheson in the Declaration of Independence in *Inventing America: Jefferson's Declaration of Independence*, Garden City, NY, Doubleday, 1978, esp. 192–205, 228–39, 250–5. See also Caroline Robbins, ' "When it is that colonies may turn independent": an analysis of the environment and politics of Francis Hutcheson (1694–1746)' in *William and Mary Quarterly*, 3rd ser., XI (1954), 214–51.

91 *Belfast Monthly Magazine*, XI (1813), 113.

92 Gilbert Kennedy, *The Wicked Ruler: or, The Mischiefs of Absolute Abitrary Power*, Belfast, 1745.

93 [Henry Joy] *Historical Collections Relative to the Town of Belfast*, Belfast, 1817, 90–102. For the context see Declan O'Donovan, 'The Money Bill dispute of 1753', in Thomas Bartlett and D. W. Hayton (eds), *Penal Era and Golden Age: Essays in Irish History, 1690–1800*, Belfast, Ulster Historical Foundation, 1979, 55–87.

94 James Crombie, *A sermon on the love of country. Preached before the First Company of Belfast Volunteers, Sunday 19th July 1778*, Belfast, 1778; William Crawford, *The connection betwixt courage and the moral virtues considered, in a sermon preached before the Strabane Rangers, on Sunday the twelfth of September, 1779*, Strabane, 1779, 19–20; William Steel Dickson, *A sermon on the propriety and advantages of acquiring the knowledge and use of firearms in times of danger, preached before the Echlinville Volunteers on Sunday the 28th of March 1779*, Belfast, 1779, 10–11, 15; Andrew Alexander, *The use of arms: a sermon preached before the Strabane, Finwater, and Urney Volunteers and Strabane Rangers October 1779*, Strabane, 1779, 11–13, 21–2; Samuel Barber, manuscript sermon preached to the Castlewellan Rangers and Rathfriland Volunteers, 24 October 1779, in the possession of the Presbyterian Historical Society, Belfast, 3, 9.

95 See Drennan's essay 'The Volunteers of Ireland', in William Guthrie, *An Improved System of Modern Geography*, enlarged edition inscribed to the Royal Irish Academy, Dublin, 1789, 495–512.

96 A. T. Q. Stewart, ' "A stable unseen power": Dr William Drennan and the origins of the United Irishmen', in John Bossy and Peter Jupp (eds), *Essays Presented to Michael Roberts*, Belfast, Blackstaff, 1976, 88. The formula crops up elsewhere in Drennan's writings, e.g. *Letters of Orellana, an Irish Helot*, Dublin, 1785, 47.

97 This is the subject of my ' "The son of an honest man": William Drennan and the Dissenting tradition', in David Dickson, Daire Keogh and Kevin Whelan (eds), *The United Irishmen: A Bicentennial Perspective*, Lilliput Press, 1993.

98 Haliday to Charlemont, 18 February 1790, HMC, 13th Report (1894), appendix, part VIII, *The Manuscripts and Correspondence of James, First Earl of Charlemont*, II, 115.

99 Charlemont to Haliday, 9 March 1790, *Manuscripts*, 118; William Drennan, *Fugitive Pieces in Verse and Prose*, Belfast, 1815, 158.

100 'Intended defence, on a trial for sedition, in the year 1794' reprinted in J. F. Larkin (ed.), *The Trial of William Drennan*, Dublin, Irish Academic Press, 1991, 124–5.

101 Bruce employed Hutcheson's arguments in a speech against capital punishment. See PRONI, Bruce papers, D.2673 'A discourse delivered before the College Society in the University of Glasgow' dated 22 March 1777.

102 PRONI, Tennent papers, D.1748/A/3/4/8, list of books belonging to William Tennent dated 24 April 1818.
103 PRONI, T.3060/8, Hutcheson to Drennan, 15 June 1741.
104 PRONI, Bruce papers, T.3041/1/D4, Alexander Haliday to William Bruce, 27 March 1754.
105 Hutcheson, *System*, xxvi.
106 *Notices and Documents Illustrative of the Literary History of Glasgow, During the Greater Part of the Last Century*, edited by William J. Duncan for the Maitland Club, Glasgow, 1831, 21.

4 The emergence and submergence of Irish socialism, 1821–51

Vincent Geoghegan

It will be argued in this chapter that there was a much more diverse and interesting range of socialisms in Ireland during the first half of the nineteenth century than the existing literature suggests. At the risk of caricaturing the standard account, we are usually presented with Thompson, Ralahine, sundry Irish Chartists and labour activists *in England*, working-class and trade union militancy, and various non-socialist thinkers who are included because of their social radicalism (Lalor, for example). This inadequate picture does, however, reflect the marginality of early Irish socialism. The various writers and movements discussed below have been easily missed because they were relatively isolated and peripheral, and left little in the way of historical traces. Alternative ideologies triumphed in history and historiography. Where, for example, artisan socialism sought to oppose O'Connellite nationalism, it was crushed, and effectively vanished from the historical record; or when *The Irishman* sought to combine socialism with radical nationalism it was absorbed by the latter and reduced to an insignificant footnote in the rise of nationalism. It is not therefore the claim of this chapter that a major historical force has failed to receive its due, but that an historically interesting phenomenon has been the victim of inadequate treatment. The concluding year in the title of the chapter is not arbitrary because the mid-century point marks the end of a particularly turbulent period of economic, social and political dislocation. Inevitably, this means that the Fenianisn/Socialism/First International relationship, which intervenes before the socialist revival in the 1880s, is not discussed. However this relationship has already received scholarly coverage elsewhere.[1] Our own discussion will deal with the following forms of socialism: Elite Socialism, Artisan Socialism, Socialism and Nationalism, and Christian Socialism.

ELITE SOCIALISM

We will not be dealing in this section with the two examples which usually take up all of the discussion on early Irish socialism – William Thompson and the Ralahine community. Whereas a disproportionally large amount has been written on both of these, virtual silence surrounds other examples: this short chapter aims to cast light on previously dark areas, and thereby contribute to a broader picture. This is in no way to disparage these two outstanding achievements of early Irish socialism. Thompson (1775–1833)[2] was undoubtedly the greatest Irish socialist theorist of the nineteenth century. His distinctive blending of utilitarianism and socialism, his subtle analysis of the modalities of labour, and of the process of distribution and exchange, his critique of political and social exploitation, and his breadth of vision respecting alternatives, make him a socialist theorist of world stature. Similarly Ralahine (1831–33),[3] a product of the co-operation between an improving landlord, John Scott Vandeleur, the English Owenite Edward Craig, and the County Clare peasantry, was widely, and rightly, considered to be the most successful of the Owenite communities. A further omission will be any specific treatment of the early socialist feminism associated with Thompson and Anna Wheeler, again because they have been treated elsewhere.[4] The purpose of this section is to bring into the light early socialists ignored by the literature, thereby, hopefully, replacing an impoverished, distorted account.

The earliest forms of socialism in Ireland were developed by social and intellectual élites who saw themselves as benevolent agents of change, bringing social-scientific insight to bear upon the problems of the lower classes. When Robert Owen was invited to Ireland in 1822 by progressive landlords he found a sympathetic hearing in elite circles.[5] Although committed in the long term to the principles of self-sufficiency and self-government, the elite socialists claimed that existing intellectual and economic inequalities necessitated a more directive role in the short to medium term. This is particularly apparent in those variants which drew most heavily on Owen. Owen was committed to a social engineering approach, where the knowledgeable few brought about a transformation of the ignorant many. As such Owenism could easily merge with existing elite philanthropic traditions. However, even the more democratic socialism of William Thompson was still predicated on an initial need for intelligent leadership. Within these parameters extensive variations were possible. Two examples will be examined: Robert O'Brien and the Dublin Co-operative Society; and Henry MacCormac and the Belfast Co-operative Trading Association.

The Co-operative Magazine and Monthly Herald, a London-based journal, announced in its issue of April 1826 that a meeting 'of gentlemen favourable to the formation of a Co-operative Society' had recently (28 February) been held in Dublin. In the chair was Captain Robert O'Brien, RN,[6] who was then heavily involved with the Owenite community at Orbiston in Scotland, having invested money in the venture and moved from Ireland with his family to take part in the experiment. O'Brien's experience of Orbiston was not a happy one. The classic history of the community, Alexander Cullen's *Adventures in Socialism* (1910), describes

O'Brien as an 'autocrat . . . intolerant to those he considered beneath him'.[7] O'Brien objected to what he considered to be the open-door admission policy of the community, which had resulted in the importation of 'disreputable samples of humanity'.[8] He developed his critique in a long angry letter to the community magazine. The call in the community for 'equal distribution', which, he claimed, came from 'non-producers', was 'injustice and . . . fraud'. He repeated his attack on the 'most injudicious and indiscriminate admission of inmates', claiming that success required a union of developed personalities. He objected to the anti-Christian emphasis on natural religion, at the expense of revelation. He was appalled by the mismanagement of the educational facilities, and developed his long-held plan of establishing a fee-paying boarding school based upon Pestalozzian principles.[9] Such was the man who chaired the Dublin meeting.

It will come as no great surprise that the Dublin Co-operative Society, formed in 1827, was a genteel and select body. The role of the Society was that of 'collecting and disseminating information concerning the Co-operative System'; this was to be achieved by establishing libraries, 'by meetings for conversation', and 'by aiding in the establishment of Co-operative communities throughout the country'.[10] An accompanying document spoke of O'Brien's heart's desire, the possibility of a boarding school attached to a community, to which a 'nobleman' had offered to send his son, and 'procure the sons of seven other noblemen'. The eleven rules of the Society established a series of procedural, administrative and financial barriers to the admittance of the 'wrong' sort of person to the Society. In a statement of purpose published in the November issue of *The Co-operative Magazine and Monthly Herald*, the Society made clear that it sought improvements in the existing class system, not the overturning of that order. The Co-operative System was

> the only practical mode of removing permanently the poverty of the poorer orders, and of enabling others, of all ranks and means, to obtain more of the real comforts and enjoyments of life than they can at present procure, thereby relieving the wealthier orders from the mental pain they suffer, and from the weighty annual expense they are put to, by the prevalence of pauperism.[11]

It was not made clear how the communities were to be constituted, nor their relationship with the broader society. A feature of this document was the stress upon the Christian basis of co-operation. The early Christians 'lived in Co-operating Community', and the obligation to love their neighbour as themselves could only be achieved through co-operation.[12]

O'Brien was a distinctly autocratic and conservative example of early Irish socialism. His social theory did not imply equality, common ownership, nor any attack on the existing religious, social, and political hierarchy. Co-operation was the means whereby philanthropy could both improve the lot of the poor and simultaneously promote the material and cultural interests of the enlightened minority. Doing good and doing well were entirely compatible.

A more sophisticated and radical analysis can be found in the work of Henry MacCormac MD (1800–86), a Belfast physician.[13] His professional work with the poor was the foundation for his critique of capitalism, and shock, pity and real anger shine through his attempts to make theoretical sense of such squalor and degradation. On a number of occasions he seemed to despair of ever fully conveying the true nature of what he has witnessed. 'I can find no language at all adequate', he says in *An Appeal on Behalf of the Poor* (1831), 'to express the various emotions of sympathy, sorrow, and even downright horror, which the spectacle of intense human misery has often excited in my breast, or to describe that misery.'[14] He does, however, attempt such descriptions, and provides harrowing little pen-portraits which anticipate those to be found in Engels' *The Condition of the Working Class in England*, published a decade and a half later. He speaks of a spiral of disease and death: of 'ragged and starving infants, unable to understand the cause of their distress . . . beside a sick or a dying parent';[15] and of a Belfast garret, 'where there was a woman lying on a little straw; [and] there was nothing else whatever in the place – either of fire, living being, utensils, or furniture'.[16] Anecdotal evidence reveals an exceptionally warm-hearted and sympathetic person[17] (whose sympathy also extended to animals).[18] The core of Mac-Cormac's social and political writing is therefore this deeply felt humanitarianism; an outraged sympathy for the condition of the poor, developed in the course of his medical dealings with them.

His published writings are like transcripts of his attempts to think through the social problems of his time; to borrow a phrase, he conducts his education in public. In a postscript to his *A Plan for the Relief of the Unemployed Poor* (1830), he notes of this plan, with engaging honesty, 'but notwithstanding that the whole has been rewritten and repeatedly revised, I have not succeeded in expressing my views to my satisfaction';[19] he then proceeds to have a final go at it in the last two pages! He borrows widely, and explicitly, from the existing literature. In terms of his analysis of capitalism he seems to have been particularly influenced by Charles Hall's *The Effect of Civilization on the People in the European States* (1805), and by William Thompson's *An Inquiry into the Principles of the Distribution of Wealth Most Conducive to Human Happiness as Applied to the Newly Proposed System of Voluntary Equality of Wealth* (1824); in terms of political theory, the work of Robert Owen held first place. But his work abounds with references to a wide range of social and political writers, including those he intends to read next!

MacCormac's critique is very sensitive to the nature of *division* in society. We might note, for example, his work on the division of gender, race, nation and sect.

He argues that the subordinate role of women is both an obstacle to the emancipation of the working class, and of society in general. He had read William Thompson's book on women, and was in no doubt about the oppression women experienced, referring to 'their present unjust and barbarous position in the moral and political scale of society'.[20] He calls for women to 'have the same voice in society which men have, and the same liberty to go and come, with equal independence of each other, and of the other sex'.[21] Although not free of all the general assumptions of the time (a belief in natural female dispositions and functions, for example), his analysis is an impressive attempt to recognize and understand the oppression of women.

After qualifying as a doctor in 1824, MacCormac spent almost a year in West Africa, where his brother John was a magistrate. Another brother, Hamilton, married a West African woman, and their children stayed with Henry MacCormac on their visits to Belfast.[22] He thus had knowledge of Africa and its peoples, and a real liking for them. His remarks on race occur in a discussion of slavery. Again his purpose is to overcome what he sees as unnatural, artificial divisions between people. He wishes to assert the unity of people, regardless of skin colour: 'nobody here will be hardy enough to assert that a man is not to be treated as a man because he is black, any more than we should think that a white horse is more of a horse than a black one'.[23] He argues that this is of more than marginal interest, for skin colour – like any other inessential distinction – must not be allowed to become a dividing factor in the working class. He condemns those who wish to affirm 'that the black mechanic is to be excluded from the same means of improvement, which are or should be possessed by his white brother; or else that he is incapable of benefiting by them'.[24]

He also has a strong sense of Irishness. Although committed to the United Kingdom, he is aware of Ireland's particular problems and potentialities. He is scathing towards Ireland's absentee landlords, whom he sees as a net drain on the resources of the country. Their appropriations have an effect right down the social chain: 'In Ireland especially, the abstraction of capital by absentees, has disabled the farmer and others from employing as many as they would otherwise.'[25] He also noted Ireland's economic backwardness, and the consequent cost of imports; a net outgoing of money 'for those articles which our deficient or imperfect manufactures do not permit us to produce'.[26] Ireland also has to pay its share of the public revenue. Unlike England or Scotland, Ireland has no poor laws, and therefore not even a threadbare safety-net for hardship. As a result, famine is an ever-present danger to the Irish poor.[27] It is hardly surprising, he argues, that the Irish working class is especially degraded: 'I cannot conceal the melancholy fact, from you, that taking them as a body, the Irish artisans and mechanics are far inferior in point of intelligence and acquirements, to those of many of the other nations in Europe.'[28] He also demonstrates and deploys an Irish patriotism to urge his point, as in an address to Belfast mechanics in December 1829, where he speaks of 'my countrymen', of 'the bright spirits which our soil has produced', and of 'the ancient renown of Ireland, your country and your native land'.[29]

MacCormac identifies religious sectarianism as an unnecessary source of division among Ireland's poorer classes, claiming that he had witnessed 'individuals in the lowest stage of human existence abuse others, because they held a different set of religious opinions from themselves'.[30] In a discussion of possible alternative arrangements, he is at pains to guard against any sectarian feeling:

> Their religious instruction would be left to the care of their respective pastors, and at no time should any improper demonstration of party or sectarian feeling be countenanced. It is hardly necessary to state, that the possession of peculiar tenets should not make the least ground of improper difference in the treatment toward them. . . . Some of these poor people would . . . occasionally . . . show that they considered the possession of particular opinions a merit on their parts, and a source of triumph; but it is evident, that any improper demonstrations of the kind must be met by the proper remedies.[31]

MacCormac's theory of class is ill thought out, imprecise, and inconsistent. It is roughly based on productivity and wealth. Society is divided into producers and non-producers, and the latter category into rich and poor (the concept of poor non-producers is unusual within early socialism where the poor are usually deemed to be producers). He describes the existing social structure as 'those who eat, but do not work; those who eat and work; and those who are willing to work, but cannot obtain employment'.[32] Rich non-producers include 'bankers, merchants, shopkeepers and money-dealers';[33] the producers 'either cultivate the earth as labourers, fashion the articles which they get from it as artisans and mechanics, or else study, and practise the arts and sciences for the common good, or fill stations of trust and office';[34] the poor non-producers are the unemployed.

MacCormac sought to eliminate, or at least reduce, *professional* distribution, in favour of co-operative production and distribution. In the early 1830s his call is: 'let each man become a producer and distributer of wealth, as well as a consumer',[35] and in 1837 he asks: 'would it not be desirable that there were fewer distributors, and more producers?'[36] In both instances he is aware that widespread, comprehensive change will take some considerable time to occur, which, added to his concern for current suffering, meant that his *detailed* plans for social reform concern the short and medium term, and are directed at the disadvantaged sections of society.

In the early 1830s he particularly focuses on the poor non-producers, the unemployed, the 'destitute', as he sometimes calls them. He proposes that from ten to a thousand of those who are able and willing should be established in a community, and there be taught enlightened working and living patterns:

> formed upon the principle of joint-production, joint-distribution, and joint-consumption, with equal rights, and attended with every apparatus that the present theoretical and practical knowledge of mankind can suggest, for facilitating the quickest, easiest and best modes of production, and the most efficacious methods of instruction, in fine, of the application of knowledge to happiness.[37]

At the economic level the goal is the co-operative raising of material standards, and at the human, the gradual cultivation of intellectual and spiritual potential. This is spelled out in great detail, down to the content of diet, and sorts of clothing to be worn. His hope is that the government will take the lead, though he is prepared to countenance a variety of initiatives.

MacCormac set about establishing a co-operative society in Belfast. In an appendix to a published address at the Belfast Mechanics' Institute (1830) he noted that 'in conjunction with assistance' he had 'been able to induce a number of individuals (140) to act upon the suggestion', and that 'a literary friend' had 'consented to edit a small monthly miscellany for their instruction'.[38] From this journal, *The Belfast Co-operative Advocate*, Ireland's first socialist journal, we learn that the First Belfast Co-operative Trading Association was established in November and December of 1829.[39] MacCormac retained his links with this body. *The Voice of the People* reported that at the fourth quarterly meeting of the co-operative, held on 16 February 1831, 'Dr Macormac addressed the meeting, and urged the necessity of establishing schools for the education of the children of co-operators, and mutual instruction generally'.[40]

MacCormac's conception of co-operation is clearly different from that of O'Brien. His approach is much more humane and egalitarian, and is free of haughty disdain towards the poor. It is theoretically more complex, and sensitive to social divisions based not merely on class, but also on gender, race, nation and sect. Like O'Brien, however, and considerably more undeserved, he has suffered from historical neglect, with Thompson and Ralahine dominating the foreground.

ARTISAN SOCIALISM

If certain exponents of elite socialism have become invisible in the historiography of Irish socialism, this applies to the whole category of artisan socialism. Commentators on early British socialism have noted how working-class practice has tended to become eclipsed by the literary output of the 'prophets'.[41] In Ireland Owenite socialism has become entirely associated with the plans and experiments of the elite socialists. However, in the pages of the Owenite journal *The New Moral World* during the early 1840s we have evidence of what we might call 'artisan socialism'. The sequence of material opens with a discussion, in February 1840, of a parliamentary interchange between Daniel O'Connell and Lord Morpeth in which the latter claimed that an attempt had been made to introduce socialism in Ireland, 'but that it had been immediately repressed'.[42] *The New Moral World* expresses surprise at this, claiming that it knows of no such attempt or subsequent suppression. In a remark which raises interesting questions about the status of the period of elite socialism, it stated that 'no social lecturer has yet been in Ireland, nor has the Association yet taken any steps to extend its operations to that island'. The context for the discussion also emerges in this item: 'Already an earnest desire is generated among some portions of the Irish people, to know what is meant by this new *ism*, about which their newspapers are full, and the occupants of their pulpits continually raving.' To substantiate this claim the paper cites 'a private letter from a highly talented and respectable friend, who is well acquainted with Ireland and its people, from which we learn that a movement is being made among the Socialists in Ireland, who have not yet openly declared themselves'. This correspondent cites a large Sunday School in Belfast where the teachers were lectured by a clergyman on the evils of socialism, and were warned against going to England at present as one of the ablest Sunday School teachers had recently defected to the socialists. This brief item introduces a number of features which recur in later evidence: silence on the period of elite socialism; an outburst of anti-socialist feeling in the press and the churches; the small size and quasi-clandestine nature of Irish socialism; the characterization of socialism as both anti-religious and alien (i.e. an English contagion).

It is from Dublin that we next hear of the progress of Irish socialism. In April 1841 a court heard a case, brought by a man who was to become the first spokesperson of Dublin artisan socialism – John Elliott. Elliott, a lithographic printer, had taken his Friendly Society, the 'Liberal Friendly Brothers', to court for effectively expelling him from the Society. This Society, 'composed exclusively of Protestants',[43] had done this because 'the complainant had lately been in the habit of promulgating "Socialist principles"'. In a cross-examination on the issue of oath-swearing, it emerged that Elliott was a Socinian Protestant, who denied the divinity of Christ and some of the Scriptures. To the question, 'Are you not now what is called a Socialist?' Elliott replied, 'Not altogether. I have read a great number of their tracts, and approve of some of them.' He persisted in this approach, reiterating: 'I partly believe in Socialism.' Elliott then addressed himself to those aspects of socialism he found congenial: 'It is my opinion that every one should assist in the amelioration of the condition of mankind, and for that purpose there should be self-supporting

institutions which would abolish poverty, vice, and lawyers (a laugh).'
He further agreed that he did believe that there should be a community
of interest and property, with 'each person to labour and work for the
community, so that there would be no poverty'. He also accepted the
proposition that there would be no need for monarchs and peers, but
that he would not abolish the latter, as his aim was to 'bring the peasant
up to the peer, and not the peer down to the peasant'. Magistrates, judges
and laws would not be required, for 'the millennium would commence
and man would be under the government of his understanding, and
"intelligence". His "intelligence" would be the regulating principle of his
'mind and acting.' Elliott's response cut no ice with the court which found
the 'exhibition' of 'the unfortunate man' 'disgusting and disgraceful', and
dismissed the case.

In a letter to *The New Moral World* shortly after the trial, Elliott
confirms the picture of himself as a fairly recent convert to socialism. He
reported that 'my first acquaintance with Socialism was by reading some
speeches of the Bishop of Exeter'.[44] Since the Bishop had only made these
hostile speeches the previous year, Elliott's familiarity with socialism was
indeed recent. He claimed that he had a poor opinion of socialism at the
time, since it appeared to him 'a debasing, degrading, soul-destroying
heresy', but that curiosity and a desire to refute the doctrine made him
borrow, from a friend, Owen's ' "Book of the New Moral World" and
his "Six Lectures at Manchester" ', in which he found 'facts and laws,
so stubborn yet so harmonious, so strange yet so convincing, that I
yielded a reluctant consent to reasoning so profound'. Elliott therefore
confirms the belief of the Belfast clergy that as a body of ideas, socialism
had been imported from across the Irish Sea. He also confirms the
impression of the isolation of Irish socialism, noting that before his court
case 'I knew very few in this city who entertained views favourable to
Socialism', but that in the wake of his case a number of sympathetic
people had sought him out. These people, 'disciples of the venerable
Owen in this city, although very few, are men, in knowledge, in language,
and in conduct, much above the average of their class'. Therefore the
picture of a small, unselfconfident (if of above average cultivation), and
beleaguered artisan group persists:

> I think if we had one person, in Dublin, sufficiently independent of
> the world, we would be able to muster some thirty or forty intelligent
> minds, favourable to our holy cause; but it unfortunately happens that
> none dare, without imprudence, give vent to the free expression of
> their convictions without risking the loss of employment; even I myself
> am not sure whether I shall get 'leave to toil'.

The dualism of ignorance and knowledge dominates Elliott's thinking.
The multitude is ignorant of its true condition, the ruling groups are
driven by prejudice, whilst Owenism provides the necessary freedom of

mind. His plea is therefore for 'our British friends' to send books, tracts and newspapers to help pierce through the gloom of ignorance. He declares that:

> I am now more of a Protestant than ever I was – I not only protest against Popery, but I protest against mystery, monopoly, and that rotten mythology which is, I believe, the only cause of the present degraded and debased condition of society.

By the first half of 1842 Elliott could refer to fifty-two names on the socialist class roll, though he admitted that only between sixteen and twenty members attended the weekly meetings. Following the example of O'Connell they collected a penny a week per member to help buy books and pay the rent of the meeting room. Some also contributed sixpence a week to try to obtain a house.[45] Sympathetic Owenites in Britain had sent them reading material, but the new goal was to get the Central Board to send over 'some fearless, talented, and independent missionary to break the ice of public attention'.[46]

Towards the end of 1842 a new voice is heard amongst the socialist artisans of Dublin, that of Michael Groves, who eventually referred to himself as secretary, and informed *The New Moral World* readers that Elliott was now president of their small group. This period sees an acceleration in socialist activities and an increasing engagement with other ideological strands, notably Chartism, O'Connellite Repealism, orthodox Catholicisim, and Orangeism.

Groves appears to have injected new energy into the campaign. It is still true, he admits, that 'Socialism is but little known here.'[47] He confirms the artisan basis of the group – 'our class is composed of working men' – but adds that some inroads have been made into other classes: 'there are others of the superior classes favourable to our cause, who remain private'. Groves's strategy was to gain public attention for socialism. He thus argued the merits of Owenism in a couple of debating societies, and introduced a street collection for funds. Already one senses trouble is brewing with the O'Connellites, for Groves introduced Owenite arguments into a series of debates on Repeal of the Union, and saw the street collection as a way of using the O'Connellite methods to generate funds for a worthier cause.

Open hostilities with the O'Connellites broke out in December 1842. The socialists decided to hold a public meeting to propound their principles on 18 December 1842.[48] The meeting was effectively hijacked by the O'Connellite master tailor Thomas Arkins, who had cut his teeth in the service of O'Connell breaking up Chartist meetings some years earlier.[49] Arriving with a hostile mob, he used the meeting to launch a fierce attack on socialism. He detailed a familiar eclectic range of charges – blasphemy, social disorder, alien origin – but gave them an interesting twist. Thus he called upon the common Christian faith of both Protestants and Catholics to reject the 'infidelity' of the socialists. In playing the 'alien' card he used a device that was to be used extensively by O'Connell himself, namely to imply that socialism and Chartism were inextricably linked: 'It was perfectly clear that the Socialists and Chartists went hand in hand. . . . Irishmen would never tolerate English Chartists or Socialists to inflict the curse of their presence on their lovely land. (Loud cheers)'. Other speakers developed different lines of attack, with one suggesting that the socialists 'have a house' in Carlisle 'where they say there is about 500 of them living in unlimited intercourse'. In the face of threatened violence the socialists withdrew.

Arkins's equation of socialism with Chartism put the latter in a quandary, and forced them to spell out their relationship to socialism. The Chartist printer W. H. Dyott, in a dignified letter to the *Freeman's Journal*,[50] sought to make a theoretical distinction between Chartism and socialism:

> Chartism which I advocate . . . contemplates no social change but what will be effected through the present form – amended – of the British constitution. Socialism, on the contrary . . . looks upon Chartism as equally futile with any other *political* nostrum of the present day, as a remedy for the evils under which society groans. It affirms that those evils spring from the *competitive* and struggling system under which we live, and it propounds the *community* or *co-operative* principle in its stead. . . . My object is to show that there is neither relation nor connexion, but on the contrary, hostility and repulsion between the two systems.

In another letter Dyott similarly asserted that 'to be a Chartist and a Socialist is altogether impossible'.[51] This is not however the full story. There was clearly some level of personal warmth between Dyott and the socialists. Dyott made a number of favourable remarks about the character of the socialists, whilst Elliott called Dyott's first letter 'straightforward and manly' and said that he would 'prefer such a mind as his to a thousand brainless brawlers'.[52] Dyott also allowed the socialists to hire a room from him as well as having had commercial relationships with them, printing their placards and selling their tracts and books. Dyott clearly had some sympathy with the critique of the socialists, and sought in his correspondence to refute a number of the charges made against them. No doubt there was also a shared sense of adversity against the likes of Arkins – Dyott is particularly vehement in his attack on the strong-arm methods of the opponents of socialism. A further complicating factor in this complex set of patterns is that although Arkins was an O'Connellite, Dyott classed O'Connell as a supporter of the Charter. As we shall see shortly, O'Connell angrily turned on Dyott. Unfortunately we possess no remark made by a Dublin socialist on the nature of Chartism.

O'Connell himself, in public meetings, now launched a broadside against socialism.[53] He was quickly followed by the Catholic hierarchy. O'Connell had not always been an opponent of Owenism. When Robert Owen gave a series of public lectures in Dublin in 1823, O'Connell was in the audience. Subsequently the Hibernian Philanthropic Society was established to promote Owenite communal experiments. In a letter of 10 May 1823 O'Connell wrote: 'I shall become a subscriber to Owen's Society. He *may* do some good and cannot do any harm.'[54] Thus at this period Owenism appeared quite compatible with O'Connell's beliefs. In the early 1840s this was no longer deemed to be the case (not that O'Connell now mentioned the earlier flirtation!). O'Connell's attack was not, however, a sober defence of liberalism against the alternative doctrines of the socialists, but rather an inflammatory and tendentious reiteration and development of the 'religious' and xenophobic charges of Arkins. He asserted that the socialists belonged 'to the poorer class of Orangemen', were dupes of the Tories and the English, and sought 'to conciliate the poorer classes of Protestants in the towns by their abuse of the Catholic priests'. They played on the undoubted grievances of the Irish people, and sought to usurp the place of the real force for change – the Repeal Association. Furthermore, they incited people to murder and sedition, and were informers to boot. O'Connell also made a distinction between support for the Charter and Irish Chartism. Supporters of the Charter would find everything they wanted by supporting Repeal. Dyott, on the other hand, was condemned as an apologist for socialism, and all socialists were condemned as Chartist. The clergy of the country were to be warned of the dangers of the infidel doctrine of socialism. O'Connell's attack was taken up by the Archbishop of Tuam.[55] Socialism was the most recent manifestation of the English Protestant attack on Catholic Ireland, 'one of the latest and most destructive of those infidel sects, of which the English schism has been the prolific parent'. However, 'the truly conservative vigour of the Catholic faith' amongst the Irish poor would not simply sweep away socialism in Ireland but would, via the Irish in England, lead to the 'second conversion' of that country itself.

From Michael Groves's indignant response to these charges,[56] we can learn of the emerging socialist critique of both O'Connellite Repealism, and of religion. Groves appears to share Owen's strictures on religion, namely that it is based on ignorance. He therefore takes the Archbishop's attack to be a sign of fear that socialism would 'dispel the darkness and ignorance in which alone the priesthood flourish'. He thinks Ireland is particularly deeply mired in such ignorance, plaintively explaining to his British readers that socialists in Ireland 'encounter a fierce and powerful opposition, and prejudices much stronger than you ever experienced in England, among a people ardently devoted to their superstitions and their priests'. Groves was indignant at O'Connell's claim 'that we were all Orangemen'. He used the opportunity to give the first evidence in his correspondence of the religious breakdown of the Dublin socialists, and to condemn Orangeism: 'We are composed of Catholics and Protestants, about an equal number of each, and have never had anything to do with Orangeism. We have added three members since the attack, all Catholics.' O'Connell is attacked on a number of levels. He is portrayed as an arrogant bully holding 'unlimited sway over his stupid and deluded followers', who uses lies and incites violence against the socialists. His political project is also attacked. Ireland 'under his management . . . is in a worse condition now . . . than when he began'. Most importantly Groves takes an anti-Repeal stance against O'Connell, referring to the latter's 'proposals or attempts to divide the countries by a repeal of the Union'. Groves uses two different approaches, one stressing O'Connell's anti-English sentiments, the other his class sympathies. Thus O'Connell is said to be motivated by hatred of England, and it is this which 'is the real cause of his agitation for repeal'. Groves also argues that 'it would be easy to shew that all his arguments, to prove that Ireland would be benefited by repeal or separation, are false'. O'Connell's claim that an Irish nobility and gentry spending their fortunes in Ireland would lead to general wealth for the country is denounced as nonsense, since the English poor have not benefited from their own grandees. The 'superior humanity of the Irish nobility and gentry' is belied by the low wages they have paid their labourers 'before and after the Union'. Groves condemns O'Connell's politics as an attempt to promote the base interests of the rich Catholics, and even includes Catholic Emancipation in this: 'The only value in his boasted emancipation and corporate reforms, was to enable rich Catholics to share with rich Protestants the unearned revenues of office, and they have already proved themselves quite as greedy.'

Groves expressed a desire to return to this topic in a later letter. Alas this was the last item of correspondence from him. Only one further letter from the Dublin socialists appears in *The New Moral World*.[57] This is a short melancholy note from John Elliott dated 21 August 1843, noting the death by consumption of a young member, Peter Crighton, aged 22. There are no further letters from the artisan socialists of Dublin.

As with O'Brien and MacCormac, emergence gives way to submergence: irrelevance to contemporaries, invisibility to successors. Unlike the elite socialists, however, the artisan socialists had their entire project, their very political existence, forgotten. A distinctive voice is therefore lost, for, although their general theoretical perspective is drawn from the 'prophets' of Owenism, they were forced by the local context to develop this base to cope with the complexities of Irish life. They were thus developing increasing theoretical sophistication as they grappled with, for example, O'Connellite Repealism and orthodox Catholicism.

SOCIALISM AND NATIONALISM

Between the silence of the artisan socialists and the end of the decade the catastrophe of the Famine occurs, and, at the ideological level, the development of radical nationalism. In 1849 and 1850 we see the first sustained effort in Irish history to combine socialism and nationalism. Emerging out of the Irish Democratic Association and its newspaper, *The Irishman* (publisher, Bernard Fullam),[58] this attempted synthesis could plausibly claim to be the earliest ancestor of Irish socialist republicanism. Its historical context is the defeat of insurrectionary nationalism in 1848. In one sense it is firmly grounded in the most radical wing of Young Ireland. Until September 1849 *The Irishman* was edited by the young poet, Michael Joseph Brennan, a former associate of Mitchel and editor of *The Irish Felon*, whose participation, with Lalor, in the failed rising of 1849, resulted in his flight to America. Subsequently the journal saw itself as carrying the torch of Mitchel and Lalor, who were themselves seen as continuing the project of Tone and Emmet. But it moves beyond the radical rural redistributionism of Lalor into the new theoretical and political territory of socialist nationalism. This is not to say, however, that *The Irishman* created this synthesis out of thin air. One can clearly see in 1848, in journals such as the *Irish Felon*, the *Irish Tribune* and *The Irish National Guard*, a growing sense of the importance of the urban working class for the success of the national revolution. *The Irishman*, however, pulls the disparate strands together into a coherent theoretical whole.

A particularly clear expression of this new synthesis can be found in a leading article, 'Social Democracy', in *The Irishman* at the end of 1849,[59] which provided an historical account of the origins of radicalism. In medieval and early modern times 'blind outpourings' against God and King, driven by 'sheer necessity' had manifested themselves in Jack Cade's revolt, the Peasant War in Germany, and so forth. In eighteenth-century France, hunger again stimulated revolt, only this time 'Frenchmen invoked the genius of Liberty.' After much further struggling liberty was triumphant. In this new period humanity became self-conscious, because liberty was no longer founded on 'impulse' or 'blind instincts'. The victory of liberty proved inadequate, however, because it was only partial freedom. The social dimension of freedom was recognized: 'social liberty must be had, or political is useless. What use the rights of a freeman if we be the slave of the capitalist or the taskmaster?' The phase of political liberty therefore gave way to a new one: 'Communism, Socialism, Red Republicanism, sprang up to meet the difficulty.' *The Irishman* views this phase as still problematic. It is a step forward but must not be viewed uncritically:

> Perhaps better modes might have been possibly devised, less objectionable and more practical. . . . Still they were the voice of nature – the

protest of suffering against injustice. Half instinct, half reason, they were the first efforts of men trying the path that led to the remedy of an unthought-of evil. . . . It is the hammer that must break down every roughness and inequality, till man be socially as well as politically on an equal with his fellow.

At the risk of reading too much into this one could argue that a claim is being made here that historical forms of socialism have lost a vital 'liberal' dimension, and that a more adequate form of socialism requires the reintroduction of this temporarily displaced item. The *Irishman* was also aware of the opprobrium socialism invited in Ireland: phrases such as 'the principles we have suggested will be branded as Communist and anti-social' occur in a number of places in the journal. The European revolutions of 1848 added to the general demonology of socialism. Mitchel himself in his *Jail Journal* wrote that 'Socialists are something worse than wild beasts.'

The question of Ireland is now introduced into *The Irishman*'s analysis. Ireland is moving steadily towards political independence, but this in itself is not sufficient. Without social change independence is an illusion: 'she must have more than that, or independence itself will be but a tinselled plaything, a dyed garment stretched over the back of misery'. Ireland must undergo a social revolution if true independence is to be acquired. *The Irishman* develops the notion of Social Democracy to conceptualize the social aspect of the Irish revolution: 'We must become *Socially Democratic*, as well as politically so . . . no great benefit can be derived from struggling for half a victory; Ireland must be thoroughly and radically revolutionised in all her social relations.'

The analysis now explicitly puts water between itself and earlier theories of rural redistribution. Resolving the 'Land Question' is clearly vital, but it is only one part of the solution, necessary but not sufficient:

It is idle to talk of confining our views to the adjustment of the land question, the firm establishment of the occupier, and the debasement or annihilation of the agrarian aristocracy. All these are necessities, solid in themselves, and essential to our independence. . . . But we must go farther.

The further stage involves a head-on confrontation with the emerging capitalist class. This is the modern strong class, eclipsing the decaying landed aristocracy – it is the new aristocracy. *The Irishman* is sensitive to the ideological aspects of capitalism's power. The new aristocracy grows up 'partially unobserved' and is 'infinitely more formidable, because apparently more consonant with reason and sound principle'; furthermore 'the crooked maxims of a heartless political economy, elevate such a man into a demigod, a philanthropist, a patriot'.

The analysis distinguishes between the position in England and that in

Ireland. England is deemed to have a more developed capitalist economy. Although the 'case is less apparent in Ireland' it is, however, 'not less black or ruinous'. Relative underdevelopment makes exploitation more naked and intense: 'The rights of labour, are even less regarded than in the English factory, or mine, or farm. Our petty tyrants oppress on a grander scale. They make up for the fewness of the objects by the intensity of the infliction.' Independence without social revolution will merely leave the Irish people at the mercy of these native exploiters: 'This must be corrected, or nationality and independence will be but the dream of a drunkard. What will be the advantage of escaping from the wholesale tyrant, if we leave ourselves in the hands of a host of paltry oppressors.'

The clarity of this presentation should not blind us to the ambiguities of the general project. The very term 'general project' can mislead, for the Irish Democratic Association was a fairly broadly-based organization, most of whose supporters were far more interested in nationalism than socialism. Furthermore even amongst the radical elements (besides Fullam this included Andrew English, Honorary Secretary of the Association, and Thomas Moffet, Chairman of the Association Committee), views differed and evolved. The intellectual core of the Irish Democratic Association and *The Irishman* was predominantly an educated middle-class group[60] whose ideological roots lay in radical liberal-democratic nationalism, and whose central concepts were liberty, democracy and nation. One is conscious of a struggle to fashion a new perspective out of this vocabulary. They were aware of socialist theorizing – *though not of any Irish predecessors* – but had very little sympathy for the specifics of traditional schools such as Owenism, Fourierism or Saint-Simonianism. They were most sympathetic to the modern continental forms associated with the revolutions of 1848, but here again there was comparatively little direct borrowing. Thus liberal-democratic nationalism is constantly intruding. In the case of liberalism, for example, an editorial of 12 January uses social contract theory to demonstrate that Irish people owe no allegiance to England, and that Ireland has 'fallen into the state of nature'; the numerous references to the 'rights of man' should also be noted. This liberal-democratic nationalist vocabulary variously dovetails, coexists, contradicts and obscures some of the other concepts developed to cope with deep theoretical and political problems. There is undoubted tension between the concepts of 'man', 'working class', 'the masses', 'the people', 'the Democracy' and 'the nation'. It is not clear, for example, who the revolutionary agent is. At times a strict class analysis categorically rules out any help from the aristocracy, the landlords, manufacturers, shopkeepers, and even (temporarily) farmers,[61] and the refurbished Davisite slogan of 'Ourselves Alone' is deemed to refer to 'the Democracy', whilst on other occasions members of all classes are seen to be capable of backing the national struggle. Within 'the Democracy', the role of the progressive middle class is ambiguously presented, sometimes as an indistinguishable part of an undifferentiated whole, sometimes as a distinct ally of a leading working class, and sometimes as a superior educational force *vis-à-vis* the working class. On occasions 'Orangemen' are called 'volunteer mercenaries of an alien tyranny' who would become 'armed fratricides to keep their trampled country for ever in chains'; at other times the hand of friendship is extended to our 'Orange brothers',[62] and 'our great project' is described as uniting 'men of every class and religious persuasion in the resuscitation of our common country'.[63] The problems of distinguishing and reconciling 'class' and 'nation' which bedevil later socialist republicanism are prefigured here.

There is a degree of vagueness and lack of clarity as to how the social and political aspects of the revolution are to be co-ordinated in practice. The working class of Ireland is to be assisted in its struggle against capital, but there is no theory of how a struggle against capital in Ireland feeds into a struggle for national independence. The overarching conception appears to be that the primary task of the working class is to work for national independence, and that an independent Ireland will then grant them the necessary social freedom. On the question of land, for example, *The Irishman* states quite bluntly: 'It is idle to think of adjusting the land question before we have asserted the independence of Ireland. Then, and not till then, we shall decide whose is the soil.'[64] This is a two-stage theory – independence, then social revolution – lacking any notion that the weakening of Irish capital will play a material role in the independence of Ireland. Independence itself is not to be won by parliamentary means, for Parliament is a class-based and, post Union, alien institution. They are circumspect about the precise means, though their constant references to police in their meetings indicate the context of their tactics.[65] It does seem that they believed that armed strength, at the appropriate moment, would be the engine of independence. They hoped for the assistance of both the British and European working class, appealing to them to 'help us twine together the banners, green and red, in one thick cord, to bind down for ever, the demon that has oppressed us'.[66]

The Irish Democratic Association itself, after an impressive start – thousands attending its meetings, branches in many parts of Ireland, England and Scotland – fizzled out in 1850. Publication of *The Irishman* was suspended in May 1850 due to financial problems; after a brief resurrection in August of that year it was finally closed down. The fact that *The Irishman* ultimately resurfaced as a non-, even anti-socialist nationalist paper is indicative of the milieu in which the Irish Democratic Association radicals operated. As with later attempts to synthesize socialism and nationalism, the former was constantly in danger of being swallowed up by the latter; of having its social dimension eliminated, or subordinated, or tailored to the needs of nationalism. The large meetings held by the Irish Democratic Association more often echoed to the call for the return of the exiled martyrs than they did to the call for social democracy. The distinctive *socialist* aspect soon disappeared and the predominant memory created, such as it was, was of a recherché *nationalist* sect.

The Irishman provides a rich and interesting body of ideas. The most notable aspect of its brief life is undoubtedly the attempt, admittedly problematic, to synthesize socialism and nationalism. It made the crucial move from the nationalist rural redistributionism of Lalor to a broader, socialist and nationalist critique of urban and rural capitalism. It clearly did not emerge out of a vacuum – these types of ideas were clearly developing in these revolutionary years. But *The Irishman* marks the first sustained effort to work out the theoretical parameters of such a synthesis. In this sense it can, with some justification, be called the creator of the earliest form of Irish socialist republicanism.

CHRISTIAN SOCIALISM

November and December of 1851 saw the birth and death of Ireland's first Christian Socialist journal, *The Christian Social Economist*. It was the creation of a Catholic priest, Thaddeus O'Malley.[67] O'Malley was born in Garryowen, County Cork in 1796. After ordination, and educational work in America, he became Rector of Malta University. On returning to Ireland he threw himself into the various political controversies of the day, and also did sterling work on the Central Relief Committee during the Famine. He was constantly falling foul of the Church hierarchy in both Rome and Ireland, and was twice suspended from the priesthood. He died in Dublin in 1877. In the revolutionary times of 1848 O'Malley contributed 'The Working Man's Bill of Rights' to the radical nationalist paper *The Irish National Guard*, where he is described as 'the workman's tried friend'. Although the 'Bill of Rights' combines elements of nationalism, socialism and democracy, it is of a very different character from the synthesis developed in *The Irishman*. The theological grounding of O'Malley's approach is apparent in the very first point of the Bill: 'God has given this fertile land to the people, who under his providence are born on it, for their plentiful sustenance – and what God has given no man or set of men shall take away, or any part thereof.' From this he argues that the land may only be held by 'Irishmen' or by persons adopting Ireland as their home and 'residing habitually in it'. In the fairly detailed programme for rural regeneration O'Malley displays an abiding feature of his socialism, a desire for moderate consensual change. Thus absentee landowners will only lose their property through due process of law, and will be compensated. Boards bringing together the various rural classes will establish prices. O'Malley is particularly keen to help the agricultural labourers, 'they who are the real producers of the whole', and argues for a minimum wage, housing provision, a garden rent free, etc. For those who have no work he proposes a national body, 'The Administration of Public Succour', to provide work and help labourers to become independent farmers. This body will also have the responsibility of promoting 'the comforts, and enjoyments, and intellectual culture of the whole body of the working classes'[68] through the provision of public fountains, baths and libraries. His moderate approach is also apparent in his suggestions for industry. Trades are to be regulated by committees of employers, workers and neutrals; minimum wages are to be set, though more skilful workers can apply for higher rates; a ten-hour day is to be established for skilled workers (eleven for unskilled), and overtime paid above this. As with the rural provisions, 'The Administration of Public Succour' will act as a safety net. O'Malley was also sensitive to the rights of women in employment:

> These regulations . . . shall apply in all their force, and in every particular, to female employers and female workers, or to male employers of workwomen . . . – that is to say, females . . . shall be protected by regulations, in the drawing up of which they must themselves be parties.

Unfortunately this enlightened approach did not extend to the franchise, from which women appear to be excluded.

In his own journal, *The Christian Social Economist* (first issue 22 November 1851), we can see O'Malley developing his Christian Socialist perspective. It does seem that he had quite a sophisticated knowledge of contemporary socialism, particularly French varieties, and was well aware of the deep divisions between different schools: 'each of them has . . . his own theory not only different from, but even in essentials, opposed to the others'. He acknowledges that ignorance and fear shroud the issue of socialism in Ireland: 'never, perhaps, was there a confusion of ideas, so utterly confounded as that which prevails, in the mind of this country upon the subject of Socialism'.[69] Explicitly basing himself on a distinction made by the Archbishop of Paris, he distinguishes true from false socialism. The first element he finds true is the longing of socialism for 'such large practical reforms as will greatly improve the social condition of the masses'. 'In this sense', he argues, 'we are all Socialists', all that is, except 'those miserable few (alas! are they but few?) who never give a thought to any one, or anything but themselves.' Secondly, he commends the socialism embodied in co-operative labour schemes, which he sees as the workers' equivalent of the capitalist joint-stock company. Where he takes issue with existing socialism is in what he takes to be its scientific and religious pretensions. The 'scientific Socialists', he argues, not only underestimate the obstacles to change, but are insensitive to the value of some of these obstacles:

They would derange and upset, and reconstruct, *all at once*, the whole complicated system of human society, without regard to the invincible obstacles opposed by old laws, old institutions, old customs, old manners, old ingrained habits of thinking, of feeling and of acting.

This in turn leads it 'to assume the lofty dogmatism of a new religion'. O'Malley also partly concedes the perennial charge levied against socialism in Ireland – that it is an atheist doctrine. He talks of *'socialistic* writings of a mischievous tendency', which are 'deeply stained with the hue of infidelity', and whilst 'insidiously flattering the poor man's world hopes, destroy his religious faith'. That this is not deemed to be a condemnation of all forms of socialism is clear in his statement that it is not possible to find 'the germs of a purer and a nobler socialism than those scattered in every page of the Christian's Gospel'.

O'Malley terms his own true socialism 'Christian Social Economy'. Its goal is to have 'the laws regulating the society . . . imbued with a Christian morality', thereby attacking the 'pagan spirit' which treats working people 'as if mere beasts of burthen, or two-armed machines of iron or wood'. In a characteristically ecumenical manner he cites as a fellow believer in a practical social morality 'that able man of whom the English Protestant Church of our time might well be proud, the late Rev. Dr Arnold'. The choice of Arnold is also interesting for another reason; although seeing himself as a friend of the workers, O'Malley takes a rather lofty, school-masterly tone towards them. Thus, for example, in an attack on what he takes to be the fatalism of the people, he waspishly refers to 'that stupid desponding tone . . . which is everlasting whining – "'tis fate, 'tis fate, 'tis fate, a wayward fate – 'tis Providence itself that wills our misery, 'twere vain to struggle with it".' He conceives of himself as an impartial referee between the contending classes, an 'interpreter' or 'mediator'. As with the 'Bill of Rights' the tone is moderate and consensual. A call is made for 'a calm and measured method, which proposes to make the most of the materials at hand, and which, in its step-by-step progress, may, perhaps, arrive sooner at the desired goal than the more adventurous teaching of the too rapid logicians'. Furthermore 'the rich and the poor should be alike persuaded that there is a *solidarity* of interests between them'. He poses his own vision of the future against what he takes to be the crude levelling conception of communism, and proposes a

> Social order . . . which makes room for the happiness of all, not upon the same flat level, as is idly dreamt of in the communistic philosophy, but, more agreeably to all the great analogies of nature, in an infinite variety of gradations, according to the infinite variety of individual tastes, and aptitudes and capacities.[70]

His nationalism is also very different from that of *The Irishman* since he firmly repudiates separatism in favour of a federalist solution: 'an Irish

Parliament elected *exclusively* for the enactment of purely Irish measures, and constructed so as *not* to interfere with the free action of imperial legislation. . . . This is the great principle of federalism.'[71]

O'Malley, besides producing Ireland's first Christian Socialist journal, is also of interest for his attempt to craft a fairly conservative socialism which would be more in tune, as he conceived of it, with the nature of Irish society and history. He thus confronts the equations in which socialism equals infidelity, and unrealistic, catastrophic change. Rooted in Irish Catholicism, but with a critical and fairly latitudinarian disposition, he is concerned to show both what is possible and what is valuable in Ireland.

These then are some of the socialisms to be found in the first half of the nineteenth century in Ireland. Such a short chapter can necessarily only scratch the surface. Each of the four forms of socialism discussed would repay a considerably more detailed examination. There are undoubtedly other forms to be explored which are not even mentioned here. None could be deemed a success: elite socialism was confined to a rather narrow social group and could only point to the ephemeral success of Ralahine as an example of a practical achievement; artisan socialism led a brief, almost fugitive existence amongst a very small number of Dublin artisans; the Irish Democratic Association, although it initially attracted some public support, rapidly collapsed, and O'Malley's *The Christian Social Economist* could only manage six issues. Each group appears to have been ignorant of their Irish predecessors: the artisan socialists make no mention of the elite socialists, and the socialists at the end of the 1840s make no reference to either of the earlier two – there is no sense of a native tradition to draw upon. The reasons for their failure to make ideological, political and social progress would require a separate chapter in itself. Descriptively all we can say here is that socialism was quite unable to challenge effectively the grip of established ideologies – conservatism, liberal nationalism, orthodox Catholicism, and Orangeism. Historical 'failures', these socialisms have almost disappeared from the historical account, resulting in the patchy historiography of Irish socialism to which we referred at the beginning of the chapter – submerged in both history and the historical record. Not only are these ideas interesting in themselves, they also need to take their place in a new comprehensive history of Irish socialism.

NOTES

I would like to thank the following for their comments on earlier drafts: Bob Eccleshall, Richard English and Gregory Claeys.

1 See: S. Daley, *Ireland and the First International*, Cork, Tower Books, 1984; J. W. Boyle, *The Irish Labor Movement in the Nineteenth Century*, Washington, DC, The Catholic University of America Press, 1988, ch. 4.

2 Thompson's works include: *An Inquiry into the Principles of the Distribution of Wealth* (1824), New York, Kelley, 1963; *Labor Rewarded*, London, Hunt & Clarke, 1827; also see: R. K. P. Pankhurst, *William Thompson*, London, Watts, 1954; G. Claeys, *Machinery, Money and the Millennium*, Cambridge, Polity Press, 1987, ch. 4.

3 See: R. G. Garnett, *Cooperation and the Owenite Socialist Communities in Britain, 1825–45*, Manchester, Manchester University Press, 1972, ch. 4; V. Geoghegan, 'Ralahine: Ireland's lost utopia', *Communal Societies*, 9, (1989), 91–104, and 'Ralahine: an Irish Owenite community (1831–1833)', *International Review of Social History*, XXXVI, 3, (1991), 377–411.

4 See: W. Thompson, *An Appeal of One-half the Human Race, Women*, London, Virago, 1983; B. Taylor, *Eve and the New Jerusalem*, London, Virago, 1983.

5 R. Owen, *Report of the Proceedings at the Several Public Meetings Held in Dublin*, Dublin, J. Carrick & Son, 1823.

6 *The Co-operative Magazine and Monthly Herald*, 1, 4 (April 1826).

7 A. Cullen, *Adventures in Socialism*, Clifton NJ, Kelley, 1972, 258.

8 ibid.

9 ibid., 258–62.

10 *The Co-operative Magazine and Monthly Herald*, 2, 4 (June 1827).

11 ibid., 2, 11 (November 1827).

12 ibid.

13 Some details of MacCormac's life can be found in I. Fraser, 'Father and son – a tale of two cities'. *The Ulster Medical Journal*, XXXVII, (1968), 1.

14 H. M'Cormac, *An Appeal in Behalf of the Poor; Submitted to the Consideration of Those who take an Interest in Bettering their Condition*, Belfast, S. Archer, J. Hodgson & M. Jellett, 1831, 15.

15 ibid., 13.

16 'Co-Operation, Association Joint-Agency, Co-Partnership Mutual-Assurance', *The Belfast Co-Operative Advocate*, 1 (January 1830), 13.

17 Fraser, 'Father and son', 12, 11.

18 H. M'Cormac, *A Plan for the Relief of the Unemployed Poor*, Belfast, Stuart & Gregg, 1830, 22.

19 ibid., 31.

20 H. M'Cormac, *On the Best Means of Improving the Moral and Physical Condition of the Working Classes; Being an Address, Delivered on the Opening of the First Monthly Scientific Meetings, of the Belfast Mechanics' Institute*, London, Longman, Rees, Orme, Browne & Green, 1830, 12.

21 ibid., 13.

22 Fraser, 'Father and son', 4–6.

23 *On the Best Means*, 11.

24 ibid.

25 *An Appeal*, 5.

26 *A Plan*, 29.

27 *An Appeal*, 6.

28 *On the Best Means*, 9.

29 ibid., 9–10.

30 *A Plan*, 17.

31 ibid.

32 ibid., 7.

33 H. M'Cormac, *The Philosophy of Human Nature in its Physical, Intellectual and Moral Relations; With an Attempt to Demonstrate the Order of Providence in the Three-Fold Constitution of our Being*, London, Longman, Rees, Orme, Brown, Green, & Longman, 1837, 118.

34 *On the Best Means*, 10–11.
35 *An Appeal*, 18.
36 *The Philosophy of Human Nature*, 118.
37 *An Appeal*, 22.
38 *On the Best Means*, 23.
39 *The Belfast Co-operative Advocate*, 1 (January 1830), 15–22. This journal in fact seems to have come out in January 1831, not 1830 as printed. A letter from James Kennedy, Corresponding Secretary of the First Belfast Co-operative Society, to the Glasgow Co-operative Society, dated 'December 21st 1830' and published in the *Herald to the Trades' Advocate, and Co-operative Journal* (January 1831) says that the first number of the journal 'will appear, we expect, next month'.
40 *The Voice of the People*, 26 February 1831. *The Lancashire and Yorkshire Co-operator* (May 1832) gives an account of 'the Second Social, or Anniversary Meeting' which 'consisted of about two hundred persons, about one half of which were females, and, with the exception of a few, they were all of the working or mechanical classes'. MacCormac is not mentioned.
41 See A. Durr's chapter 'William King of Brighton: Co-operation's prophet?' (and S. Yeo's introduction to it), in S. Yeo (ed.), *New Views of Co-Operation*, London, Routledge, 1988.
42 *The New Moral World*, 22 February 1840.
43 ibid., 24 April 1841.
44 ibid., 29 May 1841.
45 ibid., 5 February 1842.
46 ibid., 12 March 1842.
47 ibid., 5 November 1842.
48 For various accounts of the following see *The New Moral World*, 7 January 1843.
49 For Arkins see: F. D'Arcy, 'Dublin artisan activity, opinion and organisation, 1820–1850, unpublished MA thesis, University College, Dublin , 1968, Appendix XVI.
50 Reprinted in *The New Moral World*, 7 January 1843.
51 *Freeman's Journal*, 28 January 1843.
52 *The New Moral World*, 7 January 1843.
53 ibid., 4 February, 11 February 1843.
54 M. O'Connell (ed.) *The Correspondence of Daniel O'Connell*, Shannon, Irish University Press, 1972, 2, 471.
55 *The New Moral World*, 18 March 1843.
56 ibid., 11 March, 22 April, 27 May 1843.
57 ibid., 2 September 1843.
58 A few interesting memories of *The Irishman* and the Irish Democratic Association can be found in R. Pigott, *Personal Recollections of an Irish National Journalist*, Dublin, Hodges, Figgis, 1882, 30–40. Piggot, who was a young journalist on the paper, describes the Irish Democratic Association as 'a combination with aims almost entirely socialistic and revolutionary' (31).
59 *The Irishman*, 29 December 1849.
60 Pigott says that Fullam 'had the able aid of a number of young students of Trinity College' on the paper. Pigott, *Personal Recollections*, 30.
61 *The Irishman*, 9 March 1850.
62 ibid., 18 May 1850.
63 ibid., 2 March 1850.
64 ibid., 12 January 1850.
65 Pigott says that *The Irishman* 'went as far in the direction of advocating Mitchel's policy as it was safe to do in those days. I believe there is little

doubt that the proprietor was obliged to give a pledge to the Viceroy that the paper would not teach revolutionary doctrines, before it would be permitted to appear' (*Personal Recollections*, 31).

66 *The Irishman*, 6 April 1850.
67 For the scanty biographical details on O'Malley see: J. Crone, *A Concise Dictionary of Irish Biography*, Nedeln/Liechtenstein, Kraus Reprint, 1970, 193; D. Gwynn, *Young Ireland and 1848*, Cork, Cork University Press, 1949, 119; D. Kerr, *Peel, Priests and Politics*, Oxford, Clarendon Press, 1982, 148, 167–9.
68 *The Irish National Guard*, 29 April 1848.
69 *The Christian Socialist Economist*, 22 November 1851.
70 ibid., 6 December 1851.
71 ibid., 27 December 1851.

5 Trembling solicitude

Irish conservatism, nationality and public opinion, 1833–86

D. George Boyce

In the study of Irish political ideas the terms 'nationality', 'nationalism' and 'nation' are usually taken as having the same meaning. Likewise, the expression 'public opinion' is used indiscriminately to cover any political manifestation of the popular will, whether it is Daniel O'Connell's mass movement or the Roman Catholic response to Gladstone's disestablishment of the Church of Ireland. If these terms are indeed regarded thus, then Irish conservatism can hardly lay claim to any connection with them; and their usage must seem a contradiction, even a perverse and misleading use of language. Irish conservatism, long before it became subsumed in Irish Unionism, appears the very antithesis of nationality, let alone nationalism. It was fervently – at times rabidly – anti-Catholic; it was dedicated to the maintenance of the British connection (on the face of it surely nothing to do with the idea of nationhood); and it was the ideology of a minority of Irishmen, one not even shared by all Protestants, for the Whiggish and Liberal tradition, found especially among Presbyterians of the north of Ireland, held its own until the home rule crisis of 1886. Irish conservatives set their faces against nearly every reform demanded by the Catholic majority's political representatives, be it emancipation, repeal, tithe reform, land reform, or disestablishment.

But Irish conservatism was more inventive than this would imply. Irish conservatives between 1789 and 1850 lived, as did European conservatives generally, in a period of rapid change, and faced a future full of uncertainty. The tensions and fears that accompanied political, social and religious change produced their own kind of creative energy.[1] Irish conservatives, in particular, had forfeited the exclusive political title of the 'Irish nation' which they had assumed and held with pride in the eighteenth century; but some believed that this need not deprive them of a sense of nationality. Some went further, and sought flexibility in their political thinking, looking for a means whereby a sense of nationality and loyalty might be reconciled; and this launched them on the search, not only for some constitutional means to reconcile these apparent opposites, but for the creation in Ireland of what they liked to call 'public opinion'; not, as is so often implied by that expression, the opinion of all; but the opinion of the most enlightened, responsible and patriotic part of the nation: the Irish Protestant middle class and gentry.

Thus began the long, and not always explicit, engagement between Irish conservatives and the political thought of Edmund Burke. Burke wrote specifically on Ireland;[2] but it was not so much his Irish writings as his more general discussion of politics and society that underpinned the political ideas of the more philosophical Irish Tories. His defence of 'an established church, an established monarchy, an established aristocracy, and an established democracy', each preserved 'in the degree it exists, and no other',[3] was the cause of Irish conservatism. Irish conservatives' fear of the tyranny of numbers; their objection to what Burke called the reducing of a constitution to 'a problem of arithmetic'[4] haunted them as it did him. His belief in preserving checks and balances of the constitution was shared by them. They even hoped, despite all the evidence against them, to create a nation as an 'idea of continuity, which extends in time as well as in numbers and in space',[5] looking back to the Kingdom of Ireland and especially to its apogee in the eighteenth century.

And yet all this was to be achieved in a country where the discontinuities of history were more in evidence than the continuities; where, indeed, the most recent discontinuity was the Act of Union of 1800 which merged Ireland and Great Britain, and which seemed to end for ever the tradition of the Kingdom of Ireland, with its rights and privileges secreted in medieval institutions. And whereas Irish conservatives started out believing, like Burke, in the necessity of keeping Ireland within the empire,[6] they, unlike him, were obliged to admit that Protestants, as much as Roman Catholics, suffered from what they identified as English ignorance of the special conditions of life in Ireland; this included soulless Benthamism, and English dismissal of all things Irish as, at best, quaint, and at worst alien and repulsive. Irish conservatism would almost certainly find itself in strange waters when it sought to establish the *Dublin University Magazine* (*DUM*) as a periodical founded upon 'genuine Tory principles'.[7]

The *Dublin University Magazine* was founded in the wake of two great British and Irish crises: the granting of Catholic Emancipation (the right of Roman Catholics to sit in Parliament) in 1829; and the Reform Act of 1832, which reduced aristocratic influence in the boroughs. Irish Tories 'showed signs of having developed a persecution complex; and a few even contemplated the ultimate political option of ceasing to oppose Repeal (of the Union) since (one of them alleged) in a Repeal Parliament, freed from English interference, Protestants could reduce Ireland to peace – after something of a struggle'.[8] But they might yet find a better, less suicidal option: that of creating a distinctive political theory, one that would suit their peculiar circumstances, and enable them to play what they regarded as their rightful part in Irish society. The Protestant middle classes – the lawyers, writers, newspapermen, businessmen, clergy – whose educational bastion was Trinity College Dublin, knew that they must, by and large, live in Ireland and make the best of it. But this need not mean adopting a passive stance in the face of Catholic democratic power, (the 'frantic democracy'[9] so disliked by Burke); nor did it mean clinging abjectly to the coat-tails of England and accepting her blows or her kisses as the occasion demanded. Protestant Ireland, Tory Ireland could yet reveal its real depth, its rootedness in Ireland, its belief that Ireland was not a province but a nation, its intellectual qualities, and, above all, its patriotic tradition, one which it would not allow Daniel O'Connell to usurp and pervert in the name of the Catholic nation.

This was an ambitious and attractive idea. It enabled Irish Toryism to expose the hollowness of Irish Whiggery; it offered a vigorous defence of Protestant interests; but it demonstrated that Irish Tories could and should associate themselves with Irish themes, ways of life and thought, character, history. They could make contact with the national culture of Ireland – and yet remain loyal to Britain. This was the cultural equivalent of the home rule movement of Isaac Butt, which, some forty years later, aspired to create a form of Irish self-government, federal in character, that would secure Irish Protestants and reconcile nationality with the Union. This cultural movement, like the later political one, had the added advantage of removing prejudice and misunderstanding about Ireland from the minds of the English.

The *Dublin University Magazine* was a staunch and determined defender of the Protestant interest, and especially of the Protestant Church establishment. It attacked the vacillation and uncertainty of British policy. But this was only one aspect of its concern. It also wanted to convince England that Ireland was not merely the home of what the 'generality of writers' supposed: of Irishmen who 'if he be named Pat, if his conversation be overloaded with those figures of speech commonly called Irish Bulls' was then demonstrably Irish.[10] This moved *DUM* to embrace and promote Irish culture, by which it meant not only the systematic study of Ireland's past, her language, literature and history, but also the encouragement of the Irish writer to explore Irish themes: to make his name in Ireland, instead of looking to the English cultural scene. *DUM* promoted the work of William Carleton, which it described as doing 'full justice to our people', who despite their 'many faults' also possessed 'great and noble instincts'.[11] This literary effort, *DUM* declared when it took stock of its first twenty years in January 1853, was 'national'. National,

> not in the narrow sense of the term, but in the larger sense which endeavours to raise ourselves, our interests, and our institutions from the politics of mere provincialism to that of a component part of the greatest and most exalted empire the sun has ever shone upon.[12]

DUM showed its mettle when it demonstrated that membership of this empire did not imply subservience to England. On the contrary, it launched a sustained criticism of English ignorance of Ireland. In December 1835, in an article entitled 'English theories and Irish facts', it asked 'Who ever expected knowledge of Ireland from an Englishman? They know no more of Siberia and Caffreland than they do of their next door neighbours.' In September 1834 *DUM* quoted a speech by a Mr Charles Boyton (a rising conservative and a Fellow of Trinity College Dublin) at a great Protestant meeting, in which he declared that

> There is no government of Ireland or for Ireland. Ireland is considered only so far as it furnishes a price or a pretext to English parties. Irish questions, with English parties, are a weapon to assail an adversary, or a means to remunerate an auxiliary; but a government with a view to the real interests of the country . . . Ireland has none.

It commented that 'these few words contain an abstract of the conduct of all the British governments towards Ireland. This country has never yet been governed with reference to a principle.'[13] This was, on the face of it, dangerous ground, since the logical conclusion of such an argument might well be the modification of the Anglo-Irish constitutional relationship to allow the Irish to govern themselves. Certainly Isaac Butt, who became editor of *DUM* in the summer of 1834, was not slow to attack the Whigs for their misconceived inquiry into the poor law in Ireland with its conclusion that the English remedy was appropriate in Ireland also,[14] but denounced as 'absurd' the idea of two 'independent parliaments, in an empire intended to be one and indivisible'.[15] What Ireland needed was the development of 'public opinion':

> There is an unalterable law of creation, by which matter is subjected to mind, and force is made subservient to reason; then let intellect now assert its native, its unalienable superiority, and direct and control that public opinion which can never, with impunity, be set at nought; and directed, and controlled, we believe it can be. If the Conservative will but reason with the people, and instruct the people, they will guide the people – magna est veritas et praevalebit. Even the multitude are not inaccessible to conviction.

DUM, not for the first or the only time, quoted Edmund Burke: 'the multitude may fling from them all these garments of religion and of morals, "that decent drapery of life that covers the defects of our naked, shivering, nature" '; but 'let the voice of religion – the language of reason be addressed even to their madness, and all will yet be well again', and the people would sit at the feet of God, 'because at the feet of social order which He has ordained, "clothed and in their right mind".'[16]

Irish Conservatives' thinking was not as insular as it has often been portrayed: and their use of Burke to defend their position is not surprising. Burke was anxious that the brute facts of human nature should not be shirked; and he argued that they could only be controlled by a whole series of institutions, beliefs and practices that set restraints upon men.[17] Irish politics between 1832 and 1847 seemed to confirm the dangers that beset a country whose people were not subject to restraints. It was all very well to regard reform and democracy as synonymous; but this was not necessarily the case. Democracy was no more exempt from abuse than any other form of government; and, while an infusion of democracy would do good where it had been deficient, it would also do harm where there had already been an excess. It was 'all very well to subject our institutions to popular control – but it is very ill to leave them exposed to popular caprice'. Government in all its branches benefited from the ventilation of public opinion; but

> we hold that there is not more difference between the trade wind and the hurricane, than between the action of popular influence in its legitimate character, and the pressure of democratic violence, in the degree for which it is contended by modern reformers.[18]

When dealing with venerable institutions like the Irish municipal corporations, *DUM* felt, like Burke, a 'trembling solicitude'. The great mass of the Irish population was 'under the direct influence of the popish religion'; and reform in England bore a very different stamp from reform in Ireland.[19] One of the chief restraints on the excesses of Irish politics was of course the Union with England, which, like that between Scotland and England, could teach the people their duties as well as their rights: 'treat them as rational beings'. Scotland furnished proof that nationality 'in the fullest meaning of the term, may remain' even though Scotland's representatives sat in London: in all the arts of war, peace, culture and industry, Scotland excelled.[20]

DUM stood for nationality, not nationalism. Yet its belief in Ireland, its demand that Irish writers, in particular, attend to their own country and write for their own people, was a deeply influential one, and one that found an echo in the mind of Thomas Davis, who, like *DUM*, employed the word 'nationality' rather than nationalism, but who was prepared to go a stage further and embrace the concept of a 'Domestic legislation'. Davis had been brought up a 'High Tory and Episcopalian Protestant', and he urged the same advice on his people as did *DUM*: Protestants must concern themselves with the Irish past, and Irish themes.[21] He believed that the Church of Ireland was a national church; he hoped to see the divines of Trinity College Dublin seeking out monastic remains on the Continent. His newspaper, the *Nation*, acknowledged in 1844 that *DUM* was indeed 'thoroughly Tory', but also 'kindly, grave and Irish'.[22] And it is hard to tell whether it was the *Nation* or *DUM* speaking when the sentiment was expressed that 'the general estimate of our moral and intellectual condition is of the very lowest', and that 'the vast capabilities of this country for literary pursuit, are in fact concealed by the overpowering demand of the English marts. What is produced here is consumed there.' And which concluded that the Irish should seek to 'retain at home a large proportion of our native genius and learning'.[23]

DUM never travelled further than this concept of nationality: it called for an Irish literature, and an Irish press, to 'supply the place which a national legislature once held – a focus of talent; or a nursery for the production of eminent men'.[24] But there were those in conservative ranks who at least considered what other options were available to the Protestants of Ireland, and who laid the foundations for the branch of conservative opinion that led towards the home government association. Two leading examples are Charles Lever, the novelist, and W. E. H. Lecky, the historian. Lever, whose works have not survived changing taste, looked back to a golden age of the Protestant people. In his best-seller, *Jack Hinton the Guardsman* (published in *DUM* in serial form in 1842, and in book form in 1843), Lever described the Irish country house where the names of 'Burke, Sheridan, Grattan and Curran' were heard. Lever reflected upon the brightest period of Ireland's history, when wealth and genius were rife in the land and when the 'joyous traits of Irish character were elicited in all their force by prosperity and happiness'. 'Alas', he mused, 'they have no inheritors of their fame; they have left no successors behind them.'[25]

Lever edited *DUM* from April 1842 until 1845. He first involved himself in political journalism in the Catholic Emancipation crisis of 1827–9, when he managed to salvage for the press a splendid anti-Emancipation speech by Charles Boyton, whose resolution at a Tory meeting in Dublin was mangled by the Marquis of Downshire; when Downshire read the revamped product, he was heard to remark that he didn't 'do these sort of things often; but when my blood is up I get along without knowing it, never wanting a word'.[26] Yet, Tory though he was, Lever declared to Thackeray in 1842 that 'I am an Irishman, body, soul and spirit; my good name and fame, such as they are, are also Irish, and I think that my duties lie in Ireland.' Thackeray replied that there was no fame to be got in Ireland, simply because there was no public opinion there: 'Dublin is split up into factions, coteries and classes, jealous of each other, and engaged in miserable squabbles . . . the Magazine, if carried across the water, would be more Irish than it is, for many Irishmen of real genius can be had in London, and none in Ireland.'[27]

Lever's biographer, W. J. Fitzpatrick, analysed Lever's brand of Tory nationalism, which he attributed to Lever's father's conversation with his guests, many of whom were ruined by the Union, who spoke of 'the brilliant past, of the orators whom they had seen and heard, and the thrilling scenes enacted in the great drama, when the curtain fell on what was regarded as the extinction of a nation'.[28] It was an easy step for Lever to move from his admiration of the Irish gentry of Grattan's era to a criticism of the dire consequences for Ireland of the neglect of their station and duties. In 'St Patrick's Eve', he appealed through the *DUM* to the 'good feeling' felt towards landlords which they 'could only convert into an attack by convicting themselves'. He warned that he would 'not spare the owners of property who prefer factitious political influence to a position of credit and honour, and self-indulgence to the higher duties of their station'.[29] Lever's editorship raised the circulation of *DUM* to the unprecedented number of four thousand copies a month: but his criticism of the gentry, and his novel *The O'Donoghue*, set in the times of the United Irishmen, provoked some reviewers to charge him with Repealism. Lever denied the charge, pointing out that the 'old Tories . . . have derided Ireland, and cried it down; and as Wesley said that the Church left all the good music to the Devil, so the Tory aristocracy left all the nationality, all the unction and fervour of fatherland, to the dare-devils of democracy'. It was his purpose, he continued, to 'bring Irish gentlemen into better repute, not by exaggerated pictures of good quali-ties so much as by correct delineation of the state of society in which they live, where there are abundant apologies for many failings'. He was, he confessed to a friend, by now as sick of the ignorant stupidity of the High Tory as he was of the sordid conduct of O'Connell;[30] Irish public opinion, then, had failed to materialize.

Charles Lever's attitude to the Union was an integral part of the Tory nationalist tradition. Lever attacked the Repealers; but he was also a critic of the bribery and corruption by which the Union, in his view, had been passed, though he was 'unwilling to apply for a divorce'. Yet after 1845, when he moved away from Ireland and lived abroad, he redis-covered his 'early national instincts'.[31] In the last years of his life, in Trieste, he reflected on the eighteenth century, when Ireland enjoyed a period

> rich in the men we are proud of as a people, and peculiarly abounding in traits of self-denial and devotion which, in the corruption of a few, have been totally lost sight of; the very patriotism of the time having been stigmatised as factious opposition.

He noted that 'nearly every man of ability was against the Minister [Pitt the Younger, who carried the Union], that not only all the intellect of Ireland, but all the high spirit of its squirarchy and the generous impulses of its people, were opposed to the Union'.[32] Lever in 1866 was still hoping for some recognition or preferment from the Conservative government led by Disraeli: he had 'done good service in novels and other ways' for thirty years,[33] and it might seem inconsistent in him that he should seek the very advantages that he condemned in others in the passing of the Irish Act of Union. But he was sincere enough in finding his final political resting place: that of favouring 'home rule' but not 'Rabble Rule'; and looking still to England to

Cheer by its presence, and guide by its light
the people that long to be free.[34]

A love of the English constitution, and yet a call for Irish home
government; a love of Ireland, a desire to end its divisive politics, and
yet a fear of democracy: these were the pillars of the Protestant Tory
nationalism that was developed by the conservative historian, W. E. H.
Lecky, the forerunner of Isaac Butt and the flowering of Tory
nationalism.

In a review of the works of Charles Lever, published in *Blackwell's
Magazine* in April 1862, the anonymous writer noted an important aspect
of Lever's Irishness: it was

> That conviction which is entertained by Irishmen, not without a certain
> self satisfaction, that their characters are all but incomprehensible to
> Englishmen . . . and a certain sense of not unnatural resentment, with
> which, some years ago, the Irish people must have been disposed to
> regard every attempt on the part of Government to shape out or
> constrain the pattern of their national life into formal accordance with
> the modes and manners of an alien and dominant race.[35]

This feeling of resentment against the levelling and insensitive nature of
English government struck a response in Lecky, whose attitude to Irish
politics was, like that of all Tory nationalists, deeply influenced by his
concern for the implications for Ireland of an age of democracy. Lecky's
politics were not unambiguously conservative. As his biographer, J. J.
Auchmuty, noted

> He looked on himself as a Liberal, but emphatically not as a radical,
> and in truth he was all his days an old style Whig but never an extreme
> Tory, though it was as a follower of Salisbury that he was finally
> elected for Dublin University.[36]

Yet, in his approach to nationalism and democracy, he was essentially
an Irish Tory. His approach to Irish history was marked by his love of
the eighteenth century, when Ireland enjoyed a balanced constitution and
a genuine public opinion. In 1860 he was convinced that Ireland had but
two choices: a complete fusion with England; or the creation of a healthy
national feeling in Ireland uniting its people, a national feeling that would
transcend sectarianism and produce a public opinion, which in turn would
overcome the 'obstacle' to both fusion and nationality: the Roman Catholic priesthood.[37] Under Swift, 'public opinion first acquired a definite
form and an imposing influence'; but by the time of O'Connell its
'dominion became still wider, but its spirit more narrow'. It seems that
Lecky saw himself as the possible leader of that public opinion which
Henry Grattan represented so well.[38] In 1874 he refuted J. A. Froude's
calumnies on Ireland,[39] and he was convinced that English policy towards

Ireland between 1782 and 1800 undermined that public opinion which Grattan had laboured so hard to create.[40]

Lecky's view of public opinion was that it was patriotic, constitutional, national and ecumenic; and, above all, upper class in its origins. Hence his praise of the Volunteer Movement of the late eighteenth century which always remained within the control of the Irish gentry.[41] And from this he concluded naturally that a healthy national feeling must be one in which Protestants would play the key role. He also hoped that education would direct the Irish people towards this end. But he had the sense to realize that his idea of a political settlement depended upon Ireland not becoming a democracy; or at least not assuming the character of a 'pure' democracy, especially as that democracy would be susceptible to clerical influences. Thus, while he favoured Gladstone's Land Act of 1870 as a conservative measure, settling the peasant on the land and restoring good relations with the landlord,[42] he could not regard Ireland as fit for the restoration of national institutions: especially after the Fenian uprising of 1867. 'What a perfectly hopeless country Ireland is! And what complete fools, how utterly incapable of every vestige of self-government our respectable fellow countrymen are!' Fenianism, however, only emphasized the point of his earlier views: that public opinion, and Irish nationality, must be guided by the upper class.[43] In 1793 the Catholic people of Ireland were cut adrift from the beneficial influence of property by untimely franchise reform: and the result was the disastrous rebellion of 1798. Lecky's opinion of franchise reform in general was that it must end up with a balance, and must ensure that different social classes act in harmony.[44] This was difficult to achieve in Ireland, however, where there was not, as there was in England, the means of producing a healthy, well-informed public opinion. In 1879 he denounced Parnell and Parnellism as having 'killed Home Rule by demonstrating . . . that the classes who possess political power in Ireland are radically and profoundly unfit for self-government'. Home rule in a democratic Ireland was impossible, for it was incompatible with the English connection, and would lead to civil war and a 'Jacobin revolution in property'.[45]

This central concern for Protestant Ireland, this keen desire to give the Irish gentry a role in Irish political life, was, in Lecky's view, enhanced by the fact that the Protestant gentry had a dual responsibility: they had to fulfil their own proper place in society, and also stand in for the Irish Catholic gentry, for the natural leaders of Catholic Ireland. Ireland needed a ruling class, loyal both to Ireland and to the British Empire. In this, Lecky was close to Burke, whose concern was to preserve Ireland's place in the Kingdom and the Empire, and who had no time for a separate independent Irish Parliament. But it was one of Burke's axioms that society constituted an organism, possessed a natural unity, unforced and unmade by the hand of man. This involved and indeed required a view of history that centred on continuity as well as change;

on change that, if properly managed and skilfully controlled by the political elite, would contribute towards continuity. But Irish history seemed to bear witness against this view of history; Ireland's past was marked by her lack of common inheritance, by the failure of any group of her people to establish an agreed constitution for a harmoniously working society, and to pass it on to posterity.

Sir Samuel Ferguson addressed this problem, and sought a means of securing for the Irish Protestant, and especially the gentry, a full and ungrudging place in Irish national life. Ferguson used the pages of *DUM* to promulgate his view that the Protestant, 'even the newest comers amongst us', possessed 'as good a claim, now, to the name of Irishmen, as had the Norman invaders to that of Englishmen at the time of the Edwards'.[46] The unity of Irishmen could be achieved through the study of the rich materials left by the Irish past: and he asked the 'noble fortunate persons' what it was to 'buy the applause of the race-course, or excitement of the hazard table',

> at the cost of whole estates in comparison with the cheap purchase, at the cost of a few weeks' or even days' revenues of the fame of having contributed the first foundation stones to a nation's history, and the satisfaction and solace of having won a nation's thanks and the sympathies of all the educated classes of the nation, for them and theirs, to the third and fourth generation.[47]

Had the upper classes not fallen below the standards of their predecessors, then they would not be in their present helpless and humiliating position. 'So long as the populace are set against the gentry, and the gentry, attaching themselves to external associations, refuse to know their own country and its people, that state of things must continue.' But Ferguson pointed to the great achievements of the 'grandfathers' of the gentry: and he pointed to 'their mansion houses, their libraries, their collections of painting and sculpture' as evidence that 'the spurious civlization of little economists and quibbling logicians is not an improvement on the solid and elegant acquirements, and constitutional and legal learning, of the Irish noblemen and gentlemen of the last century'.[48]

Here was Burke's educated, cultured and experienced gentry now given a place in an Irish context. They must lead the quest for 'national self-knowledge', for 'whether a man seek for change or for continuance of existing institutions, he must ground a great part of his reasoning on historical experience.'[49] But there was a special Irish dimension here. Burke was convinced that Ireland could only prosper within the Empire; but in Ferguson's day it was increasingly irritating to discover that the 'empire' (that is, England) was offering Ireland what Ferguson called 'frequent provocation to resentment which the self-respecting gentry of this part of the Empire receive from the insolence and folly of writers in the metropolitan press'. Such abuse was a danger to the Empire, for 'if the Conservative gentry of Ireland thought fit to unite their friends and tenants to meet them at a new Dungannon, there is no power in Britain which could prevent the severance of the two islands'. Thomas Davis, he wrote, a gentleman 'both in feeling and in judgement', was

> opposed to all designs for destroying the legitimate power of the gentry. He would, if he could, have won them to his opinion, and through his agency have sought 'to mould, to multiply, and to consolidate' the brute mass beneath; but he never lent himself to the anarchical project of exterminating because he could not influence them, and of reducing all society to one base level of peasants.

Had Davis lived to witness the 'servile war' waged on the Irish gentry since his death, he would not be found a glorious volunteer among those waging that war.[50]

Ferguson wrote these words in 1847, a year in which he believed he saw the gentry entering a more hopeful era, one when they would play a full part in Irish national life, with consequent 'new guarantees for the stability of the whole social edifice'.[51] But the inability or reluctance of the British government to deal quickly or effectively with the great Irish famine occasioned another example of a recurring theme in Irish Protestant history: a group of Protestants founded the Protestant Repeal Association in Dublin, with the resolution that

> While we maintain loyalty to our Sovereign, we deem it our duty as Irishmen to testify our attachment to our country; and inasmuch as the Imperial Parliament has failed to make Union a source of prosperity to Ireland – and it is certain that Ireland was eminently prosperous previous to the Union – we desire to return to our ancient constitutions, and pledge ourselves not to desist from our efforts until we are governed by the Queen, Lords and Commons of Ireland.[52]

Ferguson was quick to warn that, while many of the Irish were still attached to the Union, the 'tone of the English press would lead careless observers to suppose that these Irish adherents took a morbid pleasure in avenging their quarrel with Mr. O'Connell in their common country, the reverse is the fact'.

> For it may be said of these Irish Unionists, that while becoming every day more sensible to the advantages of connection with Britain, they are also *pari passu* becoming more attached to their own country and more sensitive to every reflection on her honour.

The 'habitual contempts' heaped on Ireland, where the 'nobility and chief gentry, as well as a large proportion of the professional and commercial classes, are animated by sentiments such as these, cannot be indulged in without excitement of irritation and the creation of danger'. For England to undermine that class upon which the Union depended was 'unbecoming as well as impolitic'.[53]

Ferguson saw even greater danger in the prospects of conflict between Catholic and Protestant in Ireland. In politics, he declared, 'I am a Conservative, but always was and am a great detestor of Party and Faction'; but he was also an opponent of 'those projectors and centralisers whose schemes appear to me to keep society in Ireland from consolidating into a settled strength and refinement'.[54] In May 1848 Ferguson made a speech to the Protestant Repeal Association in which he criticized the gross mismanagement of Irish affairs, the Viceroy, Lord Clarendon's 'centralizing' policy and the 'unworthy manner in which this ancient kingdom – this loyal, great and peaceable people – have been spoken of by English representatives in the House of Commons'. He acknowledged that he had hitherto been a supporter of the Union in all its aspects; but he acknowledged that he was mistaken. The Famine had demonstrated English ignorance of Irish conditions, but, more important, the measures envisaged by Parliament to alleviate it, and especially the taxation of landlords, were intended to exterminate and put away the Irish landed gentry. This would make Ireland a 'Draw farm' for England, by attracting all that was best in Irish life to the metropolis. The Irish gentry were in danger of succumbing to humble servitude, and this must be stopped if they were not to be eradicated for ever from Ireland. Ferguson proposed as a solution some means whereby Ireland could achieve powers of government within her own exclusive province; and he believed that once this were done, then the constituencies would return to supporting the 'best gentlemen in the country'. He had no quarrel with the English people, who helped Ireland so magnanimously in her time of distress; he said, with 'cordial sincerity, "Rule Britannia" '. But 'We are not a colony of Great Britain – we are an ancient kingdom, an aristocratic people, entitled to our nationality, and resolved on having it.'[55] But this brand of Protestant nationalism must be consistent with the survival and political leadership of the gentry. When he contemplated the Parnellite home rule movement in 1885, he was less sanguine. The people, he wrote to William Allingham, were 'idle, feckless' but still a 'game breed'. He trusted in God

> that they will yet recognise as friends the men who revolt against the present teachings given them by those who would make them knaves and cowards. They need strong hands over them – even Orangemen for want of better, if the Orangemen could only be made to feel Irish. I don't think our Whig-Liberals will ever understand them.

For Ferguson, the 'safest form of home rule' was the Parliament of 1799, one 'controlled by the House of Lords and Royal Prerogative', which would 'be much more likely to end discontents, with comparative safety to property and social security'.[56]

Home rule, then, could yet be a conservative measure; and certainly its formulation by Isaac Butt in 1870 was made on sound conservative principles, and was consistent with the Butt who had edited *DUM* when Tory nationalism was first given an authentic voice. Butt was a firm believer in prescriptive rights, and in the virtue of institutions which had demonstrated their value through their rootedness and longevity. When he argued the case against Municipal Reform in 1840 he warned that the Bill would spare no privilege, respect no franchise; the removal of free-men's rights made the Bill a 'revolution': 'The Coporation of Dublin is as ancient as British rule in Ireland.' He pointed out the 'anomaly' of a Corporation 'so directly and bitterly opposed in religion to the great majority of the gentry and professional classes', and denounced a 'democ-racy' as 'the most shameless of all shameless things'. In Ireland, unfortu-nately, 'propery and numbers are opposed – religious differences make a broad separation between the holders of property and the mass of the people'. Reform would hand the propertied classes over to a 'Jacobin Club', but, what was worse, a Jacobin Club 'on which will be engrafted the worst elements of national antipathy and religious hate'. But he also cited Henry Grattan in defence of prescriptive rights: in the Irish Parlia-ment someone dared hint that the privileges of Dublin stood on lower and less sacred grounds than those of London.

> Who was the man who rose with prompt indignation to resent this insult to the constitution of Ireland? A man . . . whose memory is still held in honour in our country – the illustrious Henry Grattan! He it was who, in the spirit of a true Irishman, indignantly denounced the attempt to place the privileges of Dublin below those of London. It was no part of that great man's patriotism to vilify and bring into contempt the institutions of his country.[57]

Butt, at this stage in his political life, still resolved upon maintaining the Union inviolate, for, as he warned in 1843 when debating Repeal with O'Connell, there was no half-way house between Union and separ-ation. Repeal would mean that Ireland would sink into the position of a 'paltry, pitiful, and subject province of England'.[58] He saw Grattanite patriotism and the defence of Protestant interests as synonymous. But two aspects of his case were significant for the development of his thought. He objected to England's lack of understanding of the position of Irish Protestants; it was not such a large step, then, to discern that England might not understand Ireland as a whole; especially when, as Butt always maintained, Ireland had indeed many real problems in need of remedy. Her poverty, for example, could not be met by the English style of *laissez-faire* policies; these did not suit Irish conditions. Much was wanted to elevate the condition of the people.[59] By the 1840s he was addressing himself to the consideration of the whole economic and social structure of Ireland; and he warned the Irish landlords that they were driving the

Catholic clergy and the mass of the people into the hands of radical demagogues. In 1847 Butt returned to the land question and attacked the government for its determination to throw the burden of famine entirely upon Irish property. He reminded the British government and public that they had a responsibility for governing Ireland. In 1848 he argued that Irishmen had the right to protest against the misgovernment of their country, even to the extent of demanding Repeal. In the 1850s and 1860s Butt (who now sat as a Tory MP) advocated tenant right reform: secure tenures at fair rents, and prompt payment of financial obligations to landlords. And, when faced with the demand of the Roman Catholic Church to turn the non-denominational national education system into a denominational one, Butt supported this on the grounds that it was consistent with Irish public opinion; he also supported the call for a Roman Catholic university, arguing the secular educational thinking of English radicalism threatened the spiritual foundations of the constitution.[60]

This brought Butt to the kernel of the Irish conservative dilemma: the problem of creating a responsible public opinion in Ireland, one that had defeated Ferguson and Lecky, and now confronted him. The question was: if the Irish people had representative government, but not responsible government, then how could a public opinion be created and expressed? When in 1870 Butt devised the idea of a federal Ireland, the essentially conservative nature of his thinking was exposed, rather than contradicted. He spoke of the 'ancient constitutional rights' of the nation. 'I abide by old traditions', he declared in 1873 in a home rule conference in Dublin,

> old traditions which have their place in the hearts of the people; I abide by them when they lead in the direction of popular power. I use them equally when they become an element of conservative strength. I am sure we would act most unwisely if in reframing a state we throw away the great elements which these old traditions give.[61]

He would not oppose a guarantee to landlords that no acts would be passed interfering with their titles to their properties.[62] And despite his reference to 'popular power' he made it clear that his Irish constitution would be far from democratic.[63] Butt proposed the old constitution of king, lords and commons, for:

> We take things as we find them – we transfer to Ireland the constitution as it is – we restore the old parliamentary system, modified by the reforms and changes which the progress of opinion, the advance of society, and the course of events have made in that system within the last seventy years. But here we take our stand.[64]

And in this constitution the landlords, free from fear of any reopening of the Acts of Settlement and Explanation (which were passed in Charles

II's reign and were the foundation of the landed power of the Protestant gentry), would find a secure place.[65]

When he turned to the details of the constitution and powers of the Irish house of commons, the conservative nature of Butt's proposals became clearer. He wanted the Irish Parliament to be elected separately from the imperial Parliament, but he did not think it necessary to propose any change in the existing franchise. And he suggested including in the representative system members from what Burke called the 'little platoons': the universities, and possibly from the Colleges of Physicians and surgeons, 'and some other bodies of that nature'. The Irish house of lords should consist of peers chosen by the Queen, including life peers, which would ensure that the resident gentry of Ireland took their place in 'the council of the nation'. The Irish Parliament (the Queen, lords and commons) should have control in Ireland except in those matters which the Federal Constitution might specially reserve to the imperial Parliament; and Butt took comfort in the reflection that such an assembly would never pass an unjust law; or, if it did, then the Irish House of Lords could veto it, and veto it in safety. The Irish people were not a democratic people; it was the English people who threatened democracy, if not revolutionary violence, and Ireland might well be the conservative, stabilizing element in the British federal constitution.[66]

Would – could – Ireland find peace and stability in a Burkean constitutional settlement, adapting the old to the new, reconciling the gentry, respecting prescriptive rights? There seemed some reason to believe, in 1870, that she could. In that year a Protestant physician and surgeon, Robert MacDonnell (under the pseudonym 'A Protestant Celt') published a pamphlet that attracted widespread attention. Entitled *Irish Nationality in 1870*,[67] the pamphlet traced the shifts and movements in Irish public opinion in recent times, noting that English policy had had the effect of uniting Catholic and Protestant: 'a sledgehammer welding Irish parties together'. England had attempted to force on Ireland English laws, customs and religion; above all, in 1869 she disestablished the Church of Ireland, thus offending Protestant sentiment deeply, and causing some conservatives to question the value of the Union itself. MacDonnell wanted to see the creation in Ireland of a 'vigorous, healthy, united lay public opinion', and he believed that he perceived the making of such an opinion in the 'remarkable metamorphosis which has changed the Orangeman into an Irish patriot'. Irish Protestants were never wanting in 'national feeling and sentiment'; now this sentiment, previously dwarfed and distorted by English pampering, was assuming a healthy growth since that pampering was withdrawn. This feeling was not confined to the lower orders, but existed also in the 'higher intelligence' of the country. So much so that a man who advocated 'Imperial Union' combined with 'local government' would be like 'a general advancing through friendly country'. Irishmen of all persuasions yearned for a 'public opinion purified from the blighting influence of priestcraft and proselytism, and soaring above the pettiness of faction'. MacDonnell did not care if this public opinion favoured the 'project of Pitt' (i.e. Union) or that of Grattan; but if it were drifting towards the latter, then it was time for patriotic men on both sides of the Channel to determine 'how much of independent government may be wisely given to Ireland, and yet retain for her the enormous advantages of close Imperial Union with the greatest nation of the earth'. Yet MacDonnell was aware that there were Tories who talked of Repeal, but – like the woodcutter in the fable who called on death – would cry, in the event of it coming, 'not yet'.[68]

MacDonnell's observations were shrewd. Protestant Tories were divided on the issue of how far their sense of nationality could take them along the road to even a modest measure of federal home rule. *DUM* still searched for a public opinion, but now wanted one that would be 'so regulated as to set both the British and Irish people right as to their relations to one another'; home rule aimed at 'breaking the solemn compact of 1800'. It still longed for an Ireland 'not the Ireland of the Protestant, nor yet that of the Catholic – the true and abiding Ireland of history, of the heart's affections, and of living people this day, as truly as in the days of St. Patrick'.[69] But there was no half-way house between union and separation; and Butt's proposals were as 'wicked and demoralising as O'Connell's', aiming at the dismemberment of the Empire. It called upon England to institute a 'complete' union, a complete incorporation of the 'two kingdoms', as had occurred in Scotland: 'Abolish the Viceroyalty, leave Dublin Castle to bats and owls.' Then national antipathies and animosities would die out, and 'sound public opinion will be formed, and the popular mind, delivered from its delusions, will no longer submit to be cheated and illured by such bubble schemes as home rule'.[70]

But, though divided – and with the majority indifferent or hostile to home rule – Protestant conservatives could still take a pride in their nationality. In May 1870 the *Dublin Daily Express* replied to an attack upon Protestant home-rulers by the London *Standard*. The *Standard* had declared that it was 'at a loss to understand how such men . . . can be so careless of their own obvious interests, even if they are indifferent to the welfare of the great empire of which they are subjects'. It asked how long an Irish Parliament would allow the landlords to retain their estates acquired two centuries ago by conquest, and how long Protestant worship would be tolerated. 'Repeal would be a fatal blow to the greatness of England; it would be an irreparable calamity to Ireland . . . but to the Protestants, above all, it means nothing short of utter ruin.'[71] The *Dublin Daily Express* countered this outburst with surprising confidence. It welcomed the 'practical expression of the growing spirit of Nationalism', and pointed to the meeting that would be held in a few days to consider the creation of a royal residence in Ireland. The *Express* feared, not nationalism, but its 'perversion': 'National feeling in itself is an unmixed good.'

National Irishmen in the imperial Parliament had important tasks, especially to secure 'the recognition of the just claims of Ireland to a treatment just, at least, if not generous'. A resident sovereign would be essential: 'No Irishman likes to see his country treated and governed as a mere colony or dependency of the British Empire.'[72]

When the *Express* came to analyse national feeling, it returned to the notion of a public opinion free from 'priestcraft' – Protestant or Catholic; and it complained, again in traditional style, of the dangers of English selfishness. It set out to refute the *Standard*'s claim that there could be no such thing as 'Tory nationalism'. Ireland was an integral part of the United Kingdom – 'a position which we accept with pride:

> But it is something more. It is an island whose natural capabilities, climate, soil and conformation differ from those of England. It is inhabited, moreover, by a race which, however mixed, nevertheless preserves strong traits of dissimilarity to their Saxon neighbours; whose history, political, social and religious, and habits of thought differ widely from those of England. In short it is a Nation, and not a district of England.

Such a nation might be governed in one of three ways: in accordance with the advantage of the United Kingdom (such as was the case when Ireland was excluded from the advantages of trading with the continent); as a province of England, which simply meant to pay no attention to her special wants and capabilities (which had converted many honest patriots into Repealers); or – a policy which had never yet been tried – the government of Ireland by the imperial Parliament for Ireland's own sake, and in accordance with its true requirements, as interpreted by a trustworthy and independent Irish public opinion. The Scottish Members of Parliament – a mere handful – succeeded in carrying out this policy for their own country; the Irish MPs had double the power, if they were but united. This was a concept of nationalism that did not commend itself to Irish agitators or English parties; 'but in the same degree in which it is condemned by them it is approved by the patriotric Irishman who desires to see the interests of his native country attended to . . . who desires, in short, a truly National policy'.[73]

The possibility of reconciling the Union with nationality, and the gentry with the people, must become more difficult as Ireland, like England, moved towards a wider and more democratic franchise. Sir Samuel Ferguson warned in 1885, in the wake of Gladstone's franchise reforms, that 'the electoral pack has been swelled by the introduction of such an addition of non-court cards that, shuffle them as we may, we never can hold the same hands again'.[74] But Standish O'Grady, a firm supporter of Randolph Churchill's concept of 'Tory Democracy', looked to the possibilities of adapting the old to the new in the, admittedly more fraught, Irish context. Tory Democracy aimed at promoting the welfare of the country by means of attaching the masses to the Throne, the Church and the House of Lords. O'Grady admired Disraeli, whom he described in his book, *Toryism and Tory Democracy* (1886) as 'the first amongst our public men honestly to acknowledge the political and social transformations effected by the rapid advance of Democracy in the present age'.[75] But how could Ireland, with its sectarian divisions, with the slow but inexorable growth of the Catholic democracy, adjust to the new age? He castigated the Irish landlords for their abject surrender to the raucous demands of the Land League, and reminded them of the courage and resolution of their ancestors, the Desmonds, Red Hugh, and those who in the past had rallied to themselves bands of loyal retainers, workers and labourers on their lands; and he praised them as still the 'best class we have, and so far better than the rest that there is none fit to mention as the next best'. Yet the landlords – the rulers of the land and the people – 'have not ruled'. The landlords must make themselves the masters of the people 'or, as sure as I live and you live, you will be their prey'.[76] The landlords had reason for hope, for 'no landlord in Ireland ever drove his tenants so hard as do the average employers of labour'.[77] In the past, Irish nobles had 'never provoked a servile revolt, or one that they could not quell'.[78] In Irish history lay the 'key of safety', for the Land League had no representative in history, 'not even a Tyler or Cade', whereas 'Red Hugh, I think, would have offered but a short shrift to a committee of modern patriots going down to organise his tenantry on National League principles.' A few great individuals might yet awaken the landlords from their slumber.[79]

Ferguson, Butt and O'Grady were equally mistaken in their belief that they could reconcile Protestants, nationalism and mass politics. Irish conservatism was never able to mobilize men, to create the necessary political energy to construct the kind of public opinion, gentry led, that it believed was essential for the good of Ireland. Conservative national thought had obvious flaws. It sought to base itself on sound, Burkean, historical grounds, looking to kings and princes to justify gentry leadership of modern Ireland. Burke, for his part, held that Roman Catholics could be granted political rights since Protestant titles to property were protected by prescription; history was a complete guarantee against any claim by Catholics to legitimate appropriation.[80] But while Ireland had a glorious revolution as did England, she had also a prescriptive memory that long predated 1690, and which spoke of the events of the mid-seventeenth century in terms of recent confiscations. Butt, for his part, grappled with these discontinuities when he shifted from declaring in 1843, in opposition to Repeal, that all so-called Irish institutions were of English origin, that there were no 'ancient landmarks to abide by'; to claiming in 1873 that the restoration of the 'right of domestic legislation in all Irish affairs' was 'in accordance with the ancient institutional rights of the Irish nation'. The Irish kings who submitted to English dominion had a right to the same parliamentary constitution as enjoyed by England.[81]

Irish conservative nationalism was, necessarily, anti-democratic, or at least non-democratic; as Butt put it, the Irish constitution must be based on 'existing orders . . . exisiting franchises . . . existing powers'.[82] This was consistent with Burke's teaching, for to admit the supremacy of numbers was to invite the demise of Protestantism; but Burke's advice – that the Irish Protestants should 'raise an aristocratic interest, that is, an interest of property and education' amongst the Catholics[83] was unrealizable. The only hope lay in re-creating or reviving the deference which the Irish protestant gentry could reasonably look for (it was believed) through the making of a gentry-led public opinion, and – some conservatives came to believe – possibly through home rule; or the founding of a cultural revival which would imbue the gentry with a spirit of patriotism, and which would find common ground between them and the people. The failure of Sir Samuel Ferguson and *DUM* to achieve the latter, and the speedy development of the home rule movement into a Catholic party for a Catholic people, dashed these hopes, at least for the time being.

And yet they were not without powerful effect in the shaping of Irish politics. Charles Stewart Parnell took up the cause of home rule, a home rule based on his (misconceived) notion of what Grattan's Parliament and the constitution of 1782 had achieved. The maintenance of the Irish Parliament, he declared,

> would have been . . . better for both the people and the owners of the land – the landowners in Ireland. They would have been taught to conciliate the people towards them: they would have learned to govern the people justly and uprightly, and to give them by degrees those larger privileges, the extension of the franchise to the masses of the people . . . much mischief would have been spared, and . . . instead of occupying the humiliating position which the landlord class now do, they would have a better and happier one.[84]

When, inspired by the fall of Parnell in 1891, W. B. Yeats sought to create an Irish public opinion, Protestant led, from the 'soft wax' and to create it through the medium of a national literature (but not a nationalist one), he took as his inspiration the Tory cultural nationalism of Sir Samuel Ferguson, and thus of *DUM*, and he was mindful of the heroic claims made for the Irish aristocracy by Standish O'Grady.

In their search for an Irish history, culture and political institutions that would reflect the distinct character of Ireland, and yet enable the Irish Protestant gentry and middle classes to play a full role in Irish life, Irish conservative nationalists only succeeded in laying the foundations for a political and cultural revival that marginalized the very people they hoped to save. They did worse: if they claimed, as they did, that Ireland was very different from England, and yet tried to draw the line at the acknowledgement of those differences in separatist terms, they nevertheless opened themselves to the accusation that they were reneging on the Union to which they professed their undying loyalty. For in the eyes of British conservatives, the Union was the symbol of the elimination of all distinctions between England and Ireland, and in this view the idea of Ireland as different was a sign that Irish Protestant conservatives wanted to live in two worlds at once. They must decide whether or not they were British or Irish; 'loyalty' and 'Irishness' were not compatible. Irish Catholic nationalists were equally convinced of this incompatibility. This was a stark demand that most Irish Protestants, in the end, succumbed to, as they professed their Britishness as distinct from Irishness. It was a sign of the absolutism that came to characterize Irish political thought in the later nineteenth and early twentieth century. In the end, Protestant conservatives might be accused of acting as a midwife to an Ireland that rejected their 'trembling solicitude'; but without their cultural and political explorations, the birth of modern Ireland would have resulted in a very different issue.

NOTES

1 John Weiss, *Conservatism in Europe, 1770–1945: Traditionalism, Reaction and Counter-revolution*, London, Thames & Hudson, 1977, 37.
2 Matthew Arnold (ed.), *Letters, Speeches and Tracts on Irish Affairs by Edmund Burke*, London, 1881.
3 Frank O'Gorman, *British Conservatism: Conservative Thought from Burke to Thatcher*, London, Longman, 1986, 14.
4 ibid., 75.
5 ibid., 101.
6 J. C. Beckett, *The Anglo-Irish Tradition*, London, Faber & Faber, 1976, 56–7.
7 *DUM*, January 1833, 1.
8 R. B. MacDowell, *Public Opinion and Government Policy in Ireland, 1801–1846*, London, Routledge, 1952, 112.
9 Arnold, (ed.), *Letters, Speeches and Tracts*, 211.
10 *DUM*, January 1833, 32.
11 *DUM*, January 1841, 69–72.
12 *DUM*, January 1853, 1–8.
13 *DUM*, September 1834, 342.
14 Joseph Spence, 'Nationality and Irish Toryism: the case of the *Dublin University Magazine*, 1833–52', paper read at the fifth conference of Irish historians in Britain, Liverpool, April 1986, 13.
15 *DUM*, March 1836, 43–4.
16 *DUM*, September 1834, 347.
17 Edmund Burke, *Reflections on the Revolution in France*, ed. with an introduction by C. C. O'Brien, London, Penguin, 1983, 151.
18 *DUM*, April 1836, 426–7.
19 *DUM*, April 1836, 429; see also December 1835, 682–96.
20 *DUM*, October 1846, 456.
21 Mary Buckley, 'Thomas Davis: a study in nationalist philosophy', unpublished

Ph.D. thesis, University College Cork, 1980, 91; D. G. Boyce, *Nationalism in Ireland*, 2nd edn, London, Routledge, 1991, 155.

22 Buckley, 'Thomas Davis', 166–7.

23 *DUM*, March 1837, 365–76.

24 ibid., 375.

25 Charles Lever, *Jack Hinton, the Guardsman*, London, 1897 edn, 365. First published in *DUM*, 1842, and in book form in 1843.

26 Lionel Stevenson, *Dr Quicksilver: The Life of Charles Lever*, London, Chapman & Hall, 1937, 33–4.

27 Stevenson, *Dr Quicksilver*, 116–17.

28 W. J. Fitzpatrick, *The Life of Charles Lever*, London, n.d. (1884?), 12.

29 ibid., 236.

30 Stevenson, *Dr Quicksilver*, 142–3.

31 Fitzpatrick, *Lever*, 256–7.

32 Stevenson, *Dr Quicksilver*, 151.

33 ibid., 270–1.

34 Fitzpatrick, *Lever*, 259.

35 *Blackwoods' Magazine*, 91 (1862), 459.

36 James Johnston Auchmuty, *Lecky: A Biographical and Critical Essay*, Dublin, Hodges, Figgis & Co., 1945, 23.

37 Yvonne Dineen, 'The problem of political stability in a democratic age: the ideas of W. E. H. Lecky', unpublished Ph.D. thesis, University of Wales (Swansea), 1986, 37.

38 Donal MacCartney, 'Lecky's *Leaders of Public Opinion in Ireland*', *Irish Historical Studies*, XIV, 1964–5, 120–3.

39 Auchmuty, *Lecky*, 77.

40 Dineen, 'Lecky', 43.

41 ibid., 51.

42 Auchmuty, *Lecky*, 24.

43 Dineen, 'Lecky', 24; W. E. H. Lecky, *Leaders of Public Opinion in Ireland*, London, Longman, Green & Co., 1912 edn, I, 15, 18, 22, 26, 149–55.

44 ibid., 185–9.

45 ibid., 191–2.

46 Lady Ferguson, *Sir Samuel Ferguson in the Ireland of his Day*, London, 1896, I, 39–42.

47 ibid., 83.

48 ibid., 84.

49 ibid., 94–5.

50 ibid., 140–4.

51 ibid., 144.

52 *United Irishman*, 13 May 1848.

53 Lady Ferguson, *Sir Samuel Ferguson*, 140–4, 238–9.

54 ibid., 241.

55 ibid., 245–55.

56 ibid., 361.

57 Isaac Butt, *Irish Corporation Bill; a speech delivered at the Bar of the House of Lords on Friday, 13th May, 1840, in Defence of the City of Dublin*, London, 1840, 9, 11, 13–14, 65–9, 87, 89, 94.

58 Isaac Butt, *Repeal of the Union. A speech delivered in the Corporation of Dublin, on 28th February, 1843, on Mr. O'Connell's Motion....*, Dublin, 1843, 14, 17.

59 Laurence, J. McCaffrey, 'Irish federalism in the 1870s', in *Transactions of the American Philosophical Society*, new ser., vol. 52, part 6 (1962), 7.

60 ibid., 7–8.

61 Karen B. Stroup, 'Ending the quarrel of centuries: a rhetorical analysis of the persuasion of Isaac Butt and Charles Stewart Parnell, leaders of the Irish', unpublished Ph.D. thesis, Indiana University, 1984, 59.
62 Isaac Butt, *Proceedings of the Home Rule Conference Held at the Rotunda, 18, 19, 20 and 12 November, 1873*, Dublin 1874, 31.
63 Stroup, 'Ending the quarrel', 60.
64 Butt, *Proceedings*, 1874, 31.
65 ibid., 34.
66 Isaac Butt, *Home Government for Ireland, Irish Federalism: Its Meaning, its Objects and its Hopes*, 4th edn, Dublin, 1874, 35, 37, 39.
67 *Irish Nationality in 1870, By a Protestant Celt*, 2nd. edn, Dublin and London, 1870. For MacDonell's authorship see *Irish Book Lover*, VII (Dec. 1915), 101.
68 MacDonnell, 7, 10, 34–5, 38–40, 61–2, 65.
69 *DUM*, June 1873, 631–75.
70 *DUM*, April 1874, 466–78. See also July 1874, 117–19.
71 *Standard*, 14 May, 1870.
72 *Dublin Daily Express*, 21 May 1870.
73 ibid., 25 May 1870. See also 17 June 1870.
74 Lady Ferguson, *Sir Samuel Ferguson*, II, 233.
75 Standish O'Grady, *Toryism and the Tory Democracy*, London, 1886, v.
76 ibid., 216–18. See also his *Crisis in Ireland*, Dublin, 1882, 5, 18–19.
77 O'Grady, *Tory Democracy*, 221.
78 ibid., 227.
79 ibid., 238, 242. O'Grady had earlier advocated landlords to adopt a Land League style organization; see *Crisis in Ireland*, 54–5.
80 P. Lucas, 'On Edmund Burke's doctrine of prescription: or, an appeal from the new to the old lawyers', *Historial Journal*, XI, 1, 1968, 47.
81 Butt, *Proceedings of the Home Rule Conference*, 6–7.
82 ibid., 31.
83 Arnold, (ed.), *Letters, Speeches and Tracts*, 211.
84 *Freeman's Journal*, 24 January 1885.

6 Denis Patrick Moran and 'the Irish colonial condition', 1891–1921

Margaret O'Callaghan

> – Up the Boers!
> – Three cheers for De Wet!
> – We'll hang Joe Chamberlain on a sourapple tree.
> Silly billies: mob of young cubs yelling their guts out. Vinegar hill.
> The Butter exchange band. Few years' time half of them magistrates
> and civil servants. War comes on: into the army helterskelter: same
> fellows used to whether on the scaffold high.
> > (James Joyce, *Ulysses*, Harmondsworth, Penguin Books, 1992, 206)

> We now have a literary movement, it is not very important; it will be
> followed by a political movement, that will not be very important;
> then must come a military movement, that will be important indeed.
> > (Standish James O'Grady, 1899, in W. B. Yeats, *Autobiographies*,
> > New York, Macmillan, 1955, 424)

> All efforts to render politics aesthetic culminate in one thing: war.
> > (Walter Benjamin, 'The work of art in the age of mechanical
> > reproduction', in *Illuminations*, trans. Harry Zohn, London,
> > Fontana, 1973, 243)

The political thought of Ireland in the 1890s has been characterized in a
variety of ways.[1] The first and most significant foray into the period was
made by Conor Cruise O'Brien in his essay 'Passion and cunning', an
analysis of the politics of W. B. Yeats which argued towards the fascistic
impulses of Yeats's later years. Its significance for the 1890s was in an
insistence that politics after the fall of Parnell was characterized by a
rejection of the tedium of parliamentary and land obsessions by a generation preoccupied by the rich potential of a cultural politics. So at least
Yeats had said.[2]

F. S. L. Lyons substantially accepted this analysis. His Ford Lectures
to the University of Oxford delivered in the Hilary term of 1978
developed on this ground a theory of cultural politics in the period
constituting a battle between competing visions of what 'Ireland' should

be – Irish Ireland versus Anglo-Irish Ireland.[3] The politics of Gaelicization and Catholicity were the ground of the debate.

Significant work by a variety of scholars – Paul Bew and Tom Garvin, in particular – emphasizes the persistence of the politics of land, class and economic preoccupation in the period.[4] Roy Foster in an address to the British Academy in 1986 suggested that the marginalization of *actual* politics in interpretations of the period emerged from a willingness to view the years before 1916 through the telescope of that year's cathartic action. The work of Andrew Gailey and others on aspects of Tory, Liberal and Irish Parliamentary Party policy on land, Dublin Castle and the Constabulary in the years from 1890 to 1910 underline the endurance of the prevailing preoccupations.[5] There is a divide between historians on the one hand, and literary critics of the Irish Literary Renaissance on the other, who live in apparently unexchanging particularities. The Yeats and Joyce critical industries, with their complex transatlantic trajectories, compound the problem. A figure like Canon Sheehan, crucial for an understanding of the period – he was the most widely read novelist of the early 1900s – though superbly written about by Terence Brown in a recently published pioneering volume that attempts to bridge the literary/historical divide, is not integrated into narratives of the political thought of the period.[6]

The 1798 centenary commemorations, the anti-Boer War resistance and the vibrancy of certain Irish Parliamentary Party branches – particularly the crucial Dublin nexus around Kettle – make one wonder about the precise relation between 'culture', cultural-political thought and day-to-day Irish Parliamentary Party manoeuvrings in the period.

Crude lumpen-materialist displacement theories that see the period as one during which battles economic, social and agrarian metamorphosed into battles cultural and stylistic have to be guardedly approached. The relations between politics and culture are never easily read. Even as superb a critic as Edward Said has had problems with the politics of Yeats.[7]

In this context D. P. Moran presents himself as an inviting lens through which to attempt an analysis of cultural politics that is rooted in the political and immediate. Born in Waterford in 1872, Denis Patrick Moran spent the years from 1888 to 1898 as a minor London journalist, Gaelic League and Irish Literary Society activist. He arrived on the Dublin journalistic scene in the late 1890s and immediately plunged into a knockabout career during which he determined a language of cultural engagement.[8] From 1898 he edited the *New Ireland Review*, a crucial forum for political exchange. In 1900, on 1 September, he initiated *The Leader*, which he was to edit for nearly forty years.[9]

Most of Moran's enduring preoccupations were articulated in a series of articles published in the *New Ireland Review* between 1898 and 1900, and published in collected form as *The Philosophy of Irish Ireland* in

1905.[10] The final essay in the collection had been published in a volume edited by Lady Gregory in 1901, entitled *Ideals in Ireland*.[11]

Moran's thesis was not as simple as later commentators have suggested. His prime identification was with Douglas Hyde's 1892 address to the Irish Literary Society which was published as 'The necessity for de-Anglicizing Ireland'.[12] Hyde wrote as an Anglo-Irish Gaelic scholar, grounded in the Irish language remnants and folklore of his native Roscommon.[13] He also wrote out of a *fin de siècle* anti-modernism, a fear of the universal, the democratic and the post-aristocratic. Hyde's thesis was that as political Irish nationalism seemed likely to succeed (a tacit understanding despite Parnell's fall in 1891) the terms of debate ought to return to a re-examination of the basis of Irish nationality. Hyde's suggestion was that the Irish language and the 'Gaelic tradition' constituted the ground of separateness, the basis of nationality. His cultural essentialism built on the romantic nationalism of Young Ireland, the philological scholarship of the Royal Irish Academy, and repudiated the pragmatic legalism – the language of 'right' – articulated by O'Connell and Parnell.[14]

Hyde saw English 'music hall' culture as the essence of modern vulgarity, and the Irish language and 'tradition' as the lodestone of the nation and the bulwark against degeneracy. This was a simultaneity that the Catholic Church was more than willing to endorse when it threw its weight behind Hyde's construction – the Gaelic League.[15] For Anglo-Irish Ireland, however, this identification of the Gaelic as the national was to have enduring consequences.[16] If the language and culture were the ground of 'the Gael' and not 'the Planter', Anglo-Irish Ireland's antiquarian control of Gaelic culture could easily slip back through a racial as well as a cultural essentialism. Hyde's weapon was a double-edged sword. It was Moran who honed the other side of the blade.

The romanticization of 'the peasant' was central to the Anglo-Irish Literary Renaissance.[17] Moran, however, became the voice of the peasant as jumped-up literary hack. His position involved an insistence that the terms of the debate would be set by 'the Gael', the post-peasant. His tone was hectoring, his message ominous, and his urgency millennial. Was, he asked, 'all national life to be let to bleed out of us, until we came by our right to make laws for the corpse'?[18] He preached a language of hope, based on an analysis of despair. For many the Land and National Leagues had been the forcing-ground of politicization. The politics of the next field and the politics of the independent land of Ireland had been hammered into an equivalence by the hand-grafting rhetoric and organization of the 1880s.[19] Moran mirrored Hyde in announcing that the Land and Home Rule battles had been no more than an excrescence of 'the sunburstry songs'. Pride in the achievement of these years had been cut across by Parnell's fall – to Moran it had always been illusory – 'Whilst it bellowed and sent its schools all over the world, the real national life was asleep or else gliding away.'[20] It was, after all, 'only a material movement'. What Moran shares with Yeats, Hyde, A. E. and those allegedly opposed to him in an Irish Ireland versus Anglo-Irish Ireland dichotomy is greater than what divides him from them.[21]

For they all succumbed to a rejection of the pragmatic for variations on a language of cultural essentialism. It was Moran's mission to polemicize and inform the people of Ireland that their sense of self was faulty and inadequate, unless linguistically and culturally grounded. He claimed to battle against a sense of national inferiority which he contributed to voicing, and in many ways creating. Ireland was, he alleged, sunken in 'the feminine' and in need of 'the masculine' principle. Joe Chamberlain often echoes through Moran's prose. Politics as understood by the Irish Parliamentary Party was represented as debased, pragmatic and utilitarian. Ireland was a place 'where conditions are never normal' where class was distorted by race, by an alien aristocracy, 'a satellite of Mayfair'.[22] He claimed that the rhetorical polemic of post-Parnellite politics was a baseless incantation of formulaic abuse. The Wolfe Tone demonstration was an unfocused, ambiguous affair:

> Violent undefined passions of love or hate probably filled most of the great mass who took – I don't know how many hours – to pass a given point.[23]

It was this inchoateness that Moran saw as his invitation. He wished to replace it with clarity, and mark constitutional politics as the refuge of the morally dubious.

In 'The future of the Irish nation' Moran identified three options for Irish culture in the face of the powers of 'the English speaking races' – opposition to them, isolation or defeat. Remaining within the terms of the relationship as given in 1900 was 'like a huxter's shop in competition with a monster store'.[24] Ireland's chances of competition and survival in the face of English culture were analogous to the naïve hopes of a Fenian who had marched out with a rifle on his shoulder to Tallaght in 1867, and who still believed that he could threaten the complex technology of a modern army.

Moran identified the late eighteenth century and Grattan's colonial nationalism as the base error of national self-articulation.[25] This was the liberation text of the colony, not of the mass of the Gaelic nation. The articulation of this colonial nationalism, redefined by the Gaelic peasant mass in the nineteenth century, sat uneasily on remembered popular history. That disjunctive connection led, according to Moran, to a political infantilism that expressed itself in a willingness to evince blind submission to an adored leader. In such a context did he place O'Connell and Parnell. O'Connell had, he claimed, flattered and cajoled his sunken people. Anticipating O'Faolain he recognized O'Connell's priorities as

'King of the Beggars' but described him as feeding 'the elemental appetite of the Irish gallery'.

Moran's language is essentialist, organic, nominalist. In this he resembles Yeats, Lady Gregory and the other societal obsessives and cultural nationalists of his time. They share the same symbolic capital and arguably belong to the same cultural formation – they merely spend the capital and decline the formation differently.[26] In this context it is debatable if class or race can be placed at the centre of their later disagreements.

His disagreement with those, like Yeats, who marketed 'the Celtic note' was economic and competitive. Though they shared his essentialism, theirs was of Fergus, of Fergal and of the shadowy past.[27] For Moran, this was constructed for the jaded literary appetites of London. They 'earn their fame and their livelihood by supplying the demand which they have honourably and with much advertising created'.[28] For Moran their vision could only encompass a future for Ireland as a touristic Celtic theme park. His analysis included an economic imperative and an attempted engagement with the anti-rhetorical.

Irish parliamentary leaders were sunken in a 'speeches from the dock' oratory and an economic unreality. Their insistence on sitting for 'God Save The Queen', and scrupulous avoidance of Dublin Castle, were empty gestures that created anti-Irish prejudice in England and little else.[29] He rejected that respectable nationalist Ireland that Joyce found tedious, but insisted that 'the real Ireland' was not the land of heart's desire or of Arthur Griffith's Hungarian drama. He wanted a bilingual country based upon the Gaelic League, because such a wide and popular movement could not be betrayed by any single leader, would not be 'a cone upon its apex with one man holding it in place'.[30] Such a structure would be impervious to 'economic tendencies, battering rams or the Queen's soldiers'.[31] Parnell, he believed, would have seen the wisdom of annexing the Gaelic League since he was 'a master of tactics'. His successors were too incompetent to see its force.

Moran rejected the notion that he was anti-political:

> I hope no one will take away the impression that in my eagerness to dethrone political agitation from its present false position as the begin-all and end-all of Irish nationhood, I wish in any way to belittle its necessity and importance in its relative place.[32]

In 'The Pale and the Gael' he announced that Gaelic Ireland had been broken at Limerick; 1782 fixed Ireland 'not as an Irish nation, but as an English province'.

> When we look back upon 1782 from 1899 we see it not in the halo of a glorious victory, but in the shape of an animated skull grinning at us, an emblem of victory perhaps – the victory of death. . . . It sent

us adrift in a new world by which we were first corrupted and then eaten away; it set up a new temple before which we have burned incense, and have made the greatest sacrifice in our power – the sacrifice of our national character.

Grattan truly put a *new* soul into Ireland, but what he vivified with it was not the once illustrious Gael, but an English-speaking, English-imitating mongrel, a people without a past, a people who, we were afterwards to see, could not by any chance, carve out a future of its own. . . . It is sickening to contemplate the smug satisfaction with which at the present day Irishmen reflect on and gloat over the Dublin of those decadent 'Independent Parliament' days, on its duellings, its fire-eating bucks, its dissipation, its clubs, its cock fights, and the rest of the excrescences which the first feverish rush to turn English threw up on the surface of the polite society of those days. All the while they have no thought for the leaderless, powerless millions, the real historic Irish race – hunted to the hills, and clinging to the language which should have been that of all Irishmen; those millions that were to be slowly, insidiously conquered by all this Anglo-Irish parade of sentimental Paleism.[33]

Moran spoke of 'the children that we have allowed ourselves to become' who 'look nervously to our masters to find out how much good we may believe of ourselves. England did not flatter us; so today we are a mean race in our own estimation'.

Edward Said has written in his study of the colonial, *Orientalism*, of the imaginative construction of the object by the subject, of the conquered by the conqueror.[34] Over the past decade there has been an intense debate in Irish literary, philosophical and historical scholarship as to the validity of applying a colonial model to Ireland.[35] Was Ireland England's first colony, or is it merely an imperfectly assimilated backward fringe area within the United Kingdom? Said's emphasis, like that of Franz Fanon, is on the internalization of the eye of the conqueror in the self-perception of the conquered.[36] It is not a litmus test, but it has a validity. If perceptions are as valid as material actuality, then clearly it must be acknowledged that Moran at least constructs himself as a classic colonial case. Writers like Elie Kedourie[37] and Ernest Gellner[38] have conceived of nationalism and colonialism in ways utterly at variance with Said. Benedict Anderson, in *Imagined Communities*, seems to respect the actuality of an imagined past.[39]

But Said's delineation of the dilemma into which a colonized self-analysis can lead seems compelling in some Irish cases. His argument is subtle and difficult, but clearly articulated in a recent essay on Yeats. Said represents Yeats as an Irish nationalist endeavouring to transcend the limitations of an anti-colonial politics.[40] Moran he would see as suffocated within it.

For Moran insists upon historical discontinuities. His analysis rests upon the assumption that the years since 1782, if not since 1691, have been 'a wrong turning'. In effect he requires an abnegation of history as lived, for history and the past as it *ought* to have been. He sees 1798 as the fall-out of the 'false note' of 1782. 'What did the peasants know of Republics?'[41] These were crushed, ignorant and conservative, capable only of a *jacquerie*:

> the appeal (in 1798) should have been in Irish, the object held out not an academic Republic but the re-conquest of the land, the re-establishment of old ways and manners, and the sweeping away not only of the English connection but, I fear, of the Paleman as well.[42]

Moran concluded that since the majority of people in *any* society were unconcerned by the political, they required to be seduced by their snobbery. In 'Politics, nationality and snobs' he marked out his territory. Irish political nationalism as practised was hollow and thin – a cheap reversal of English stereotyping rather than an alternative. If, as Moran claimed, 'the seduction of the average snob' was a national imperative, then the agenda would have to be altered from 'wild talk, village demagogues, lip patriotism, petty tyranny'[43] to an alternative vision. Irish political nationalism rested upon the 'hysterical and artificial stimulation of racial hatred', adventure stories 'concerning the Wexford rising', 'hyperbole and screech' and diminishing political disabilities.

The official political nationalist hegemony was narrow, riven by camp hatreds, tyranny and loss of individuality.

> The people may do anything but think for once they do commence to do that, and call things by their proper names, the game is up.

For Moran the 1880s had been an anomaly:

> the coincidence of a few years ago when an extraordinary leader synchronized with an extraordinary and desperate economic grievance.[44]

But Parnell had ensured the success of his purpose by surrounding himself with 'second-rate politicians competent to lead sheep', whom he had no choice but to rule with an iron hand. In his wake:

> to ask a question or make an independent remark is an outrage upon the sacred cause of Irish nationality.[45]

It was through the Gaelic revival that this shell of a political culture was to reconstitute itself and 'seduce the average snob'. Ireland, personified as usual as a woman (presumably *en route* to a liberated masculinity), was 'either in a wild carnival of screech or in a drowsy state of Oriental fatalism'. The Gaelic League would be the engine to remould the national character which 'as much as an individual character, can be moulded and

changed. I see in the Gaelic revival a means to effect such a change.'
But Moran feared 'that there is already too much reason to dread that
we may carry the methods of heroic politics into the altogether different
field of social and intellectual revival'.[46] The Gaelic League was to be
non-partisan, a national regeneration, a movement that ended factional-
ism and permitted a recognition that Sir Horace Plunkett was a greater
patriot than an anti-Boer War polemicist. It would end the politics of a
'ra ta ta tat on the Emerald drum'.

> If the Unionist papers or the Unionist party strike a practical note –
> as they often do – it is of little or no avail. For various reasons, which
> I need not go into, all the backs of us mere Irish go up at once, and
> we all agree to have a flying kick at any practicality that comes from
> such quarters.[47]

The League offered hope to Unionists, 'sensible and thinking extremists',
and those interested in industrial advance and economic reform.[48]

In 'The battle of two civilizations' Moran insisted that the League
would undermine 'the false proposition that politics was nationality':

> Irish popular oratory was corrupted under these influences into one
> string of uncomplimentary adjectives applied to England and the Eng-
> lish, and another string of an opposite description applied to Ireland.[49]

Yeats, intent on defining a national identity through a parallel route, was
condemned for failing to recognize that there 'is manifestly no essential
difference between first-class literary work executed by an English-speaking man born in Ireland, and that executed by an English-speaking man
born in England'.[50] Above all Yeats was attacked for being seduced by
Matthew Arnold's 'Celtic note'.

Moran's disagreement with Yeats was of agreed agendas, not a battle
in analysis between Anglo-Irish and Gaelic Ireland, but a disagreement
about method. Moran condemned the 'literariness' of Yeats on cultural
nationalist grounds; yet Yeats protested that his passion too was for a
national movement, theatre, voice. His desire to de-Davisize Irish culture
is not dissimilar to Moran's plea to rid it of cant. For Yeats 'the literary'
dominated 'the national', but in his writings the two are inextricably
bound.[51] Moran, condemning literature and polemic in the English language, was a master of the English verbal polemic he claimed to despise
and be shackled by. *Odi et amo* – I hate and I love.

The post–1890s generation had been formed by the politics of Parnellism. The Special Commission and the divorce court had shadowed the
revolution of the 1880s.[52] The stymied Liberal alliance deglamourized
constitutional politics. The sophistication of the connection between high
and low politics from 1879 to 1891 had found a median in Parnell's austere
rhetoric. But the Plan of Campaign, the Conservative anatomization of
'Parnellism and Crime', the divorce court and the parodic agrarian insist-

ence of William O'Brien's campaign in the west after 1898, brought rhetoric to the ground.[53]

Moran's response was pragmatic, petit-bourgeois, practical. He clung to Hyde's idea of renewal like a drowning man, as did a generation of his class.[54] Joyce alone, as the voice of urbanized post-peasant Ireland, rejected the offered dichotomies.[55] For though Stephen Dedalus is quoted for the words 'History is a nightmare from which I am trying to escape',[56] Joyce in fact chose to engage with the historical experience of English-speaking nationalist Ireland as lived.[57] Joyce as modernist eschewed practical politics but succeeded in his ambition to 'forge in the smithy of my soul the *uncreated* conscience of my race'.[58] The cultural formation of the post–1891 generation who lived in Ireland was not permitted the luxury of genius or distance.

Yeats did not cease to be a nationalist after 1902; he simply became bored by Dublin's in-fights and the solidity of its earnest debates. The mature nationalist of the 1920s *can* be set against the senator who protests at divorce disabilities.[59] His autobiographies have been ransacked to read the political and cultural history of Ireland from 1891 to 1937, but really they tell us primarily of Yeats.

The shape and identity of the independent Irish state was determined by the cultural debates of the years after 1891. For the first generation who ruled, and who opposed the rule of the state, had their mentality formed by Gaelic revivalist ideas. The tension that this engendered was acute. Irish independence was not to be what O'Connell and Parnell had pursued – *mere* self-government.[60] It was to be a messianic quest for the grail of true Irishness as delineated by the analysts of the preceding generation. This was not 'political thought' as a hermetically sealed intellectual abstraction. It was a complex emotional, intellectual and spiritual formation that shaped twentieth-century Irish history. Irish independence, achieved by a bloody revolution in the name of a republic, carried searing contradictions into the future.[61] It became not the Republic, but the Free State. It achieved a part of the partitioned island. It retained the imagery of Pearse's 1916 proclamation as a republic of all who inhabited the island.[62] It initially expressed its separate identity through Catholicity and Gaelicism.[63]

George Bernard Shaw in 'On throwing out dirty water' insisted that Irish independence should be based on the premise that, after all, Ireland was merely ordinary.[64] The extraordinariness of *fin-de-siècle* Dublin precluded that possibility. Nineteenth-century Ireland had been the ground of Gaelic Catholic Ireland's re-emergence – emancipation, disestablishment of the Church of Ireland, the displacement of a landlord class through a language of right *and* retrieval or reconquest. But the politics of the next field and the independent ground of Ireland was deemed to be insufficient.

The contention of Moran, Hyde and those who flocked to join the

Gaelic League was that an independent Ireland demanded a cultural differentiation from the phase in which they lived. The only choices that Moran could see were opposition, isolation or defeat by 'the dominant culture'. What those choices denied was the actuality of the complex and sophisticated internal relations of the lived life of nineteenth-century Ireland. Moran wished to escape from the dilemma of being defined by what he opposed. Such an escape incorporated 'the modern' through a radical economic policy and a desire to transcend anti-Englishness. It also demanded a language of retrieval, recovery, return.

Yeats too, demanded a romantic, anti-scientific Celtic actuality for the freedom ahead. The demands of his intellectual and creative life precluded practicality.

The politicization of Irish nationalism took place during the 1880s through the brutality of the Land War, the sophistication of the home rule high political game and the ensuing revolution in land ownership. William O'Brien's *United Ireland* had, together with the *Freeman's Journal*, created the anti-landlord rhetoric that fuelled the home rule struggle. Tom Garvin has talked about the role of young men in the Gaelic revival. The revolutionaries of the early 1880s were comfortable parliamentarians by 1900. The association of the parliamentary party with ranching, profiteering, small-town respectability and clericalism is a cliché, but an important one. It is easy, therefore, to forget that they had won the moral battle for political independence. Not merely that but the 'land battle' was not finished, at least not until the Dunraven Land Conference of 1903. George Wyndham, in consultation with Balfour, believed the construction of controlled rural ideality was possible. In the 1920s Balfour was to say that the Irish Free State was nothing more than 'the Ireland that we made'. The aim of the Parnellite party had been to create through their rhetoric a situation to conclude the British political presence. The 1880s had been the crucible; the politics of the years after 1890 were to be concerned with constructing new agendas.

NOTES

1 'Political thought' suggests a category of analysis removed from the politics of the mundane. By 'political thought' I mean the articulations of the political in public and literary discourse, rather than in works which declare themselves to be works of political philosophy; what historians of the *Annales* school refer to as 'histoire des mentalités'. James Joyce, *Ulysses*, Harmondsworth, Penguin Books, 1968, provides the best insight into the complex political mentality of Dublin in the late 1890s and the early 1900s. See Dominic Manganiello, *Joyce's Politics*, London, Routledge & Kegan Paul, 1980.
2 Conor Cruise O'Brien, 'Passion and cunning: an essay on the politics of W. B. Yeats', in Conor Cruise O'Brien (ed.), *Passion and Cunning*, London, Weidenfeld & Nicolson, 1988. Originally published in *Writers and Politics*, New York, Pantheon Books, 1965.

3 F. S. L. Lyons, *Culture and Anarchy in Ireland 1890–1939*, Oxford, Clarendon Press, 1979.

4 Paul Bew, *Conflict and Conciliation in Ireland 1890–1910; Parnellites and Agrarian Radicals*, Oxford, Clarendon Press, 1987. Tom Garvin, *Nationalist Revolutionaries in Ireland 1858–1928*, Oxford, Clarendon Press, 1987.

5 On the political history of the years after 1890 see Andrew Gailey, *Ireland and the Death of Kindness: The Experience of Constructive Unionism 1890–1905*, Cork, Cork University Press, 1987.

6 Terence Brown, 'Canon Sheehan and the Catholic intellectual', in Terence Brown (ed.), *Ireland's Literature, Selected Essays*, Dublin, Lilliput Press, 1988. See too W. J. McCormack, *Ascendancy and Tradition in Anglo-Irish Literary History from 1789 to 1939*, Oxford, Clarendon Pess, 1985. Also John Hutchinson, *The Dymamics of Cultural Nationalism; the Gaelic Revival and the Creation of the Irish Nation State*, London, Allen & Unwin, 1987.

7 Edward W. Said, *Nationalism, Colonialism and Literature: Yeats and Decolonization*, Field Day Pamphlet, no. 15, Derry, Field Day, 1988.

8 There is no comprehensive study of Moran, though he is mentioned in all mainstream accounts of the 1900s. The most direct treatment of Moran is by Brian Inglis, 'Moran of the *Leader* and Ryan of the *Irish Peasant*', in Conor Cruise O'Brien (ed.), *The Shaping of Modern Ireland*, London, Routledge & Kegan Paul, 1960, and by F. S. L. Lyons in *Culture and Anarchy*, 'Irish Ireland versus Anglo-Irish Ireland', 57–83.

9 Its successor, edited by T. Desmond Williams in the 1950s was an equally important, though rather different, sounding board.

10 D. P. Moran, *The Philosophy of Irish Ireland*, Dublin, James Duffy, 1905.

11 D. P. Moran, 'The battle of two civilizations', in Lady Gregory (ed.), *Ideals in Ireland*, London, Unicorn, 1901.

12 Douglas Hyde, 'The necessity for de-Anglicizing Ireland', in Sir Charles Gavan Duffy, George Sigensen and Douglas Hyde, *The Revival of Irish Literature*, London, 1894.

13 There is no comprehensive recent study of Hyde. For a study of philological curiosity about the Irish language in the 1890s, see Sean O'Luing, *Kuno Meyer, 1858–1919, A Bibliography*, Dublin, Geography Publications, 1991.

14 For an analysis of the politics of the Irish language and its engagement with nationality in the years before 1800, see Joseph T. W. Leerssen, *Mere Irish and Fior Gael; Studies in the Idea of Irish Nationality, its Development and Expression prior to the Nineteenth Century*, Amsterdam and Philadelphia, John Benjamins Publishing Co., 1986.

15 For an analysis of the development of the Catholic Church in the late nineteenth century, see David Miller, *Church, State and Nation in Ireland 1889–1921*, Dublin, Gill & Macmillan, 1973. For an understanding of the Church's self-image as an alternative spiritual empire to the decadent material empire of Great Britain see Patrick Farrell, *Ireland's English Question: Anglo-Irish Relations 1534–1970*, London, Batsford, 1971. For the Catholic hierarchy's response to that self-image during the years of violence, see M. O'Callaghan, 'The church and Irish independence', *The Crane Bag*, 7, 2 (1983). For a view of the cultural stereotyping against which these heroic self-constructions set themselves see L. P. Curtis, Jr, *Apes and Angels: The Irishman in Victorian Caricature*, Newton Abbot, David & Charles, 1972.

16 For Lyons it represented the basis for 'the final round of the battle of two civilizations'. For a contrary view see M. O'Callaghan, 'Language, nationality and cultural identity; the *Catholic Bulletin* and *Irish Statesman* "reappraised" ', *Irish Historical Studies*, XXIV, 94 (November 1984), 226–45.

17 For a recent treatment of the stereotype and its political consequences see

Edward Hirsh, 'The imaginary Irish peasant', *Proceedings of the Modern Language Association of America*, 106 (October 1991), 1116–33.

18 Moran, *The Philosophy of Irish Ireland*, 3.

19 The historical literature of the 1880s is vast and excellent. A limited sample of the most accessible works for the politics of land and Parnellism is as follows: S. Clark, *Social Origins of the Irish Land War*, Princeton and Guildford, Princeton University Press, 1979; P. Bew, *Land and the National Question in Ireland 1858–82*, Dublin, Gill & Macmillan, 1980; Conor Cruise O'Brien, *Parnell and His Party*, Oxford, Clarendon Press, 1957; A. B. Cooke and J. R. Vincent, *The Governing Passion: Cabinet Government and Party Politics in Britain 1885–6*, Brighton, Harvester, 1974; L. P. Curtis, *Coercion and Conciliation in Ireland 1880–92; A Study in Conservative Unionism*, Princeton, Princeton University Press, 1963; Donal McCartney (ed.), *Parnell: The Politics of Power*, Dublin, Wolfhound, 1991; D. George Boyce and Alan O'Day (eds), *Parnell in Perspective*, London, Routledge, 1991; Frank Callanan, *The Parnell Split, 1890–91*, Cork, Cork University Press, 1992; Margaret O'Callaghan, 'Crime, nationality and the law; the politics of land in late Victorian Ireland', unpublished Ph.D. thesis, University of Cambridge, 1989.

20 Moran, *Irish Ireland*, 4.

21 The essence of the debate as defined by Lyons in *Culture and Anarchy* is whether or not the cultural politics of the period should be understood primarily in terms of a battle between Anglo-Irish and Irish-Ireland. See W. J. McCormack, *Ascendancy and Tradition* for a discussion of the problematic nature of the term 'Anglo-Irish'. See also his *The Battle of the Books, Two Decades of Irish Cultural Debate*, Mullingar, Lilliput Press, 1986.

22 Moran, *Irish Ireland*, 7.

23 ibid, 8–9.

24 ibid, 13.

25 This theme was developed and institutionalized by Daniel Corkery in two widely read and profoundly influential works: Daniel Corkery, *The Hidden Ireland, A Study of Gaelic Munster in the Eighteenth Century*, Dublin, M. H. Gill and Son, 1925 (1989), and *Synge and Anglo-Irish Literature*, Cork, Cork University Press, 1931. For an attack on Daniel Corkery's view of eighteenth-century Ireland, see Louis Cullen, 'The hidden Ireland: reassessment of a concept', *Studia Hibernica*, ix (1969).

26 For a discussion of the notion of 'cultural capital' see Pierre Bourdieu, *Outline for a Theory of Practice*, Cambridge, Cambridge University Press, 1977, and Bourdieu, 'Symbolic power', in P. Bourdieu, *Two Bourdieu Texts*, trans. R. Nice, Birmingham, Centre for Contemporary Cultural Studies, 1977. See also Nicholas Garnham and Raymond Williams, 'Pierre Bourdieu and the sociology of culture: an introduction', *Media, Culture and Society*, 2, 3 (July 1980), 208–23.

27 Moran's objection to the 'Celtic note' school was based upon its romanticization of an ethereal past – but also to its existence as a literary enterprise in the English language, drawing on 'foreign' models. Yeats's view was as follows:

> All literature in every country is derived from models, and as often as not these are foreign models, and it is the presence of a personal element alone that can give it nationality in a fine sense, the nationality of its maker. It is only before personality has been attained that a race struggling towards self-consciousness is the better for having, as in primitive times, nothing but native models, for before this has been attained it can neither

assimilate nor reject. It was precisely at this passive moment, attainment approaching but not yet come, that the Irish heart and mind surrendered to England, or rather to what is most temporary in England; and Irish patriotism, content that the names and opinions should be Irish, was deceived and satisfied. It is always necessary to affirm and to reaffirm that nationality is in the things that escape analysis. We discover it, as we do the quality of saltness or sweetness, by the taste, and literature is a cultivation of taste.

(W. B. Yeats, 'Samhain' (1908), in *Explorations*, New York, Macmillan, 1962, 233–4)

28 Moran, *Irish Ireland*, 22. This is precisely the argument that Desmond Fennell has used to attack Seamus Heaney almost one hundred years later. See Desmond Fennell, *'Whatever You Say, Say Nothing'. Why Seamus Heaney is No. 1*, Dublin, ELO Publications, 1991.
29 Joyce's parody of nationalist public utterance endorses Moran's analysis, but incorporates him in its savagery. The Citizen in *Ulysses*, modelled on Michael Cusack, is an amalgam of what Moran despises, and what Moran is.
30 Moran, *Irish Ireland*, 27. See also Joyce (*Ulysses*, 421) on the Dublin City Hall's putative decision to give recognition to the Irish language:

> O'Nolan, clad in shining armour, low bending made obeisance to the puissant and high and mighty chief of all Erin and did him to wit of that which had befallen, how that the grave elders of the most obedient city, second of the realm, had met them in the tholsel, and there, after due prayers to the gods who dwell in ether supernal, had taken solemn counsel whereby they might, if so be it might be, bring more into honour among mortal men the winged speech of the seadivided Gael.
>
> – It's on the march, says the citizen. To hell with the bloody brutal Sassenachs and their *patois*.

31 Moran, *Irish Ireland*, 30.
32 ibid, 35.
33 ibid, 36.
34 Edward Said, *Orientalism*, London, Routledge & Kegan Paul, 1978.
35 No comprehensive account of the recent debate in Irish historiography has as yet been written. Roy Foster's 'We are all revisionists now', *The Irish Review*, 1986, represents the most comprehensive conclusion to date; W. J. McCormack, *Battle of the Books*, is a brief account of the shifting interpretations of the past represented by different literary and philosophical positions during the 1980s. Events in Northern Ireland since 1969 have affected all areas of Irish historical scholarship in ways that have scarcely begun to be assessed.
36 Franz Fanon, *The Wretched of the Earth*, London, MacGibbon & Kee, 1965.
37 Elie Kedourie has consistently depicted nationalism as a regressive and destructive force. See E. Kedourie, *Nationalism*, London, Hutchinson, 1960; and *Nationalism in Asia and Africa*, London, Weidenfeld & Nicolson, 1971. For a sympathetic analysis of Kedourie see Maurice Cowling, *Religion and Public Doctrine in Modern England*, Cambridge, Cambridge University Press, 1980, 315–38.
38 Ernest Gellner too has an intellectually alarmed perspective on nationalism, which he primarily sees in terms of the disintegration of the Austro-Hungarian empire, the rise of German militarism, and its ensuing European anti-semitic horrors. He sees nationalism, intellectually constructed in late eighteenth-century German culture, as later manifested in the economic drive of peripheral intellectuals for centrality; hence their construction of a 'national identity'

in the marginalized periphery of Ruritania. See Ernest Gellner, *Nations and Nationalism*, Oxford, Basil Blackwell, 1983.

39 Benedict Anderson, *Imagined Communities: Reflections on the Origin and Spread of Nationalism*, London, Verso, 1983.

40 Said, *Yeats and Decolonization*.

41 Moran, *Irish Ireland*, 40.

42 For a brilliant study of nationalist representations of the past as the validatory texts of contemporary politics, see Oliver MacDonagh, *States of Mind: A Study of Anglo-Irish Conflict 1780–1980*, London, Allen & Unwin, 1983.

43 Moran, *Irish Ireland*, 66.

44 ibid, 68.

45 ibid, 70.

46 ibid, 76–7.

47 ibid, 87.

48 ibid, 92.

49 ibid, 100.

50 ibid, 103.

51 For a recent examination of Yeats and politics see Elizabeth Cullingford, *Yeats, Ireland and Fascism*, New York, New York University Press, 1981. The bibliography of Yeats studies is vast, but for an introduction see Richard Ellman, *Yeats: The Man and the Masks*, London, Faber & Faber, 1949; Joseph Hone, *W. B. Yeats 1865–1939*, 2nd edn, London, Macmillan, 1967. See also Michael Steinmam, *Yeats's Heroic Figures: Wilde, Parnell, Swift, Casement*, Albany, N. Y., State University of New York Press, 1984, and Denis Donoghue, *Yeats*, London, Fontana, 1971. Roy Foster is currently working on the authorized biography of Yeats.

52 See M. O'Callaghan, 'Parnellism and crime: constructing a Conservative strategy of containment', in McCartney (ed.), *Parnell: The Politics of Power*, pp. 102–24.

53 Bew, *Conflict and Conciliation*.

54 Garvin, *Nationalist Revolutionaries*.

55 For a critical response to this reading of Joyce see Terence Brown 'Yeats, Joyce and the Irish critical debate', in Brown, *Ireland's Literature*, 77–90. See also Seamus Deane, 'Parnell: the lost leader', in McCartney (ed.), *Parnell: Politics of Power*, 183–91.

56 James Joyce, *Ulysses*, p. 42.

57 On Joyce as anti-colonial modernist see Fredric Jameson, *Nationalism, Colonialism and Literature: Modernism and Imperialism*, Field Day Pamphlet no. 14, Derry, Field Day, 1988.

58 Joyce, *Portrait*.

59 Such a reading of Yeats rests upon a class/Anglo-Irish analysis and sees him as a manifestation of Anglo-Irish Ireland in 'the battle of civilizations'.

60 Deane, 'Parnell', pp. 183–91.

61 For an analysis of independent Ireland see Ronan Fanning, *Independent Ireland*, Dublin, Helicon, 1983; R. F. Foster, *Modern Ireland 1600–1972*, London, Allen Lane, 1988; Joseph Lee, *Ireland 1912–1985: Politics and Society*, Cambridge, Cambridge University Press, 1990.

62 On the regenerative imperatives of 1916 see William Irwin Thompson, *The Imagination of an Insurrection: Dublin, Easter 1916*, Oxford, Oxford University Press, 1967. See also Ruth Dudley Edwards, *Patrick Pearse, The Triumph of Failure*, London, Gollancz, 1978. On the divisions within the Free State see Jeffrey Prager, *Building Democracy in Ireland: Political Order and Cultural Integration in a Newly Independent Nation*, Cambridge, Cambridge University Press, 1986.

63 The themes raised in this chapter are explored in greater detail in my unpublished MA thesis 'Language and religion; the quest for identity in the Irish Free State', University College, Dublin, 1981.
64 George Bernard Shaw, 'On throwing out dirty water', *Irish Statesman*, 15 September 1923.

7 Green on red

Two case studies in early twentieth-century Irish republican thought

Richard English

'I'm afraid I have not one idea in my head as to policy. I know nothing of the application of freedom as I know nothing of the application of tyranny.'[1] So wrote Ernie O'Malley, a leading member of the Irish Republican Army (IRA), in December 1923. He had spent the years since 1918 as a full-time republican rebel, fighting first against the forces of the British Crown in Ireland and subsequently against the authority of the Irish Free State. The first conflict (the Anglo-Irish war) had resulted in a treaty offering partial independence for a part of Ireland. Though a significant offer, this had failed to satisfy O'Malley's separatist aspirations[2] and he had sided with the anti-treatyite republicans in the civil war of 1922–3. Captured by Free State forces in November 1922, he was imprisoned until July 1924. Though badly wounded, O'Malley participated in the republican prisoners' hunger strike for unconditional release which took place in October/November 1923.

During his post-strike recuperation he was nursed by fellow republican prisoner, Peadar O'Donnell.[3] Like O'Malley, O'Donnell had fought with the IRA during the Anglo-Irish war and had rejected the 1921 treaty. Their political ideas overlapped, but were significant in their differences. O'Malley's political violence during the 1916–24 Irish revolution was founded on republican *faith* and not on extended political *analysis*. An uncompromising and simple belief in the rectitude of the Irish republican cause served as sufficient justification, in his view, for paramilitary political expression. O'Donnell's republican career, by contrast, was focused on an elaborately articulated social reading of Irish and Anglo-Irish politics. O'Malley was a republican soldier, O'Donnell a republican socialist.

Both men were important in Irish republican politics in the early part of the twentieth century.[4] Yet despite their significance and the richness of the sources which they each left behind them, neither man has yet been the subject of a thorough biography.[5] Their value as guides to republican political thinking has been recognized in the work of numerous authors.[6] But their failure to gain even a place in the index of Joseph Lee's justly acclaimed *Ireland 1912–1985* reflects the fact that neither O'Malley nor O'Donnell has yet become accepted as a figure of primary significance in our understanding of modern republican political thinking. This chapter will use O'Malley and O'Donnell as case studies in republican thought. In doing so it draws on much material which has not been discussed in the existing literature on Irish republican politics. In particular, it is important to note the use made: of papers which have recently been published in a volume of O'Malley's civil war letters; of the unpublished material contained in the papers of Sheila Humphreys and of Mabel FitzGerald; and of Peadar O'Donnell's novels as a guide to his political thinking.[7] Furthermore, the chapter will concentrate on the two men's arguments, ideas and political mentalities in a more concentrated way than has hitherto been the case. In terms both of sources and of method, therefore, this chapter represents a more detailed and more serious study of these two men's ideas than has yet been published. O'Malley and O'Donnell provide focal points around which to build a picture of early twentieth-century republican and republican socialist ideas in Ireland. Their massive legacy of published and unpublished material makes them particularly valuable in illuminating our reading of this period, and by drawing out the ideological family resemblances between these two individuals and the broader republican community a clear portrait will emerge.

In the first section of the chapter it will be argued, with reference to the 1916–24 period, that there existed a tension between the uncompromising simplicity of Ernie O'Malley's republican ideas and the actual complexity of contemporary Irish and Anglo-Irish political reality. This point is underlined by the fact that O'Malley's *own* individual culture during the revolutionary period reflected the complexities which his political ideas fought zealously to obscure. The second section of the chapter will concentrate on Peadar O'Donnell. It will be demonstrated that, contrary to the common assumption that O'Donnell's political ideas were those of an iconoclast, he should rather be seen as one whose ideas were *not iconoclastic enough* to deal with the situation which he sought to confront. Republicanism (whether in its non-socialist *or* in its socialist form) proved a powerful, catalytic but ultimately bankrupt ideology.

I

Ernie O'Malley's political ideas were uncompromising. In his posthumously published account of the 1921–4 period he wrote of himself and his comrades that 'We had given ourselves to this land, with death or imprisonment as a reward.'[8] In his account of the Anglo-Irish war he cited Sinn Fein's 1917 declaration of intent with regard to the achieving of an Irish republic: 'Sinn Fein aims at securing the recognition of an Independent Irish Republic.'[9] But he *omitted* to quote that part of the Sinn Fein statement which reflected the tension within the movement as to whether or not a fully separatist, republican stand should have been taken. The actual, more equivocal, 1917 statement had read: 'Sinn Fein aims at securing the international recognition of Ireland as an independent Irish Republic. Having achieved that status, the Irish people may, by referendum, freely choose their own form of government.'[10]

It was typical of O'Malley to simplify the issue. The certainty of his commitment manifested itself in an absolute adherence to the full republican position: 'We had taken the oath of allegiance to the Republic; we meant to keep it.'[11] Faced with what he perceived to have been the betrayal of the pure republic in 1921, he held unwaveringly to the republican ideal. With respective reference to the anti- and pro-treaty factions he observed: 'There were two parties now, Republican and Free State. Those who believed in an absolutely independent Ireland and those who wished to become a dominion of the British Empire.'[12] An absolutely independent, all-island republic was the objective to which he flintily held. In fact there existed within the 1917–21 independence movement a variety of opinion on the issue of exactly what form of Irish autonomy might be judged acceptable. The leading Sinn Feiner, Arthur Griffith, and the incomparably symbolic Eamon de Valera provide powerful examples. But neither Griffith – whom one commentator has described as 'a monarchist by political nature'[13] – nor de Valera were cut from the same stone as O'Malley. Griffith had influentially backed the 1921 treaty against which O'Malley raged. De Valera's Document No. 2 – an alternative to the treaty – was held by O'Malley to be unsatisfactory.[14]

In the post-treaty period O'Malley displayed pessimism about the immediate prospects of achieving the republic: 'certainly we will never get a Republic out of the present fight'.[15] But he retained both his stand by the republic and also his millenarian conviction that it would one day be realized: 'we're going to beat them [the Free Staters] in the long run so I suppose we should not question the time we do it in too closely'.[16] And in adhering to this purist republican position he had to side-step the opposition or hesitation of those within Ireland who did not share his convictions. This was attempted by means of an emphasis upon *Britain's* role in dividing Irish opinion. In his account of the civil war split he referred to 'the British who had divided our nation'.[17] He explicitly cited the role of Lloyd George and of Churchill in bringing pressure to bear on the pro-treaty authorities to launch an attack on the anti-treaty headquarters in Dublin in 1922.[18]

While British opposition to the Irish republican position should not be ignored, it is also vital to recognize the shades and divisions of opinion which existed *within* Ireland on the question of nationalist aspirations. There was the fierce anti-republicanism of unionists, particularly (though not exclusively) in Ulster. O'Malley had virtually nothing to say regarding the problems which Ulster unionism represented for republicans. He casually accepted the idea that one island implied one nation and that the appropriate unit for government should, inevitably, be a thirty-two county Ireland. If people did not want to endorse the new Irish republic then the message was clear: 'The people of this country would have to give allegiance to it or if they wanted to support the Empire they would have to clear out and support the Empire elsewhere.'[19] A republican blind spot with regard to Ulster unionism was hardly unique to O'Malley. Many failed to take unionism seriously at all. Thus IRA leader, Dan Breen, later dismissed the 1912–14 threat of Ulster resistance to home rule by force of arms, with the lazy remark: 'Of course, it was bluff.'[20] Unwavering Irish republicans failed, in this period, adequately to address the question of exactly whom their nation comprised.[21] On the very day of Ernie O'Malley's capture in Dublin in November 1922 the *Irish Times* carried a report of Edward Carson which reflected the sturdy unionist outlook which O'Malley's uncompromising republicanism failed to comprehend. On 3 November Carson had stated 'that any idea of driving Ulster under a Southern Government was absolutely out of the question. It was a harmful and a dangerous dream.'[22]

If the harmful and dangerous dreamers failed to appreciate the significance of the unionist obstacle, they also underplayed the importance of divisions within *nationalist* ranks over the republican ideal. O'Malley read the events of 1921 as marking the British provocation of Irish disagreement; he largely ignored the issue of a pre-existing continuum of opinion within nationalist Ireland over the question of independence. Recent scholarship has rightly stressed the importance of the ideological diversity which existed within nationalist Ireland before and during the 1916–21 independence struggle. The work of Jeffrey Prager, for example, has underlined 'the profound cultural antinomies that had long existed in Irish society'.[23] But for O'Malley the question was essentially a simple one: ambiguities within Irish opinion could not be allowed to undermine the legitimate republican stance. He repeatedly stressed the importance of people's oath-bound pledge to the republic. 'The Volunteers were to become the Irish Republican Army and they would take the oath to the Republic.'[24] 'The members of the Dail took an oath of allegiance to the Irish Republic.'[25]

> TD's had in 1919, as had all members of the Army, taken the Oath of Allegiance: 'I will support and defend the Irish Republic and the Government of the Irish Republic, which is Dail Eireann, against all enemies foreign and domestic.'[26]

The oath was held to be prescriptive of future allegiance: once committed, there should be no withdrawal of support from the republic to which one had become pledged.

Thus the question was one of legitimacy. The republic had been declared, fought for, voted for, and backed up by an oath. It could not subsequently be jettisoned. Those who opted for the 1921 treaty in defiance of the republic were traitors. Writing of 1922 O'Malley stated

that: 'a proclamation was being prepared [by the anti-treatyites], outlaw-
ing the [pro-treaty] Provisional Government and declaring them traitors
to the Irish Republic'.[27] In a letter written in 1922 O'Malley denied that
he and his comrades were 'in rebellion against the lawful Government':
'Whence does that Government derive its authority? Is it from the second
Dail? Was not that Dail elected to preserve and defend the Republic?'[28]
There was a simple principle involved, that of the legitimacy of the Irish
republic which had been proclaimed in the 1916 rebellion and voted for
in the 1918 general election; with O'Casey's Mary Boyle, O'Malley held
straightforwardly that 'a principle's a principle'.[29]

The essential point is the simplicity of this approach. There is a Pearsean resonance here. 'We have the strength and the peace of mind of
those who never compromise' asserted Pearse[30], and (no less tellingly)
his biographer has referred to 'the essential simplicity of Pearse's mind'.[31]
The similarity between the uncompromising republicanism of O'Malley
and that of the 1916 Pearse is unsurprising. O'Malley had been converted
to republicanism by Pearse's rebellion: 'Then came like a thunderclap
the 1916 Rising.'[32] And he repeatedly alluded, in favourable terms, to
the rebellious post office messiah. Writing in December 1923, O'Malley
stated:

> I'm afraid it will take a big length of time to make up for the personal
> loss of the '16 [1916] group. [Patrick] Pearse and his group set out to
> minister to the spiritual side of the nation. They were replaced by
> [Michael] Collins and [Richard] Mulcahy neither of whom, from what
> I could see of them during the 1918–21 fighting, were spiritual; they
> had genius for work though.[33]

In an earlier letter O'Malley had referred to his keenness for a monthly
paper 'to deal with articles such as Pearse might write',[34] and he elsewhere
stressed Pearse's virtues and sought to compare his own struggle with
that of the 1916 leader.[35]

Like Pearse, O'Malley was a charismatic, compelling and complex
character. But the uncompromising republican separatism of the 1916
Pearse and of the post–1916 O'Malley bore unhappy resemblances in
terms of their rigidity and of their simplification. Ulster serves as an
example. O'Malley's inability to address the question of Ulster unionism
has already been mentioned. And a similar point could be made with
regard to Pearse. Joseph Lee, for example, has recently observed that,
'Generous and inclusive though Pearse's definition of Irish nationalism
was, there was no place for a distinctive Ulster room in the house of his
thought.'[36]

The rigid definition of legitimate authority lay at the root of irreconcilable republican thinking. O'Malley later acknowledged that his republican
ideal of freedom had never been realized in practice: 'I had given
allegiance to a certain ideal of freedom as personified by the Irish Repub-

lic. It had not been realized except in the mind.'[37] But he held to the purity of this republican commitment even after it became clear that a messy compromise had won majority support within Ireland. O'Malley recognized republican legitimacy as embodied in the pre-treaty republican Parliaments. But when the Dail voted against his republic and (more significantly) when a *popular* pro-treaty majority became clear, O'Malley effectively rejected the right of the Parliament or of the people to confer political legitimacy. As Tom Garvin has observed, 'The electorate repeatedly gave the [treaty] settlement huge majorities in 1922 and 1923 in the general elections.'[38] But this did not convince O'Malley that the treaty settlement deserved his allegiance.

For at root O'Malley's political ideas were self-referential and galvanic. Republican legitimacy was an article of personal faith. And while the people could be invoked in defence of this legitimacy their support was not essential to continued republican commitment. For it could always be argued that the action of the republican faithful would have a galvanic effect upon the people, bringing them round to the rightful republican position. This is why the 1916 myth was so central; it could be used to imply the possibilities of republican action awakening latent national feeling. As Townshend notes, the notion of rousing a dormant nation is a questionable one, resting as it does 'on the romantic assumption of innate national consciousness'.[39] But traces of this dubious assumption can certainly be found in O'Malley.

> In general [he wrote of the Anglo-Irish war], the local IRA companies made or marred the morale of the people. If the officers were keen and daring, if organisation was good, if the flying columns had been established, and if the people had become accustomed to seeing our men bearing arms openly, the resistance was stiffened. When the fighting took place, the people entered into the spirit of the fight even if they were not Republican, their emotions were stirred, and the little spark of nationality which is borne by everyone who lives in Ireland was fanned and given expression to in one of many ways.[40]

Whether it was perceived to be the *reawakening* or the *creation* of the right national feeling, this notion of galvanic republican activity was crucial to O'Malley's political ideas. There was no doubt that 1916 *had* substantially altered popular opinion.[41] O'Malley sought to repeat the process. It was not necessary to have a popular mandate prior to action; the important thing was to act and thus to bring the people with you. 'If [we had consulted the feelings of the people], we would never have fired a shot. If we gave them a good strong lead, they would follow.'[42] With reference to 1922 he wrote that 'Deep down [the people] could be stirred by something they would adjudge as heroic.'[43] Acts of violence would have a symbolic quality, drawing people in their wake.

Every man who was contributing in any way to the event [an attack during the Anglo-Irish war] would help to build up in the minds of the neighbourhood, and strengthen in the thoughts of the IRA, the symbol of an unarmed people emerging to fight for freedom against a formidable enemy which had successfully come through the greatest war in history.[44]

During the Anglo-Irish war the catalyst was also intended to work through its negative qualities. There was the negative impetus of IRA intimidation and pressure.[45] And there was also the effect of British reaction. In responding to IRA activity the authorities provoked considerable resentment, their ostensibly anti-republican security measures in fact contributing to the legitimation of the republican cause. In O'Malley's view, 'Their campaign of terror was defeating itself.'[46] He also recognized the tension between the various agencies of the Crown and held that this was heightened by the repressive violence employed in the fight against the republicans.[47]

O'Malley stressed the importance of those influences which consciously worked *against* the republic. The Irish representatives had signed the 1921 treaty 'under Lloyd George's threat of "immediate and terrible war" on the Irish people'; the press and the Catholic clergy influentially backed the treaty.[48] Similarly, an important part of his political thinking was the conviction that action should be taken with the conscious aim of leading or coercing people into support for (or acquiescence under) the republic. This approach could have a distinctly menacing quality. Writing as Acting Assistant Chief of Staff of the IRA in 1922, O'Malley threatened the *Irish Times* in relation to its presentation of contemporary affairs.

A warning recently addressed to certain newspapers in Dublin has been ignored and no change has been observed in the tone of these Journals since the warning was delivered. The Staff of this Command has now finally and carefully considered the whole question of the Dublin Press and have decided that by allowing the present paper campaign to continue they would be committing a crime against the REPUBLIC.
    The following alternatives are open to you:–
    1. Conduct your paper as a genuine Free Press, or
    2. Hand over your Journal to the Free State Authorities to be conducted officially by them.
Failure to comply with either of the above alternatives will be regarded as a determination on your part to use the Press as a military weapon against the REPUBLIC and will involve the same risks for you as are run by armed soldiers of the Free State Provisional Government.[49]

O'Malley was undoubtedly right in recognizing the importance of competing catalysts. But his adherence to a galvanic theory involved him in a circularity of argument. The people were invoked as the justification of the republican crusade; yet the crusade was judged necessary in order to create and sustain a people sympathetic to the republic. O'Malley constantly alluded to the idea of a popular root to the republican struggle. Looking back on 1921 he commented of his area, 'The people were staunch. Every house supported the Republic.'[50] Similarly, 'Our area was improving daily, the people were becoming more staunch in their allegiance to the Republic.'[51] In the course of a later description of events which had occurred in County Tipperary during the Anglo-Irish war, O'Malley commented that 'The district took its share of the burden. The people complained when it irked, but their loyalty was not breached.'[52] Writing in 1923, he observed of the Anglo-Irish war that 'The people learned to look out for, and to be particularly kind to, all [IRA] Column men and to fight amongst themselves to see who would put them up.'[53] With reference to the alternative republican government, O'Malley claimed that 'We had built up a government that the people respected and trusted.'[54]

The image cultivated by such claims is one of popular sanction for the republic. The people are presented as the foundation of the republic and of republicanism. Thus O'Malley described his distinctive account of the pre-treaty republican struggle as 'an attempt to show the background of the struggle from 1916 to 1921 between an Empire and an unarmed people.'[55] Yet even on the basis of his own evidence the attitude of the people appears rather more equivocal. With reference to 1920 he recognized that 'the people of Mallow . . . were not very friendly'.[56] And the picture he painted of 1921 hardly suggests a movement which assumed (or even liked) popular sympathy. He subsequently asserted that, shortly before the July 1921 Anglo-Irish truce, 'We were becoming almost popular.'[57] Again, the truce having come into effect, 'The Irish Republican Army was in danger of becoming popular.'[58] Writing in August 1921 he asserted that 'the IRA are popular and popularity is harder to face than contempt; the crowd cheering you to-day would cut your throat to-morrow, if they had the pluck'.[59]

There was, indeed, a significant distance between O'Malley and the people in whose name he fought. He found aspects of 'the people's' life distasteful when he actually lived amongst them[60] and he subsequently admitted that 'our merging in what we were glad to call "the people" was a figment'.[61] And after the 1921 treaty the people became an extremely problematic political concept for those of O'Malley's irreconcilable ilk. Writing of 1922 he commented on 'the hostility of the civilian population' in Dublin.[62] Later in the same account he observed, again of 1922, that 'the people as a whole were hostile'.[63] But the strength (and, ultimately, the weakness) of the galvanic theory was that, on its own terms, the republican argument could not be refuted. If the people were perceived to be in support then you acted with apparent sanction; if the people were perceived *not* to be in support then you acted in order to stimulate them into giving you their backing. Either way, you acted. Thus O'Malley argued of 1922:

> The area in a circle around Dublin had never been properly organized in the Tan fight [the Anglo-Irish war]; it was late to begin now when there was little support, but it could have been done.[64]

The difficulty was that, given the complexity of Irish and Anglo-Irish affairs, it seems implausible that O'Malley's absolutist project *could* have been realized. During the ill-defined struggle of 1917–21 it was possible for divisions within nationalist Ireland to remain obscured. But once a concrete offer had to be decided upon it was only to be expected that such divisions would come to prominence. Thus the partially satisfying 1921 treaty undermined republican legitimism. Faced with something partial but immediately available, large numbers of 'the people' accepted the bargain. As a result O'Malley's dream was scuppered. For republican legitimism and galvanism could not be employed as successfully after 1921 as had previously been the case. Where the alternative army and alternative parliament had impressively withered *British* authority during the Anglo-Irish war, it was not possible for anti-treaty republicans to do the same to *Irish* authority. During the 1920s and 1930s the legitimist argument – that the post–1921 northern and southern Irish regimes were usurpers of the pure republic and were therefore invalid – came to look increasingly absurd. O'Malley himself effectively withdrew from republican politics after 1924; but the legitimist flag continued to be flown. The IRA's constitution from 1925, for example, maintained the full republican stance. The army's primary objects were declared to be:

> (1) To guard the honour and uphold the Sovereignity [*sic*] and Unity of the Republic of Ireland.
> (2) To establish and uphold a lawful Government in sole and absolute control of the Republic.[65]

Nine years later the IRA still held to the legitimacy of a non-existent, all-island, fully independent republic:

> The national sovereignty of the Republic of Ireland resides under God in the citizens of the entire nation. It is non-judicable and inalienable. It cannot be surrendered or transferred to an external authority or power; any attempt made to surrender or transfer it shall be treason.[66]

By this stage (1934) the uncompromising legitimist argument had been further marginalized by important political developments. In 1926 Eamon de Valera – 'the tall, professorial figure of nationalist Ireland's conscience'[67] – had spearheaded the formation of Fianna Fail, the political party which was to inherit the anti-treatyite mantle. As one of de Valera's followers recognized, outdated adherence to republican purism acted as an obstacle to practical influence:

> [On the eve of his split from Sinn Fein] De Valera was still President of the Irish Republic, a shadow government which governed nothing. He was President of Sinn Fein, a shadow political party which took no part in practical politics. He decided that this situation must end.[68]

Fianna Fail were to bury hard-line republicanism in the twenty-six county Irish state. The defections from the pure republic of legitimist thinking to the more realistic politics of Fianna Fail nationalism were to prove fatal to uncompromising republicanism. In 1927 de Valera's party entered the Free State Dail, a move which was to have 'momentous implications' for the state and for Anglo-Irish relations.[69]

Fianna Fail made pragmatic virtue out of twenty-six county necessity. Unable to offer any serious challenge to the partition of the island, they sought to rid the Free State of those other aspects of the treaty arrangement which they found unacceptable. During the 1930s numerous features of the treaty state were abolished – the land annuities payments to Britain, the oath of allegiance to the British Crown, the office of governor-general, the senate – and in 1937 de Valera's constitution sealed the new non-republic. The importance of all this for legitimist republicanism was that Fianna Fail managed to woo such large numbers of twenty-six county nationalists that the less compromising outlook became increasingly marginalized. De Valera's party brought anti-treaty opinion into the Free State's constitutional arena. In doing so it effectively validated the twenty-six county state and de-legitimized the republic. Between 1923 and 1933 the percentage of the electorate actually voting increased in successive elections. And Fianna Fail's *share* of the votes cast rose at successive elections between June 1927 and 1933. In the 1923 election republicans had been supported by 27.4 per cent of those who voted. Fianna Fail won 26.1 per cent of the vote in June 1927, but this figure increased to 35.2 per cent in September 1927 and to 44.5 per cent in 1932. In 1933 49.7 per cent of those who voted supported de Valera's party, in 1937 the figure was 45.2 per cent and in 1938 it reached 51.9 per cent. In 1923 only 58.7 per cent of the electorate had voted, and only 27.4 per cent of these people had voted republican. In the 1938 election 75.7 per cent of the electorate voted, and 51.9 per cent of these votes were cast in favour of Fianna Fail.[70] In the words of one of Ernie O'Malley's closest associates (leading republican Sheila Humphreys), 'There were a lot of people that thought [de Valera] was going slowly, but he was going somewhere – and they were happy with it.'[71] As Ronan Fanning has put it:

> While de Valera was withholding the land annuities, tearing up the oath, degrading the office of Governor-General, taking the crown out

of the constitution, getting back the ports and defending neutrality against all comers, the IRA had scant hope of winning ground among the unconverted.[72]

Brian Murphy has recently disputed the notion that those republicans who refused to compromise the republican ideal – and who, as a result, did not follow de Valera's Fianna Fail initiative – were 'of inferior calibre' when compared with de Valera's adherents. 'Given the opportunity, there is no reason to believe that this body of people would, at the very least, have performed any worse than the Fianna Fail party that came to power in 1932.'[73] But this misses the point. Purist republicans were not given 'the opportunity' to demonstrate their ability precisely *because* they themselves persisted in a legitimist fiction which prevented them from participating in practical, governmental politics. The crucial fact was that by opting for a pragmatic, parliamentary path the Fianna Fail people gave *themselves* the opportunity to achieve things in practice. The point is underlined by the increasingly pathetic nature of hard-line republican claims during the 1930s. In January 1930 the IRA Army Council made the following grandiose claim: 'The Army Council recognises itself as the Supreme National Authority in Ireland, and is not subservient to, or subject in any way to any other body.' The Council also recognized 'that it has the right, at any time, to proclaim itself the provisional Government of the Republic of Ireland'.[74] But self-recognition was plainly an insufficient basis upon which to build powerful political action. While the IRA relied on its self-referential legitimacy, Fianna Fail built sturdier foundations in the form of majoritarian endorsement. De Valera informed the IRA's Sean MacBride during the early 1930s that, if the IRA objected to his (de Valera's) policy, then they 'could go and seek the votes of the people, to put [their] policy into effect'.[75] The Fianna Fail leader could rely on the fact that the IRA would not and could not achieve a popular mandate for their uncompromising approach.

The IRA could jab and sneer at Fianna Fail,[76] but only with increasing impotence. In 1936 Sean Russell (soon to become the IRA's chief of staff) asserted that the Free State government 'depends for its very existence on the British parliament whose puppet it is'; in the same letter he claimed to represent the 'government of the Irish Republic'.[77] But the Free State authorities in fact depended for their existence on endorsement from the Free State people. And the government which Russell claimed to represent was a fictional regime, claiming to embody legitimate republican authority long after such a claim had become meaningless for all but a handful of marginalized zealots. When this republican rump of a Dail handed to the IRA the keys to legitimacy in 1938, the announcement was pathetically pompous: '[On 8 December 1938] the Government of the Republic of Ireland was taken over from the Executive Council of Dail Eireann by the Council of the Irish Republican Army.'[78]

The legitimist argument, therefore, became increasingly irrelevant during the early years of the southern Irish state. Uncompromising theory failed. But the mismatch between the simplicity of republican argument and the complexity of Irish reality was evident even before the series of splits which demolished hard-line republicanism in the post-treaty period. And this is where Ernie O'Malley's ideas *during* the revolutionary period prove particularly revealing. As noted, O'Malley's political thinking was characterized by a simple aim: the establishment of a totally independent, all-Ireland republic. In support of this he alluded to the discreteness and distinctiveness of Irish culture, in particular suggesting that English/British culture was alien. 'We had fought a civilization which did not suit us. We had striven to give complete expression to the genius of the race.'[79] Of the Anglo-Irish war he claimed that 'the people saw the clash between two mentalities, two trends in direction, and two philosophies of life; between exploiters and exploited'.[80] The system against which he had fought was one

> which had stifled the spiritual expression of nationhood and had retarded our development; which had dammed back strength, vigour and imagination needed in solving our problems in our own way. The spirit of the race was warped until it could express its type of genius.[81]

Anglicized Ireland had been eclipsed, so O'Malley contended, by a distinct, discrete Irishness: 'The enemies [*sic*] anglicization and snobbery, almost synonymous terms, had given way before a national zeal and the development of national consciousness.'[82] British civilization did not suit Ireland; the genius of the Irish race needed to be given room for its own, distinctive development; there was a clash between two mentalities/ philosophies; the spirit of the Irish race needed to be set free. This (subsequently imposed) cultural interpretation provided a simple and useful foundation stone upon which to build a justification of the uncompromising republican argument. If Irish culture was discrete and distinctive then the separatist struggle might appear appropriate.

Of relevance here was the politics of Gaelicism. The English language had 'virtually replaced Gaelic' in Ireland,[83] but a striking renaissance movement had developed prior to O'Malley's political conversion. Whether or not one accepts the view sustained by people like Tom Garvin that 'culture became a surrogate for politics' during the post-Parnell period,[84] it remains the case that Gaelicism significantly influenced the thinking of early twentieth-century Irish republicans. In accordance with Thomas Davis's theory that 'A people without a language of its own is only half a nation',[85] Gaelicism could be seen simultaneously to provide republicans with definition and justification. O'Malley repeatedly stressed the importance of Gaelicism. 'Most of the officers and men in the recent rising [the 1916 rebellion] had had some knowledge of, or had been students of, Irish.'[86] Most of his post-rising colleagues in the Volunteers had, he stated, joined the Gaelic League.[87] Gaelic Leaguers, he asserted, 'stressed the incentive of the language towards propagandist nationality; few had disinterested literary values'.[88] From O'Malley's contemporary and subsequent accounts of the revolution there do indeed emerge traces of a definite Gaelic flavour.[89]

O'Malley did not come to republicanism through a Gaelic route.[90] But after his conversion to republicanism through the military events of 1916 he did adopt parts of the Gaelic package. Christened Ernest Malley, he came (on occasions) to sign his name during the early 1920s as Earnan Ó Maille.[91] As noted, he recognized the importance of Gaelicism in the lives of the 1916 rebels who had influenced him; and after the rebellion he himself joined the Gaelic League.[92] Yet his Gaelic self was a re-invented one. Furthermore, as O'Malley himself acknowledged, it was only a partially convincing re-invention. In January 1923 he referred to his 'lack of Gaelic tradition and outlook'.[93] With reference to 1922 he observed that, 'My Irish was poor.'[94] Of 1919 he later claimed: 'I regretted I had not studied Irish thoroughly.'[95]

The phenomenon of nationalists seeking authentication by means of spurious historical argument is one which has been widely noted.[96] The particularly interesting thing about O'Malley is this: that *according to his own evidence* he can himself be seen to demonstrate the complexity of the cultural world which his aforementioned discrete civilizations thesis fought so hard to obscure. His political project (pure, unambiguous, separatist republicanism) conflicted with the complexities and diversity of Irish opinion. So, too, his portrait of a discrete Irish culture to which British civilization was alien was contradicted by the fact that his own personal culture during the revolution was so heavily informed by British influences. Rather than the clash of two civilizations, it was their mingling to which O'Malley bore witness. Thus, writing in April 1923 from prison, he asserted, 'I have a decent library now and have ample time to browse deep in Chaucer, Shakesp[eare], Dante and Milton.'[97] In July of the same year he wrote, 'I have mapped out a course in English literature and am endeavouring to follow it.'[98] Like fellow prisoner Peadar O'Donnell, he loved Shakespeare[99] and, indeed, referred regularly to him or to works about him.[100] He loved Robert Louis Stevenson,[101] and enjoyed Austen, Buchan, Scott, Dickens, Shelley, Keats, Browning, Blake, Chaucer, Milton, Lamb, Hazlitt, Johnson, Bennett and Galsworthy.[102] Writing in 1923, he listed the material which he had read and in doing so cited roughly four times as many English/British authors as he did Irish ones.[103] Moreover the authors over whom he most enthused were British.[104]

O'Malley's intellectual framework also took in influences which were neither British nor Irish.[105] But the point remains that his own mind was deeply informed by British/English influences – influences which he himself celebrated. He had drunk deep – and pleasurably so – of the civilization which his cultural theory asserted to be unsuitable in Ireland.

O'Malley advocated the pursuit of a separatist republicanism which did not take account of actual Irish opinion. He likewise produced a map of Irish cultural dicreteness which did not reflect the complexities of the existing cultural landscape. The tension is particularly interesting because his own personal culture during the revolution so clearly demonstrated the inadequacy of the theory upon which his revolutionary activities were founded.

At heart, however, O'Malley's revolution was about political violence rather than political ideas. He demonstrated a neo-fenian distaste for politics.[106] He later recognized himself to have shared 'the pseudo-military mind of the IRA and its fear of constitutional respectability'.[107] He disliked the idea of being a member of the Dail.[108] He admitted that at IRA Executive meetings and the like he had 'not the faintest ideas on policy or statesmanship'.[109] Of the Anglo-Irish war he later observed that 'We could not see any definite social shape or direction to our efforts. We were not critical of our leaders and our work absorbed our judgment in its immediate local use.'[110] This is a vital point. Thought and energy were directed toward the military struggle – *soldiership* became a surrogate for politics. It was 'as a soldier'[111] that O'Malley identified himself during this period. In August 1921 he even asserted that he was 'anxiously looking forward to war for a slight rest in the line of active service'.[112]

Here, too, the questions of British influence and context manifested themselves. When the First World War began, O'Malley was pro-British and intended, like his brother, to join the British army.[113] And even after 1916 converted him to an alternative patriotism in an alternative army, the British resonances remained. In his zeal to acquire military knowledge he read official British military books and enjoyed discussions with his British army brother.[114] And in his military method O'Malley was as uncompromising as in his political aim or his theoretical justification. Writing in April 1923 he stated: 'Personally I can see either a complete surrender or an ultimate victory. I would infinitely prefer the former to a compromise.'[115] Reflecting later on the treaty split he acknowledged that his sympathies would have been with the irreconcilables, however the pattern of alliances had emerged:

> I had doubts about our course of action in resisting the attack of the [Free] Staters on the Four Courts; I wondered if any other solution could have been reached. Doubts did not last. Whatever alliance could have been made with [Michael] Collins, civil or military, some section of the country would possibly have fought, and I knew that I would have joined them.[116]

O'Malley's absorption in military action enabled him, in effect, to turn away from the intricacies of political theory. In doing so he ignored the fatal tension at the heart of his political ideas: between the simplicity of his vision and the complexity of Irish reality. He stood uncompromisingly by a rigid republic, and as a consequence was unable to cope ideologically with the actual diversity of Irish opinion. In cultural terms his simple reading of a discrete Ireland was inadequate. That this inadequacy was highlighted by the complexity of his *own* culture renders him a fascinating case study. It does nothing to make his republican argument any less flawed.

II

Writing subsequently, Ernie O'Malley observed of the post–1916 Volunteers that their 'spirit in essentials was hostile to Labour, afraid that any attention to its needs or direction would weaken the one-sided thrust of force'.[117] This observation had depressing implications for O'Malley's equally charismatic republican colleague, Peadar O'Donnell. For the leitmotiv of O'Donnell's political career was that social struggle and national struggle must be interwoven.

Speaking in Belfast in 1984 O'Donnell referred to a telephone conversation which he had had with Eamon de Valera during the latter's presidency in the Republic. ' "You've got to remember, Dev," ' – said O'Donnell – ' "that damn nearly a million Irish people left there while you were Taoiseach." "Ah, be fair now," ' – said de Valera – ' "if you had been in my place there'd have been emigration, too." "Yes, Dev, that's quite true;" ' – O'Donnell claims to have replied – ' "if I had been in your place there'd have been a great many people who would have left the country. But they would not have been the same people!" '[118] In some ways this exchange is a typically O'Donnellite one: impishly challenging the powerful and famous; personally amicable yet unrepentantly dissident; involved with and yet apart from those at the heart of Irish influence. In his brilliant memoir of civil war incarceration, O'Donnell described himself as '(above all else) a great neighbour'[119] and this is a good place to start in analysing O'Donnell's political ideas. Originating in small-farm Donegal, O'Donnell's social (and sociable) approach was deeply rooted in the community culture with which he was first familiar. His literary output repeatedly reflects this and the concept of neighbourliness was at the heart of his social and political thinking. Even his most influential political campaign – the land annuities movement which he began in the mid–1920s – he described as 'entirely an affair of neighbours'.[120] Neighbourliness for O'Donnell was rooted in the soil and in the people of the soil. But it was not a soppy parade of kindness or do-goodery – rather a tough-minded form of self-regulation. He noted that neighbours might do their best to eat in on your land[121] and one of his literary characters observes that:

> It would be a bad habit, a habit of being too plentiful with your share. To be a neighbour you have to give and you have to take, but you

have to keep an eye on yourself not to over-give. Give in your turn and ask in your turn and to be too soft is as bad as to be too hard.[122]

But the same hunger for life which counselled such self-protection was at the core of the acts of mutual, communal support which O'Donnell more regularly identified as constituting neighbourly action. In his first novel, *Storm*, the semi-autobiographical Eamonn Gallagher claims that poor rural people possess 'the strongest sympathy knitting them all together' and that 'the hardest pressed of them would somehow manage to spare a naggin of milk when a neighbour's cow was dry, or there was a sick child in the house'.[123] A similar theme is evident in O'Donnell's final novel, *Proud Island*:

> A crowded island was a special kind of townland. It was more than a scatter of houses. It was *Our* Island. *This* Island. How could it be else when one night of storm and the boats out made one heart of all its people?[124]

As one commentator has observed (of O'Donnell as novelist): 'His community can be seen to act, when at its best and most united, in ways which reinforce the deep sense of sharing and belonging.'[125] Examples abound. In *Islanders* the entire community automatically makes the Doogan family its primary priority after Nellie Doogan's death.[126] In the opening chapter of *Adrigoole* it is claimed that 'The diffused neighbourliness of the open fields collected in pools of eager folk in special houses that varied from night to night.'[127] It is also asserted that this communal spirit manifested itself through acts of practical co-operation such as 'gatherings' – the 'voluntary coming together of neighbours for part of a day to do special work without pay for some family without men-folk'.[128]

Neighbourliness – a kind of communal self-reliance – helps define the nature of O'Donnell's political ideas and vision. 'We were a needy lot in those townlands',[129] O'Donnell later observed in reference to his own background, and his creative works certainly stress poverty and suffering.[130] But if need was shared then so – according to O'Donnell – was the neighbourly resilience with which to deal with it. The Donegal society which his (creative and other) literature portrays is one inhabited by neighbours who clearly see what they want and who evince a communal toughness. Writing in the radical paper, the *Irish Democrat*, in June 1937, for example, he paid tribute to

> a colleague and a neighbour of mine in the No Rent fight in Donegal. . . . He came of a great stock of people; and in Tirconaill we are great on the breed of men. He was of a community of the sturdiest bodies and best lit minds in the small farmer world. His townland folk were among the earliest pioneers of the Land Annuity fight, and they entered it with the clearest idea of what they sought.[131]

It is interesting here to compare C. S. Andrews' comment – having been shown around the Donegal Rosses by O'Donnell – that 'what struck me most forcefully was the atmosphere of independent self-reliance'.[132] O'Donnell's Donegal experience of (what he perceived to be) capable, resilient communities played a vital role in forming his complex and ultimately unconvincing political ideas. The influences which helped to sculpt his dissident approach were intimate, forceful and varied. His mother was 'a strong Larkinite';[133] an uncle had been radically active in the United States; and both mother and uncle had, by O'Donnell's own admission, 'left their mark' on him. Then – while a teacher on Donegal's Aranmore Island – he had visited Scotland in connection with a strike involving migrant labourers. The experiences in Scotland, where he met numerous socialists, were extremely significant ones. In Glasgow, he said, 'I entered an exciting world, the world of the working class struggle.'[134]

Family radicalism and Scottish-induced socialist awareness were to be complemented by professional commitment and ideological fever. In 1918 O'Donnell became a full-time organizer with the Irish Transport and General Workers' Union [ITGWU].[135] In Liberty Hall, he later claimed, they prepared 'to fulfill [*sic*] the dream of [James] Connolly'. Having, by his own admission, discovered his ignorance he 'read omnivorously, day and night'.[136] According to one of his closest associates, 'Somebody . . . in Liberty Hall . . . gave him [Karl] Marx to read. He just couldn't get over this.'[137] O'Donnell's ideas were fed, therefore, by a combination of potent influences. Family, community and intellectual absorption all impelled him in the same (revolutionary) direction.

Mention of Connolly is important. O'Donnell expressed a healthy sense of the need for appropriate historical context. In relation to Pearse and Connolly, for example, he commented that:

> the habit we have in this country of taking the name and making it a slogan and attempting to revive something that has passed through history and to revive that effort in totally different conditions is one of our weaknesses[138]

– but in fact O'Donnell could himself be accused and convicted of having done precisely what he criticizes here. The Republican Congress movement of the 1930s – in which he was a vitally influential figure – overdosed on Connolly as hero and rhetorician.[139] And it did so in circumstances greatly different from those which had obtained during Connolly's life. There were tremendous ideological similarities between the Connollyite and the O'Donnellite approaches. Both held that an independent Irish republic must be established and that integral to the struggle to attain this republic was the class identification of that struggle. Class politics was interwoven with the politics of national freedom. Thus in April 1916 Connolly's *Workers' Republic* carried the assertion that, 'The cause of labour is the cause of Ireland, the cause of Ireland is the cause of labour.

They cannot be dissevered.'[140] Eighteen years later the manifesto which trumpeted out the approach of O'Donnell's Republican Congress stated: 'We believe that a Republic of a united Ireland will never be achieved except through a struggle which uproots capitalism on its way.'[141] Again, Connolly's masterpiece of self-deceptive brilliance, *Labour in Irish History*, claimed that 'only the Irish working class remain as the incorruptible inheritors of the fight for freedom in Ireland'.[142] Compare this with a resolution moved by Peadar O'Donnell at the Republican Congress's 1934 Rathmines convention, which stated that 'the only dependable forces for achieving the freedom of the nation' were 'the Irish working class and working farmers'.[143]

Both Connolly and O'Donnell sought the eradication of capitalism (Connolly: 'The day has passed for patching up the capitalist system; it must go''';[144] O'Donnell: 'in order to make any changes that are worthwhile, you've got to endanger or change the structures which constitute capitalism').[145] Capitalism for O'Donnell, as for Connolly before him, stood in the way of the republic. 'My quarrel [with de Valera, said O'Donnell in 1934] is that he pretends to be a Republican while actually the interests for which his Party act – Irish capitalism – are across the road to the Republic.'[146] Those classes which thrived under the capitalist system which accompanied British hegemony in Ireland could and would, O'Donnell argued, find a compromise with Britain short of the full Irish republic. This compromise would suit their economic needs. Those classes which did not thrive under capitalism were the only ones with a genuine reason for seeing the republican fight through to completion, as their economic interests were only capable of being satisfied in a post-British, post-capitalist context. Thus had argued Connolly; thus echoed O'Donnell.

But O'Donnell's ideas were not as locked into an urban context as Connolly's had been. He attempted – most notably in his land annuities campaign – to build on rural foundations. He claimed that his intellectual point of reference here was James Fintan Lalor. He had tried, he said, to find in the works of Connolly and Pearse the kind of foundations which Marx had discovered in Smith and Ricardo. Having found nothing there upon which to base a movement, he turned to Fintan Lalor: 'the most advanced thinker of the Young Irelanders'.

Fintan Lalor had a theory that the way into a national struggle was not by just shouting patriotism, but by finding some law that was part of the very nature of government, that wasn't dependent on [a] moral code, that helped to nullify itself, and set out to nullify that law and gradually force the government to come out into warfare against the people. And it struck me that he regretted there was no tax directly payable to Britain that he could get the people to refuse . . . and I could see that the land annuity payment . . . was exactly the sort of tax that Fintan Lalor regretted wasn't in existence in his day.[147]

Hence the land annuities campaign emerged – a campaign started by O'Donnell in the mid–1920s. It was directed against payments made by farmers to Britain, in repayment of the money which had been forwarded in order that Irish tenants should be enabled to buy their land.[148]

O'Donnell rightly recognized the need to sink sturdy, rural roots if his political project was to have any hope of success. He expanded the Connolly tradition in this respect. But for all his energetic endeavour, O'Donnell's ideological fusion of social and national struggle proved unable to make any serious impression on early twentieth-century Ireland. In his charming, latter-day phrase, 'I never was on the winning side in any damn thing ever I did.'[149] He fought on the losing side in the 1922–3 civil war. He tried after the civil war to steer the IRA towards a self-definition which was based upon class-struggle; and again he failed. His land annuities campaign ended up benefitting de Valera; Fianna Fail's 1932 success derived in part from its espousal of hostility towards these payments to Britain.[150] He was central to the founding of the socialist republican organization, Saor Eire, in 1931; but this swiftly drowned. He was at the heart of the Republican Congress movement established in 1934; this disintegrated and died without making any serious impact on Irish political life.

The reasons for his failure are clear enough when his political ideas are set against the context of contemporary Irish society. The explanation must start with the land. If O'Donnell's radical revolution were to succeed then he had to develop a cogent, appealing land argument. In fact there were considerable problems with his approach. Not only did he fail to address the enormous complexity and variety of early twentieth-century Irish agriculture, but he fumbled around ambiguously without reaching any clear, convincing policy. At times he endorsed the rights of the property-owning small farmer. At others he made it plain that state/collective farming represented his preferred model.[151] Peasant proprietorship provides the crucial context here. The late nineteenth and early twentieth centuries had witnessed 'an extraordinary transformation in the pattern of Irish landholding',[152] with the massive shift from tenancy to land ownership. The emergence of peasant proprietorship had, in the words of one historian, reinforced 'the post-famine tendencies to greater conservatism, unwillingness to part with land and general peasant caution'.[153] It was crucial to the failure of class-struggling republicans such as Peadar O'Donnell that so many of those to whom they looked for support existed within a small farm orbit. If small-scale proprietors or landless labourers did desire change, then such aspirations were likely to develop around the conservative theme of land ownership. This is where O'Donnell's ideas faced difficulties. If he espoused socialist, socializing land programmes he would be overwhelmingly rejected by those who owned (or wished to own) land. If he *recognized* the importance of peasant proprietorship and consequently offered more conservative suggestions, then there would be little to distinguish his ideas on the land from those of conservative nationalists. In fact he equivocated between the two positions and, predictably, achieved minimal success. The Republican Congress had espoused 'a system of peasant ownership where appropriate, but especially the development of co-operatives on a large scale'.[154] But if one's ambitions lay in the realm of land ownership then why support a figure such as O'Donnell, who had spoken menacingly of 'collectives'?[155] The irony of O'Donnell's reference to Fintan Lalor is that Lalor's sympathy for 'landlord-tenant dual ownership'[156] leaned in *precisely* the direction which later caused such problems for O'Donnell: the shift from tenancy towards ownership.

O'Donnell's urban horizon was no less depressing. As noted, the extra-constitutional fanaticism of characters such as O'Donnell was increasingly eschewed by the post–1922 southern Irish people. The more pragmatic, persuasive constitutionalism of Fianna Fail eclipsed O'Donnell's breed of republicanism just as effectively as it eclipsed that of the non-socialist Sean Russell. Thus there was a further irony. O'Donnell's idea had been that the land annuities campaign should resurrect the independence movement – a movement which he saw as leading towards the full republic: 'This skirmish we were conducting could lead into a land war which could restore the independence movement that the Treaty had wrecked.'[157] In fact the land annuities issue (brought to life by O'Donnell)[158] helped de Valera to achieve power in 1932. And it was de Valera's constitutionalizing of the nationalist constituency which buried all hope of O'Donnellite success. O'Donnell chose to remain outside the arena of practical politics, preferring the virtues of his imaginary republic to the limited but real qualities of the Free State non-republic. By doing so he confirmed his own marginalization.

In Northern Ireland – the one part of the inter-war island in which a sizeable concentration of urban workers existed – there were further problems for socialist republican ideology. Sheila Humphreys recalled an occasion on which Maurice Twomey (IRA chief of staff between 1926 and 1936) had been informed that a particular Protestant republican had converted to Catholicism. ' "That's the limit;" ' – Twomey exclaimed – ' "we *can't* keep a bloody Protestant in the movement!" '[159] The anecdote *proves* nothing. But it does nicely capture the dilemma which socialist republicans shared with their non-socialist republican allies: the inability to make any serious impression on Protestant Ireland. O'Donnell's ideas in relation to unionist difference were wholly inadequate. 'I think it is nonsense' – he claimed – 'to suggest that we [in Ireland] are two peoples. We are the same people with different relatives.'[160] In 1922 he is recorded as having thought 'unity between Ulster Specials and [the] IRA on national freedom not impossible',[161] a hopelessly optimistic attitude. *Republican Congress* argued in May 1934 that 'The natural, normal task for the Belfast workers in common with the workers of the rest of Ireland is to lead the struggle for freedom.'[162] But that which was normal and natural for the unionist workers in Belfast in fact had very little to do with the endorsement of the Congress's republican socialist 'struggle for freedom'.

An exacerbating difficulty for O'Donnell concerned Catholicism. Ireland's Catholic Church (and the Catholic ethos which prevailed in the post–1922 state) tended to solidify hostility to his ideas. O'Donnell famously locked horns with the Church over many years. Of clerical anti-republicanism in the civil war period, he wrote that:

> The Bishops' faction took the platform and dogmatized on every question within touch, associating the Gospel with their views and the devil with their opponents'. Every curate was the Holy Roman Catholic Church with infallibility complete and every Republican was an unbeliever, a heretic, an anti-Christ. The spirit of Cromwell had returned to Ireland and Maynooth was its tabernacle.[163]

That O'Donnell's republicanism was dyed red rendered him even less popular with many of the clergy.[164] O'Donnell's ideas regarding this problem are interesting. With regard to Catholic, anti-communist frenzy, he argued that while people 'on occasion . . . find an individual clergyman to go crazy with them they more often impose themselves on clergymen who abhor what they do'.[165] He also argued that people who had assaulted him on one such frenzied occasion in Dublin had done so because they 'had been driven out of their minds by a month's rabid Lenten Lectures'.[166] Both reflections are telling. The clergy did often preach anti-communism/anti-socialism; but the laity often needed no great pushing anyway in order to reach strongly anti-O'Donnellite conclusions. Godless radicalism – perceived as hostile to Church, Lord and private property – was one of the few phenomena which rivalled jazz and extra-marital sex in the league table of sins in inter-war Ireland. Thwarted by peasant proprietorship, outflanked by constitutional nationalism and powerless against northern unionist opposition, Peadar O'Donnell found that his ideas also came up against an inimical Catholic Church and ethos. It was a collection of obstacles which they simply could not overcome.[167]

Owen Dudley Edwards has argued of O'Donnell that 'Nature intended him to be an iconoclast, and he went with nature.'[168] But his problems in fact arose as a result of his not having been iconoclastic *enough*. He questioned numerous republican orthodoxies, including martyrdom[169] and physical force.[170] And in his attempt to define the republican struggle in terms of class conflict he certainly struck a dissident chord within the republican tradition (as well as within broader Irish society). But while he challenged republicanism's *multi-class* assumptions he did not apply his critical faculties sufficiently to the *socialist* republican assumptions which he sought to put in their place. He assumed – as had Connolly before him – that the only true or effective republicanism was that which fought a battle ultimately determined along class lines. But this was to underestimate – as had Connolly before him – the potential of a republicanism or of a nationalism not defined according to class conflict; witness the triumph of Fianna Fail's capitalist nationalism. O'Donnell was far from iconoclastic enough: in his failure to tear down the altars of socialist republican assumption he demonstrated an intellectual laziness which was in fact all too typical of early twentieth-century republicanism. His socialist republicanism relied ultimately on self-validating faith, as did the non-socialist republicanism of Ernie O'Malley. In O'Malley's case an uncompromising legitimist conviction spawned obdurate revolutionary action. But the rigidity of O'Malley's vision rendered it incapable of dealing adequately with the complexities of existing Irish reality. So, too, O'Donnell's political ideas were marred by his adherence to an insufficiently flexible creed. His crude class analysis was unable to cope with the true complications of Irish society,[171] and the central problem with his thinking was precisely that he did not challenge the assumptions contained within the socialist republican tradition. The cause of labour and the cause of Ireland *could* be (and indeed were) dissevered.

NOTES

1 O'Malley to Molly Childers, 17 December 1923, in R. English and C. O'Malley (eds), *Prisoners: The Civil War Letters of Ernie O'Malley*, Swords, Poolbeg, 1991, 123–4.
2 On hearing of the signing of this December 1921 Anglo-Irish treaty, O'Malley's response had been one of anger: 'I cursed loud and long. So this was what we had been fighting for'. E. O'Malley, *The Singing Flame*, Dublin, Anvil, 1978, 41.
3 'In the morning Peadar O'Donnell visited me and appointed himself my nurse and made arrangements for supplying me at regular intervals with nourishment' (O'Malley to Molly Childers, 28 November 1923, in English and O'Malley (eds), *Prisoners*, 97).
4 Ernie O'Malley (1897–1957): born in County Mayo; family moved to Dublin when he was young; began as a medical student in University College, Dublin, in 1915; powerfully influenced by the Easter rebellion of 1916; joined Irish Volunteers, going full-time in 1918 and becoming an influential IRA officer during the Anglo-Irish war and civil war; imprisoned, 1922–4; subsequently travelled extensively, and pursued research on a variety of historical, artistic and literary topics. For fuller biographical information, see: P. O'Farrell, *The Ernie O'Malley Story*, Cork, Mercier, 1983; English and O'Malley (eds), *Prisoners*.

Peadar O'Donnell (1893–1986): born in County Donegal; trained as a teacher in St Patrick's Training College, Dublin, 1911–13; school-teacher, before becoming a full-time organizer for the Irish Transport and General Workers' Union (ITGWU); IRA officer during the Anglo-Irish war and civil war; imprisoned, 1922–4; influential in the IRA's Army Council and Army Executive during the post-civil war decade; edited IRA paper, *An Phoblacht*, 1926–9; a leading founder-member of socialist republican organizations, Saor Eire (1931) and the Republican Congress (1934); helped establish (and subsequently edited) the literary/artistic/social journal, *The Bell*. For fuller biographical information, see: R. English, 'Peadar O'Donnell: socialism and the republic, 1925–37', *Saothar*, 14, (1989); R. English, 'Radicals and the republic: socialist republicanism in the Irish Free State 1925–37', unpublished Ph.D. thesis, University of Keele, 1990, ch 4; G. Freyer, *Peadar O'Donnell*, Lewisburg, Bucknell University Press, 1973; M. McInerney, *Peadar O'Donnell: Irish Social Rebel*, Dublin, O'Brien, 1974.

5 It should be noted that Henry Patterson's valuable study, *The Politics of Illusion: Republicanism and Socialism in Modern Ireland*, London, Hutchinson Radius, 1989, draws heavily on O'Donnell in its earlier stages. There is also a growing thesis literature of relevance to O'Donnell: M. M. Banta, 'The red scare in the Irish Free State 1929–37', MA thesis, University College, Dublin, 1982; S. G. Bruton, 'Peadar O'Donnell: republican socialist visionary', MA thesis, University College, Dublin, 1988; A. Crean, 'Confronting reality: social and political realism in the writings of Peadar O'Donnell 1922–1939', M. Phil. thesis, University College, Dublin, 1986; English, 'Radicals and the republic'; J. P. McHugh, 'Voices of the rearguard. A study of *An Phoblacht*: Irish republican thought in the post-revolutionary era, 1923–37', MA thesis, University College, Dublin, 1983.

6 See, for example, the references to O'Malley in M. Hopkinson, *Green Against Green: the Irish civil war*, Dublin, Gill & Macmillan, 1988; R. F. Foster, *Modern Ireland 1600–1972*, Harmondsworth, Allen Lane, 1988; D. G. Boyce, *Nineteenth-century Ireland: The Search for Stability*, Dublin, Gill & Macmillan, 1990. For O'Donnell, see P. Bew, 'Sinn Fein, agrarian radicalism and the war of independence, 1919–1921', in D. G. Boyce (ed.), *The Revolution in Ireland, 1879–1923*, Basingstoke, Macmillan, 1988.

7 J. J. Lee, *Ireland 1912–1985: Politics and Society*, Cambridge, Cambridge University Press, 1989; English and O'Malley (eds), *Prisoners*; Humphreys Papers, Archives Department, University College, Dublin (ADUCD) P106; FitzGerald Papers, ADUCD P80; Patterson's *The Politics of Illusion*, for example, offers no treatment of O'Donnell's novels, despite their importance as sources for understanding the man and his thinking.

8 O'Malley, *The Singing Flame*, 42.

9 E. O'Malley, *On Another Man's Wound*, Dublin, Anvil, 1979 edn (first published 1936), 66.

10 *Irish Times*, 26 October 1917.

11 O'Malley, *The Singing Flame*, 155.

12 ibid., 48.

13 C. Townshend, *Political Violence in Ireland: Government and Resistance since 1848*, Oxford, Clarendon Press, 1983, 328.

14 O'Malley, *The Singing Flame*, 45. Compare Townshend's observation that de Valera's alternative proposal 'lacked the transparent simplicity of absolute independence' (Townshend, *Political Violence*, 364).

15 O'Malley to Sheila Humphreys, 12 April 1923, Humphreys Papers, ADUCD P106 (not yet given a full reference number).

16 O'Malley to Sheila Humphreys, 9 April 1923, Humphreys Papers, ADUCD P106 (not yet given a full reference number). Compare his comments in a letter of December 1923:

> Years ago . . . my chums (who have all since been killed) and I tried often to look ahead and pierce the future and always we ended our discussion by saying that we hoped we would be still Republicans if we ever lived to be old. At any rate we had faith and saw ultimate victory, though not in our time. I feel the same today.
>
> (O'Malley to Sheila Humphreys, 25 December 1923, in English and O'Malley (eds), *Prisoners*, 128).

17 O'Malley, *The Singing Flame*, 82.
18 ibid., 90.
19 O'Malley, *On Another Man's Wound*, 332. Fittingly, perhaps, O'Malley (in his version of the civil war) admitted that he 'had never been in Belfast', O'Malley, *The Singing Flame*, 139.
20 D. Breen, *My Fight for Irish Freedom*, Tralee, Anvil, 1964 edn (first published 1924), 14.
21 A working assumption such as that employed by Eric Hobsbawm – 'any sufficiently large body of people whose members regard themselves as members of a "nation", will be treated as such' (E. J. Hobsbawm, *Nations and Nationalism Since 1780: Programme, Myth, Reality* Cambridge, Cambridge University Press, 1990, 8) – serves neatly to amplify the point. Such a definition would plainly allow early twentieth-century Irish nationalists their nation; but it would also recognize that there was an obdurate and problematic minority on the Irish island who clearly did not form part of that nation.
22 *Irish Times*, 4 November 1922.
23 J. Prager, *Building Democracy in Ireland: Political Order and Cultural Integration in a Newly Independent Nation*, Cambridge, Cambridge University Press, 1986, 16. The current author remains sceptical about Prager's 'ideal typical approach to Irish history' (ibid., 37). But it remains the case that *Building Democracy* amply demonstrates the long-term existence of significantly divergent assumptions and aspirations in the realm of Irish political ideology. For lengthier reflections on Prager's book, see English, 'Radicals and the republic', Prologue.
24 O'Malley, *On Another Man's Wound*, 115.
25 ibid., 163.
26 E. O'Malley, *Raids and Rallies*, Dublin, Anvil, 1982, 98.
27 O'Malley, *The Singing Flame*, 163.
28 O'Malley to P. Hooper, 24 August 1922, FitzGerald Papers, ADUCD P80/311[3].
29 S. O'Casey, *Juno and the Paycock*, in S. O'Casey, *Three Plays*, London, Pan, 1980 edn (*Juno and the Paycock* first published 1925), 9.
30 P. Pearse, *Political Writings and Speeches*, Dublin, Talbot, 1952, 121.
31 R. D. Edwards, *Patrick Pearse: The Triumph of Failure*, Swords, Poolbeg, 1990 edn (first published 1977), 70.
32 O'Malley to Molly Childers, 26 November/1 December 1923, in English and O'Malley (eds), *Prisoners*, 72–3. Compare O'Malley, *On Another Man's Wound*, ch. 3. See also the effect which IRA leader, Tom Barry, claimed that the 1916 rebellion had had upon him: 'through the blood sacrifices of the men of 1916, had one Irish youth of eighteen been awakened to Irish Nationality' (T. Barry, *Guerilla Days in Ireland*, Tralee, Anvil, 1962 edn (first published 1949), 8). Even if one were sceptical about such later claims, the very fact that people reinvented their past in order to portray 1916 as the pivotal event in their lives would *of itself* demonstrate the influence of the Pearsean rebellion within republican tradition.
33 O'Malley to Sheila Humphreys, 25 December 1923, in English and O'Malley (eds), *Prisoners*, 129.
34 O'Malley to Molly Childers, 5/7 December 1923, in English and O'Malley (eds), *Prisoners*, 110.
35 O'Malley, *The Singing Flame*, 285–6; O'Malley to P. Hooper, 24 August 1922, FitzGerald Papers, ADUCD P80/311[4].
36 J. J. Lee, 'In search of Patrick Pearse' in M. Ni Dhonnchadha and T. Dorgan (eds), *Revising the Rising*, Derry, Field Day, 1991, 137.
37 O'Malley, *The Singing Flame*, 214.

38 T. Garvin, *Nationalist Revolutionaries in Ireland 1858–1928*, Oxford, Claren-
    don Press, 1987, 142.
39 Townshend, *Political Violence*, 26.
40 O'Malley, *The Singing Flame*, 11.
41 On the growth of post-rising sympathy for the rebels, see the Cabinet memor-
    andum of 15 May 1916, 'Public attitude and opinion in Ireland as to the recent
    outbreak', Bonar Law Papers, House of Lords Record Office (HLRO), BL
    63/C/3. On the notion that the 1916-induced changes were to prove lastingly
    harmful, see P. Bew, 'The Easter Rising: lost leaders and lost opportunities',
    Irish Review, 11 (Winter 1991–2).
42 O'Malley, *The Singing Flame*, 25.
43 ibid., 132.
44 O'Malley, *Raids and Rallies*, 70–1.
45 O'Malley to Molly Childers, 26 November/1 December 1923, in English and
    O'Malley (eds), *Prisoners*, 80; O'Malley, *Raids and Rallies*, 50; O'Malley,
    On Another Man's Wound, 324.
46 ibid., 326; cf. O'Malley, *The Singing Flame*, 12. For his account of reprisals
    carried out by the Crown forces, see O'Malley, *Raids and Rallies*, 77–82.
    Compare Charles Townshend's comment that the British response to the
    IRA campaign was 'brutal, and in many ways counter-productive' (C. Town-
    shend, *The British Campaign in Ireland, 1919–1921: The Development of
    Political and Military Policies*, Oxford, Oxford University Press, 1975, 206).
47 O'Malley, *On Another Man's Wound*, 326; O'Malley, *The Singing Flame*,
    12–13. Problems of co-operation between the various arms of the state in
    Ireland were not new; see E. A. Muenger, *The British Military Dilemma in
    Ireland: Occupation Politics, 1886–1914*, Dublin, Gill & Macmillan, 1991, ch. 4.
    48 O'Malley, *The Singing Flame*, 41 and 43.
49 O'Malley to J. E. Healy, 21 September 1922, copy in the possession of
    Cormac O'Malley; cf. O'Malley Papers, ADUCD P17a/57; see also O'Mal-
    ley, *The Singing Flame*, 177. I am grateful to Cormac O'Malley for permission
    to see the archives in his personal possession.
50 O'Malley, *On Another Man's Wound*, 301; cf. O'Malley, *The Singing Flame*, 16.
    51 ibid., 11.
52 O'Malley, *Raids and Rallies*, 54.
53 O'Malley to Molly Childers, 26 November/1 December 1923, in English and
    O'Malley (eds), *Prisoners*, 81.
54 O'Malley, *The Singing Flame*, 45.
55 O'Malley, *On Another Man's Wound*, 9.
56 ibid., 190.
57 ibid., 332.
58 O'Malley, *The Singing Flame*, 15.
59 O'Malley to Mabel FitzGerald, 25 August 1921, FitzGerald Papers, ADUCD
    P80 (not yet given a full reference number).
60 O'Malley to Molly Childers, 26 November/1 December 1923, in English and
    O'Malley (eds), *Prisoners*, 78–9.
61 O'Malley, *On Another Man's Wound*, 323.
62 O'Malley, *The Singing Flame*, 148.
63 ibid., 164.
64 ibid.
65 *Constitution of Oglaigh na h-Eireann (Irish Republican Army) as Amended
    by General Army Convention 14th–15th November 1925*, copy in McGarrity
    Papers, National Library of Ireland (NLI), MS 17529.
66 Oglaigh na h-Eireann, *Constitution and Governmental Programme for the*

Republic of Ireland (1934), copy in Coyle O'Donnell Papers, ADUCD P61/11(1), p. 4.

67 D. G. Boyce, *The Irish Question and British Politics 1868–1986*, Basingstoke, Macmillan, 1988, 74.

68 R. Briscoe (with A. Hatch), *For the Life of Me*, London, Longman, 1959, 224. On the important role of Sean Lemass in stimulating the Fianna Fail initiative, see Prager, *Building Democracy*, 200.

69 D. McMahon, *Republicans and Imperialists: Anglo-Irish Relations in the 1930s*, New Haven, Yale University Press, 1984, 1.

70 T. Garvin, 'Nationalist elites, Irish voters and Irish political development: a comparative perspective', *Economic and Social Review*, 8, 3 (April 1977), 173.

71 Sheila Humphreys, interview with the author, Dublin, 26 February 1987.

72 R. Fanning, ' "The rule of order": Eamon de Valera and the IRA, 1923–1940', in J. A. Murphy and J. P. O'Carroll (eds), *De Valera and His Times*, Cork, Cork University Press, 1983, 170–1.

73 B. P. Murphy, *Patrick Pearse and the Lost Republican Ideal*, Dublin, James Duffy, 1991, 178.

74 Army Council to Joseph McGarrity, 27 January 1930, McGarrity Papers, NLI MS 17535(1).

75 MacBride to Joseph McGarrity, 19 October 1933, McGarrity Papers, NLI MS 17456.

76 See, for example, the assertion in 1934 that

> Fianna Fail's anti-Republican campaign is beginning in deeper earnest. Afraid to admit failure: national, political, economic, our ex-Republican ministers will now brook no criticism of their apostacy [*sic*]. Using all weapons which their puppet state can afford them, they wield them in the face of Republican activity.
>
> (*An Phoblacht* 6/7 January 1934)

77 Russell to Hans Luther, 25 October 1936, McGarrity Papers, NLI MS 17485.

78 *Wolfe Tone Weekly*, 17 December 1938.

79 O'Malley, *The Singing Flame*, 279.

80 O'Malley, *On Another Man's Wound*, 317.

81 O'Malley, *The Singing Flame*, 214.

82 ibid., 12.

83 Boyce, *Nineteenth-century Ireland*, 284.

84 T. Garvin, 'The politics of language and literature in pre-independence Ireland', *Irish Political Studies* 2 (1987), 51.

85 T. Davis, 'Our national language', in T. Davis, *Literary and Historical Essays*, Dublin, James Duffy, 1854, 174.

86 O'Malley, *On Another Man's Wound*, 61; cf. Garvin, *Nationalist Revolutionaries*, 78.

87 O'Malley, *On Another Man's Wound*, 57.

88 ibid., 58.

89 See, for example, O'Malley to Countess Plunkett, 15 November 1923, in English and O'Malley (eds), *Prisoners*, 50; O'Malley, *The Singing Flame*, 198 and 283; O'Malley, *Raids and Rallies*, 15. For traces of anti-modernism, see O'Malley to Molly Childers, 16 July 1923, in English and O'Malley (eds), *Prisoners*, 37, and also O'Malley to Molly Childers, 5/7 December 1923, ibid., 109–10.

90 R. F. Foster, 'Varieties of Irishness' in M. Crozier (ed.), *Cultural Traditions in Northern Ireland*, Belfast, Institute of Irish Studies, 1989, 8.

91 See, for example, English and O'Malley (eds), *Prisoners*, 26, 30, 31; O'Malley to Sean T. O'Kelly, 25 July 1922, FitzGerald Papers, ADUCD P80/298(7).

92 O'Malley to Molly Childers, 26 November/1 December 1923, in English and O'Malley (eds), *Prisoners*, 73; O'Malley, *On Another Man's Wound*, 61.

93 O'Malley to Liam Lynch, 12 January 1923, in English and O'Malley (eds), *Prisoners*, 26.

94 O'Malley, *The Singing Flame*, 161.

95 O'Malley, *On Another Man's Wound*, 104.

96 See, for example, Gellner's assertion that 'The cultures [which nationalism] claims to defend and revive are often its own inventions, or are modified out of all recognition' (E. Gellner, *Nations and Nationalism*, Oxford, Basil Blackwell, 1983, 56).

97 O'Malley to Sheila Humphreys, 12 April 1923, Humphreys Papers, ADUCD P106 (not yet given a full reference number).

98 O'Malley to Molly Childers, 16 July 1923, in English and O'Malley (eds), *Prisoners*, 37.

99 O'Malley to Molly Childers, 8 December 1923, in English and O'Malley (eds), *Prisoners*, 118; for O'Donnell, see P. O'Donnell, *The Gates Flew Open*, London, Jonathan Cape, 1932, 150–1.

100 English and O'Malley (eds), *Prisoners*, 60–1, 88–9, 114, 116, 118–19, 130; O'Malley, *The Singing Flame*, 105, 192–3.

101 O'Malley to Molly Childers, 12 November 1923, in English and O'Malley (eds), *Prisoners*, 46.

102 English and O'Malley (eds), *Prisoners*, 42–4, 49, 89–92, 118; O'Malley, *The Singing Flame*, 256 and 275.

103 O'Malley to Molly Childers, 26 November/1 December 1923, in English and O'Malley (eds), *Prisoners*, 88–92.

104 English and O'Malley (eds), *Prisoners*, 46, 89, 118.

105 See, for example, O'Malley, *On Another Man's Wound*, 107, 136, 269; O'Malley, *The Singing Flame* 190–1, 231.

106 For fenian anti-parliamentarianism (in relation to Britain) see, for example, John O'Leary's declaration in 1878 that 'Nine out of ten Irishmen entering the British Parliament with honest intentions are corrupted soon' (J. O. Ranelagh, 'The Irish Republican Brotherhood in the revolutionary period, 1879–1923', in Boyce (ed.), *The Revolution in Ireland, 1879–1923*, 137). For later, and more generalized, anti-parliamentarianism see Constance Markievicz's comments from 1917: 'I have no ambition to have a vote for an English Parliament . . . I don't think that Parliaments are much use anyhow. All authority in a country always seems to get into the hands of a clique and permanent officials' (A. Sebestyen (ed.), *Prison Letters of Countess Markievicz*, London, Virago, 1987, 174).

107 O'Malley, *On Another Man's Wound*, 213.

108 English and O'Malley (eds), *Prisoners*, 94, 130; O'Malley, *The Singing Flame*, 238.

109 O'Malley to Molly Childers, 24 November 1923, in English and O'Malley (eds), *Prisoners*, 63.

110 O'Malley, *On Another Man's Wound*, 323.

111 O'Malley to Liam Lynch, 9 January 1923, in English and O'Malley (eds), *Prisoners*, 25; cf. O'Malley, *The Singing Flame*, 141.

112 O'Malley to Mabel FitzGerald, 25 August 1921, FitzGerald Papers, ADUCD P80 (not yet given a full reference number).

113 O'Malley to Molly Childers, 26 November/1 December 1923, in English and O'Malley (eds), *Prisoners*, 71; O'Malley, *On Another Man's Wound*, 27. O'Malley fits the young, male Catholic, middle-class, educated pattern suggested by Garvin in relation to the republican élite of this period (Garvin, *Nationalist Revolutionaries*, 49–53). The alternative professionalism offered

by IRA officership matched O'Malley's social expectations and aspirations (O'Malley, *On Another Man's Wound*, 27). For a discussion of the relationship between class and the 1916–23 nationalist movement, see R. English, *Radicals and the Republic: Socialist Republicanism in the Irish Free State, 1925–37*, Oxford, Oxford University Press, forthcoming, Introduction.

114 O'Malley to Molly Childers, 26 November/1 December 1923, in English and O'Malley (eds), *Prisoners*, 75; O'Malley, *On Another Man's Wound*, 52–3.

115 O'Malley to Jim O'Donovan, 7 April 1923, in English and O'Malley (eds), *Prisoners*, 35.

116 O'Malley, *The Singing Flame*, 214.

117 O'Malley, *On Another Man's Wound*, 59.

118 P. O'Donnell, speech given in the Conway Street Mill, Belfast, 7 April 1984. I am grateful to the West Belfast branch of the Communist Party of Ireland for allowing me access to a recording of this event.

119 O'Donnell, *The Gates Flew Open*, 13.

120 *An Phoblacht*, 14 January 1927.

121 P. O'Donnell, *On the Edge of the Stream*, London, Jonathan Cape, 1934, 144.

122 P. O'Donnell, *The Big Windows*, Dublin, O'Brien, 1983 edn (first published 1955), 101.

123 P. O'Donnell, *Storm: A Story of the Irish War*, Dublin, Talbot, 1926, 55. O'Donnell's novels have a distinctly didactic flavour; cf. his comment to his publisher in 1933 that 'My pen is just a weapon' (O'Donnell to Jonathan Cape, 24 February 1933, Jonathan Cape archives, University of Reading Library). I am grateful to Jonathan Cape for permission to see archival correspondence between O'Donnell and Jonathan Cape.

124 P. O'Donnell, *Proud Island*, Dublin, O'Brien, 1977 edn; (first published 1975), 8.
125 F. Doherty, 'Windows on the world', *Fortnight* 290 (December 1990) (supplement), 10.

126 P. O'Donnell, *Islanders*, Cork, Mercier, 1963 edn (first published 1927), 47.

127 P. O'Donnell, *Adrigoole*, London, Jonathan Cape, 1929, 12.

128 ibid., 114.

129 McInerney, *Peadar O'Donnell*, 33.

130 See, for example, O'Donnell, *Islanders*, 13; O'Donnell, *Storm*, 54.

131 *Irish Democrat*, 19 June 1937.

132 C. S. Andrews, *Dublin Made Me: An Autobiography*, Cork, Mercier, 1979, 199–200. O'Donnell himself preferred to stress people's self-reliance rather than try to evoke pity on their behalf (P. O'Donnell, 'The dumb multitudinous masses', *The Bell* 2, 4 (July 1941), 67; P. O'Donnell, 'People and pawnshops', ibid. 5, 3 (December 1942), 207.

133 English, 'Peadar O'Donnell', 47.

134 McInerney, *Peadar O'Donnell*, 33–7.

135 English, 'Peadar O'Donnell', 47.

136 P. O'Donnell, *Monkeys in the Superstructure: Reminiscences of Peadar O'Donnell*, Galway, Salmon Publishing, 1986, 10.

137 Nora Harkin, interview with the author, Dublin, 4 February 1988.

138 O'Donnell, speech in Belfast, 7 April 1984.

139 R. English, 'Socialism and republican schism in Ireland: the emergence of the Republican Congress in 1934', *Irish Historical Studies*, 27, 105 (May 1990), 58–9.

140 *Workers' Republic*, 8 April 1916.

141 *Republican Congress*, 5 May 1934.

142 J. Connolly, *Labour in Irish History*, London, Bookmarks, 1987 edn (first published 1910), 24.

143 G. Gilmore, *The Irish Republican Congress*, Cork, Cork Workers' Club, 1978 edn, 48.
144 J. Connolly, 'Labour, nationality and religion', in P. B. Ellis (ed.), *James Connolly: Selected Writings*, Harmondsworth, Penguin Books, 1973 ('Labour, nationality and religion' first published 1910), 117.
145 O'Donnell, *Monkeys in the Superstructure*, 30.
146 *Republican Congress*, 6 October 1934.
147 O'Donnell, speech in Belfast, 7 April 1984.
148 For O'Donnell's version of the land annuities campaign, see P. O'Donnell, *There will be Another Day*, Dublin, Dolmen, 1963; to set the campaign in the wider context of Anglo-Irish relations, see McMahon, *Republicans and Imperialists*.
149 O'Donnell, speech in Belfast, 7 April 1984.
150 *Irish Press*, 6 February 1932, 8 February 1932, 9 February 1932, 10 February 1932.
151 English, 'Radicals and the republic', 334–6.
152 R. Fanning, *Independent Ireland*, Dublin, Helicon, 1983, 73.
153 M. E. Daly, *Social and Economic History of Ireland Since 1800*, Dublin, Educational Company of Ireland, 1981, 51.
154 Patrick Byrne to the author, 12 April 1988. Byrne was, for a time, one of the Congress's joint secretaries; see his *Memories of the Republican Congress*, London, Connolly Association, n.d.
155 *An Phoblacht*, 28 February 1931.
156 R. Davis, *The Young Ireland Movement*, Dublin, Gill & Macmillan, 1987, 189.
157 O'Donnell, *There Will be Another Day*, 52.
158 For an early acknowledgement of O'Donnell's role here, see S. O'Faolain, *De Valera*, Harmondsworth, Penguin Books, 1939, 124.
159 Sheila Humphreys, interview with the author, Dublin, 26 February 1987.
160 McInerney, *Peadar O'Donnell*, 201.
161 Frank Gallagher's prison diary, 23 December 1922, Gallagher Papers, NLI MS 18356.
162 *Republican Congress*, 5 May 1934.
163 O'Donnell, *The Gates Flew Open*, 47.
164 On clerical hostility to O'Donnell and his projects, see English, 'Radicals and the republic', 114–15, 163–4, 227–9.
165 P. O'Donnell, 'Facts and fairies', *The Bell*, 13, 1, (October 1946), 4.
166 McInerney, *Peadar O'Donnell*, 242.
167 It should also be noted that there were, on occasions, contradictions within O'Donnell's thinking when it came to questions of strategy; see, for example, English, 'Radicals and the republic', 212–16.
168 O. D. Edwards, 'Evangelical puritanism', *Fortnight*, 290 (December 1990) (supplement), 8.
169 U. MacEoin (ed.), *Survivors*, Dublin, Argenta, 1987 edn (first published 1980), 25.
170 O'Donnell, *Monkeys in the Superstructure*, 28.
171 Compare, for example, O'Donnell's reading of the 1921 treaty ('that the middle-class was getting all they wanted' (Mac Eoin (ed.), *Survivors*, 24)) with Garvin's presentation of the more complex relation which in fact existed between class and the treaty split (Garvin, *Nationalist Revolutionaries*, 142).

8 Unionist political thought, 1920–72

Jennifer Todd

INTRODUCTION

Ulster unionism – the political movement that emerged out of the home rule crises of the nineteenth century and that ruled Northern Ireland from 1920 until 1972 – has been central to Irish, and British, political life for over a century. But there is no agreement as to the broader political aims, values or assumptions that this movement embodies. For some analysts, unionism is an allegiance and a political strategy, not a theory. For some it embodies an instrumental, for others a principled view of political allegiance and authority. Some see it as essentially a form of contractual loyalty, others as a national movement – a form of British or Ulster nationalism.[1] For some there are important unifying strands in all the varieties of Ulster unionism, for others unionism is various, divided and contradictory.[2] Despite its central concern with the structure and status of the United Kingdom, it resists incorporation into the categories of British political thought – liberal or conservative or socialist.

Unionist political thought is hard to deal with because there have been few unionist intellectuals and they have not developed systematic theories of political obligation, the aims of government, the basis of citizenship or the rights and liberties of citizens. It has to be pieced together from politicians' statements – often strategic rather than principled theoretical discussions – and from the writings of unionist historians, biographers, autobiographers and novelists and the speeches of clergy.

The greatest sources of systematic writings from the unionist perspective have been in the two periods of crisis – 1886–1920 and 1970–90. During the home rule crises politicians, clergy and men of affairs stated the unionist case clearly.[3] The British political parties themselves took clear and systematic positions on the place of Ireland, and Ulster, in Kingdom and Empire.[4] Writers and novelists described the range of views and motivations that led to the mass unionist mobilization.[5] In the later period, too, articulate political and intellectual statements of the unionist case were given, while numerous autobiographies and histories presented the world as unionists perceived it.[6] In the intervening period of unionist power, systematic statements of unionist thought were few.

Yet this intervening period is important. The writings at time of crisis show the articulation of multiple, competing, contradictory versions of unionism. In the earlier period, a unity and coherence of unionist thought was only beginning to emerge out of diverse sources. In the later period, unionism itself was splintering, and with it any appearance of a unified theory. But in the intervening period, despite internal tensions, unionism had more unity, intellectually as well as politically.

Unionism never possessed a coherent theory, but, especially during the period of unionist power, it was more than a bare political allegiance to the Union of Great Britain and Northern Ireland, more than a strategic alliance of diverse groups with distinct ideologies. There was a community-based culture, with central concepts and ideals, ways of understanding political authority, and self-perceptions of its own political interests and responsibilities. The thrust towards a more coherent world view was there, given in shared meanings, concepts and reference points. Ideas of liberty, rights, modernity and prosperity fed into a British patriotism. In unionism, the contractual and the national, the instrumental and the principled, the liberal and the conservative images of society were merged.

Tensions and contradictions existed in this body of thought. They were continually brought into view as the Union itself was consistently challenged in the Irish context. That these tensions fractured into competing theories, however, has more to do with the crisis of political unionism than with any logical incompatibility. The structure of unionist political thought presupposed parallels between British and unionist interests, and a quiescent Northern nationalist population. When these assumptions proved unrealistic, ideological as well as political crisis ensued.

In this chapter I trace the diverse elements and origins of unionist political thought, and the ways unionists expressed, elided and partially transcended the tensions within this body of thought particularly in the period 1920–70.

ORIGINS 1886–1920

In this period, Ulster unionist unity was being forged out of diverse interests and concerns. Ulster unionists (like Irish nationalists) mobilized one of the great cross-class alliances: tenant farmer, farm labourer, landowner, urban working class, manufacturer, merchant and professional man, Protestants of all regions, denominations and social strata united against home rule.

The intellectual strands which merged in unionist political thought were, therefore, various and diverse. There was the settler emphasis on threat, covenant, and public banding.[7] There were the variety of

Reformation religious tendencies, which took as central concepts of religious liberty, Protestant identity, and the role of the individual conscience: within this broad framework, interpretations of political authority, liberty and the role of reason differed radically.[8] Liberals and Conservatives allied in defence of the Union, and unionism incorporated elements of liberal and conservative political thought. It incorporated, too, many of the images and much of the ideology of the new expansive phase of late nineteenth-century British imperialism. Notions of the civilizing mission of British imperialism, British subjects spanning the globe, the redefinition of freedom and patriotism in an imperial context, and of the Crown as the focus of patriotism, were used in Ulster, as in Britain, as ideas which could unite otherwise conflicting classes and interest groups.

In the initial period of mobilization, a wide variety of arguments first for the Union, then for the exclusion of Ulster from the home rule settlement, were proposed.

There were arguments based on Protestants' religious interests. Fred Crawford, who organized the gun-running of 1914, justified his actions in such terms: 'We were going to defend our faith and liberty.'[9] The religious theme could also take more secular forms. H. S. Morrison, a South Derry doctor, president of the local Unionist Association and elder in the Presbyterian Church, wrote of the secular significance of religion:

> religious difference is the basal fact that fissures from top to bottom and from side to side the whole fabric of Irish life. The dread of Rome, not as a religion, but as a political organisation, runs through Irish life and splits it into two opposing sections.[10]

Religious and settler concerns were often interrelated. The Orange Order increased its membership and influence in the wake of the home rule crises, and its rhetoric and ritual connected defence of the faith with the folk memories of 1689–90, and with defence of the Protestant position in Ireland.[11] A local settler consciousness was clearly expressed in the late nineteenth century, in the stories, widely circulated among Protestants, of Catholic 'lotteries' anticipating the redistribution of Protestant lands and property with home rule. Sometimes, however, the settler past was brought out explicitly and seen as a continuous piece with Britain's contemporary imperial project. For Thomas Sinclair, liberal Unionist MP in 1912:

> The Ulster Scot is not in Ireland today upon the conditions of an ordinary immigrant. His forefathers were 'planted' in Ulster in the troublous times of the seventeenth century . . . We Ulster Unionists who inhabit the province today, or at least the greater number of us, are descendants of these settlers. The overwhelming majority are passionately loyal to the British throne . . . These things being so, it seems to Ulster Unionists that a grave responsibility rests on their

English and Scottish fellow citizens. . . . We are in Ireland as their
trustees, having had committed to us, through their and our forefathers, the development of the material resources of Ulster, the preservation of its loyalty, and the discharge of its share of Imperial
obligations.[12]

There were economic interests and general class interests. Thomas
MacKnight, the editor of the liberal newspaper, the *Northern Whig*,
portrays home rule as commercially disastrous for Belfast, and gives the
flavour of the opposition to home rule in Belfast commercial and liberal
society. Home rule would

> place the loyal in the power of the disaffected; the wealthier, educated,
> professional and more industrious classes under their social inferiors,
> the comparatively ignorant, the comparatively idle; they who were
> attached to the Crown and to the Empire under those who made no
> secret that their ultimate object was national independence.[13]

Or, as Lord Londonderry was to put it, 'The opposition to Home Rule
is the revolt of a business and industrial community against the domination of men who have shown no aptitude for either.'[14] For MacKnight,
class interests were more important than religion: home rule was opposed
by anyone who had anything to lose.[15] Protestant trade-unionists were as
adamant on the economic benefits of the Union as were businessmen. In
a 1914 appeal they argued that

> We have won improved conditions because the workers of the three
> kingdoms were able to exert joint pressure on the Imperial Parliament.
> To leave us to the consideration of a Parliament with crippled finances,
> elected mainly from agricultural constituencies, will deprive us of par-
> ticipation in those further benefits which British workers are certain
> to secure from the Imperial Parliament in the near future.[16]

Urban, modernizing contempt for rural life was apparent in this perspective: unionists were determined to resist coming

> under the influence of a bitterly prejudiced, ignorant and disaffected
> populace in the towns south of the Boyne, and of the peasants in the
> Southern country districts, still more prejudiced and ignorant and not
> less disaffected.[17]

Contemporary postcards showed Portadown and Belfast, bustling and
prosperous under the Union, decaying – literally gone to seed – under
home rule.[18] And the contempt was not confined to those in the industrial-
ized East of the province: similar attitudes to Southern rural life were
apparent in unionist newspapers in Fermanagh.[19]

The distinction between those Irishmen loyal to the Empire and the
disloyal was central to Unionist discourse; for Sir Edward Saunderson,

first leader of the Ulster Unionists, the divisions in Ireland were not between two races or nations, but between the loyal and the disloyal.[20] Some, like Sir William Park, moderator at the 1890 Jubilee Presbyterian General Assembly, made loyalty to Britain and the Empire primary in their rhetoric.

> Seldom, if ever, have any of us been ashamed to declare we are Britons . . . whatever their views of the best solution towards the Irish problem, the sentiment of loyalty towards and pride in the British inheritance and commonwealth of peoples has been common to us all.[21]

Empire, however, could mean different things to different unionists. For Park it was a source of proto-national identification. For some socialists, empire was a progressive and internationalizing force: the *Belfast Labour Chronicle* in 1905 commented that 'Nationalism is dead or dying and Imperialism is the transition stage to international union of the proletariat all the world over.'[22] For others, the main benefit of empire was in providing an expanded market for Belfast manufacturers and ship-builders.

Empire was, of course, the central factor for the Unionist party in Britain itself: Empire, imperial defence and state authority are overriding themes in the 1912 publication *Against Home Rule: The Case for the Union*. Sir Edward Carson, in an introduction which summarizes the themes in the book, notes that

> If there were no other arguments against Home Rule, the paramount necessities of Imperial defence would demand the maintenance of the Union. But the opposition to the proposed revolution in Ireland is based not only on the considerations of Imperial safety, but also on those of national honour.[23]

Carson goes on to show the British state financial, political and economic strategies which are designed to improve conditions in Ireland.

There were, finally, Protestants who were not initially inclined to unionism. Some had purely localistic interests and loyalties: those who 'considered every question from the point of view of their own farms'.[24] And, according at least to Rev. J. D. C. Houston of the Irish Protestant Home Rule Association, there were some 'liberal minded' Protestants who might have been 'willing to acquiesce in a fairly reasonable legislative scheme for the better government of Ireland . . . [and] . . . disposed to give the scheme . . . a fair trial'.[25] By 1912, however, unionist political mobilization had led most Protestants to prioritize community interests and to stand in solidarity with other Protestants and unionists.

The different arguments were not mutually exclusive. Prominent Presbyterians emphasized them all. MacKnight is as much a representative of those who give contractual loyalty to the British Crown as he is of

Belfast commercial and industrial interests.[26] Unionist politicians tailored their rhetoric to their audiences, emphasizing Protestant interests to local Orange meetings and imperial interests in Westminster.

The emphasis of unionist arguments changed over time, in response to changes in British public opinion, to nationalist rhetoric and to internal political needs for unionist cross-class solidarity.[27] Some stressed themes which later were occluded from discussion. In 1917, Lord Ernest Hamilton tackled head-on the issues of colonization, plantation and its consequences, ending with some hopes that the secular tendencies in Sinn Fein might overcome the dominant Catholic ethos of nationalism.[28] Notions of a distinctive Ulster character, and indeed an incipient Ulster nationalism, became most important after Ulster unionism became organizationally autonomous of Irish unionism in 1912.[29] And some themes which were initially more important in English than in Ulster unionism – that partition was the product of the separation of two nations or races within Ireland, or within Ulster itself – were to become important in Northern Ireland in later years.[30]

UNIONISM BY 1920

The various elements and themes of unionist argument were welded together in conditions of war and crisis. Examples of this new, hegemonic unionism can be seen in the writings of the 1920s. Ronald McNeill, a member of the unionist gentry, integrates the themes of empire, religion and good government in his *Ulster's Stand for Union*, published in 1922. In McNeill's account, traditional Protestant loyalism and religiosity are incorporated into mainstream unionism, itself centrally concerned with imperial responsibilities. Ulster unionists, opposing home rule, were

> men who felt as if living in a beleaguered citadel, whose flag they were bound in honour to keep flying to the last . . . a populace that came more and more to regard themselves as a bulwark of the Empire, on whom destiny . . . had imposed the duty of putting into actual practice the familiar motto of the Orange Lodges – 'No Surrender'.[31]

Thus Ulster unionism was rendered respectable and assimilable to British norms.[32]

From a less patrician perspective, and one that is more conscious of egalitarian values, Morrison's *Modern Ulster* (1920) harmonizes and integrates themes of liberal unionism and Orangeism, religion and economic interest:

> The speaker and his people fought with all their force in conjunction with their Roman Catholic neighbours to secure civil and religious liberty and freedom from any ascendancy, and it was only when the Catholic Section, in demanding Home Rule, laid claim to create

another ascendancy that Presbyterians left them to maintain the old cause of equality.[33]

McNeill deals explicitly with the constitutional issue. Only a majority in the United Kingdom could democratically decide on the status of the Union – thus the Irish had no right to secession.[34] And unionist resistance to the home rule bills did not constitute disloyalty for true allegiance to the sovereign is not the same as passive obedience to an Act of Parliament.[35] Unionists were not revolutionaries or subversives, but aimed to maintain the status quo.[36] This view assumes that Parliament's sovereignty is limited. McNeill quotes Randolph Churchill speaking at the Ulster Hall: 'no portentous change such as the repeal of the Union, no change so gigantic, could be accomplished by the mere passing of a law.'[37] But McNeill is not clear exactly what limits parliamentary sovereignty: the weight of the constitutional status quo, the interests of Empire and Kingdom, the contractual guarantee of Crown to unionist people, and/or the rights of British subjects.

There has been much debate in the literature as to the importance of British nationalism and imperial loyalties – as opposed to more particularistic Ulster Protestant economic and religious interests – in unionist motivations. On the one hand, the unionist sense of political obligation has been seen as a pre-national sense of contract between Crown and people, on the other hand as a form of British or as an incipient Ulster nationalism.[38] Indeed British patriotism, Ulster identity, and Irish national feeling were by no means incompatible. Writing of the 1920s, St John Ervine states that

> An Ulster Protestant Unionist is not 'anti-Irish' because he believes that it is good for Ireland to be closely joined to the British Commonwealth and intimately allied with Great Britain. He is pro-British because he is pro-Irish and desires the welfare of his country.[39]

Such questions of regional, national and state allegiance preoccupied Henry Quinn, the hero of Ervine's 1917 novel, *Changing Winds*. Jackson notes that 'the abiding impression is one of ambiguity. For, if there were two, or even three nations in late nineteenth-century Ireland, it would appear that each of these (and every combination) was represented within loyalism.'[40]

The tensions between British loyalty and particularistic Ulster Protestant interests should be seen in this context. A sense of British patriotism typically coexisted with a sense of unionist interest, without clear distinctions being made or priorities chosen. From the start, as unionists themselves saw, there was an affinity between their particularist interests and the wider British and imperial structure. For some, the similarities were of race and colonial mission.[41] For others, it was a matter of social structure: unionists were defending British Ulster, 'the Ulster of the plains, prosperous, industrious and loyal, with Belfast as the centre'.[42] The class distinctions within unionism, and between unionists and nationalists, the dominance of industry over agriculture and the cultural, political and economic linkages of Protestants with the British centre, could be seen roughly as a microcosm of the wider British socio-political and territorial order. The parallels and interconnections permitted the coexistence within Ulster unionism of two seemingly incompatible emphases and ideologies, the British-oriented and those primarily concerned with Protestant interests. The two coexisted, albeit in tension, because the Protestant position in Northern Ireland was not only defended by but to some extent reflected British socio-political and cultural hierarchies.

The main difference between the British and the Irish order was the presence of a Catholic and nationalist population, hostile both to British and to unionist power and status. The existence of this population was treated variously in unionist arguments. Some unionists were unashamedly exclusivist, treating Catholic and nationalist interests and wishes simply as a threat to themselves. Expulsions at the shipyards and other overtly sectarian actions exemplify this sectarian unionism, at once insecure and supremacist. Some took the view that two nations existed in Ireland, each with a right to their own form of state and society.[43] This perspective ignored the existence and interests of nationalists within the unionist heartland itself. Some held that equality and good community relations existed until they were disrupted by nationalist agitation.[44] Protestant exclusivism was a reaction to nationalism. The formal inclusivism of this view – which took unionist interests to be common to all – could only take practical effect once stable unionist government was achieved.

Whatever the rationale, in practical politics only Protestant and unionist interests were considered. John Whyte noted that he nowhere found in unionist deliberations over the size of the to-be-partitioned Northern state any concern for the democratic rights or wishes of the Catholics who would be included in it.[45] The practical moral community, in whose interests and for whose benefit the Union was maintained and partition imposed, was a Protestant one. Northern Catholics were written out of unionist political theory. Self-interest and moral fervour dovetailed for the unionists, because it was in terms of the interests, rights and loyalties of their own community that the foundation of the Northern state was legitimated. Northern Ireland, in this sense, was founded on an exclusivist legitimating principle, which was impervious to more generalized and universalistic pleas for justice and democracy if these were to conflict with unionists' basic interest in the survival of the state and the union.

THE NEW STATE 1920–45

With the foundation of the new Northern Ireland state, the unionist perspective was given an institutional arena on which to work. From its inception, unionist politicians stressed the British 'ties and feelings'[46] which bound them to the United Kingdom; the identification with the Empire, with its protection of religious and political values; the material benefits of the union, for example in trade, tax and welfare legislation. The values of liberty, equality, and order were affirmed. As Carson gave up the Ulster unionist leadership, he urged fair treatment for all religions:

> From the outset . . . let us see that the Catholic minority have nothing to fear from the Protestant majority. Let us take care to win all that is best among those who have been opposed to us in the past. While maintaining intact our own religion let us give the same rights to the religion of our neighbours.[47]

Before the opening of the Northern Ireland Parliament, Craig voiced classic liberal democratic ideals:

> Remember that the rights of the minority must be sacred to the majority, and that it will only be by broad views, tolerant ideas and a real desire for liberty of conscience that we here can make an ideal of the Parliament and the executive.[48]

At the same time, the politicians asserted the rights of unionists in Ireland: they saw unionist and nationalist equally having a right to 'their own' state in Ireland. A 'two-nations' rhetoric became common, with Sir Basil Brooke, later unionist Prime Minister, a consistent exponent.[49] Initially, at least, the two-nations rhetoric was linked with the hope that the two distinct peoples and states in Ireland could develop in 'friendly rivalry'.[50] The 1921 Presbyterian General Assembly pointed out that the

> fact that two parliaments are set up need not separate the people of Ireland. It simply means that two communities which are different in many respects will each be able to carry out its own ideals with the least possible friction.[51]

For nationalists within Northern Ireland, however, the implications were less benign. The unionist state, it was taken for granted, would be unionist ruled: there was never any question but that the nationalist minority in Northern Ireland would remain without power. In 1927, a Unionist (UULA) MP, William Grant, made the position clear:

> I was one of those . . . who never cared whether there was any Opposition in the House or not. I am glad to see them here, but if they went out of the House to-day I would have no regrets. I would not care if they never came back again.[52]

In effect, the two-nations rhetoric was used to legitimate unionist rule in Northern Ireland and to justify the exclusivist foundations of the state. It provided an internationally acceptable alternative to justifications in terms of the rights of settlers or of loyal citizens or of Protestants. However, it did not replace religious justifications, and sometimes merged with them: in a much-quoted 1934 speech, James Craig contrasted Northern and Southern states: 'All I boast of is that we are a Protestant Parliament and a Protestant State.'[53]

Unionists emphasized the constraints of their situation. Foremost among them was the threat to survival of the new state posed by nationalists within Northern Ireland and in the new Southern state. Security dominated unionist discussion in the early years of the state. In March 1922, the unionist *Belfast Newsletter* claimed that 'The existence of a hostile military organisation in Northern Ireland is the crux of the whole problem' and was quick to blame Sinn Fein in the South.[54] The murders of Protestants in the South, much reported in the press, served retrospectively to justify unionist resistance to home rule. So too did Southern nationalist politicians' reluctance to accept the Treaty as a final settlement, and their gradual severance of the linkages with Britain. To the *Northern Whig* in 1932, the election which brought De Valera to power in the south, and his subsequent actions 'illustrates anew the impossibility of any sort of fusion between North and South'.[55]

The values, hopes and liberal principles voiced by the unionist leaders were always framed by the necessity to secure the survival of the state. As early as 1920, unionist leaders had noted that 'no rebel who wishes to set up a republic can be regarded merely as a "political opponent", but must be repressed'.[56] In 1934, the *Belfast Newsletter* claimed that the danger of nationalist attack 'is restrained only by the realisation that the Ulster authorities would deal ruthlessly with any revolutionary outbreak within this area.'[57] Such security was necessarily at the expense of Catholics in Northern Ireland. Unionists enacted draconian security measures – by 1921, well over 32,000 men were mobilized in the security forces under unionist government control.[58] A strong Special Powers Act was enacted in 1922 and made permanent in 1933, giving government and security forces virtually a free hand against potential subversion.

The survival of the state was threatened politically as well as militarily. Unionists feared that the Boundary Commission, set up under the terms of the Anglo-Irish Treaty, would so lessen the area under unionist control that the state would be unviable. They worried about the potential increase in the numbers of Catholics in Northern Ireland, who might eventually outvote unionists. They were aware that any breach in unionist solidarity might allow nationalist victory – unionists only needed to lose once. In consequence, unionist governments did everything to meet the demands of local unionists and to ensure unionist solidarity and unionist power at local as well as regional level: the result was the gerrymandering of constituency boundaries, a change from the PRSTV electoral system, and systematic discrimination wherever unionist power was threatened.

A justification of such measures was available from a unionist perspective. Sir Basil Brooke gave the argument bluntly in Stormont, in defence of his earlier advocacy of discrimination in employment in favour of Protestants.

> There is . . . a catholic political party which ranges from what I might call benevolent nationalism, to what I might call the extreme of the extreme . . . but the one plank in its platform is the destruction of Ulster, as a unit and as a constitution . . . That is the policy and it simply varies in method. . . . Anyone who is out to break up . . . [the] constitution . . . established by Great Britain is to my mind disloyal. . . . I shall . . . use all my energies and whatever powers I possess to defeat the aims of those who are out to destroy the constitution of Ulster, be they protestants or Roman Catholics.[59]

It was formally an argument for a strong, conservative, security state, whatever the price in civil liberties. In the context of Northern Ireland, however, it was an explicit vindication and reaffirmation of the legitimacy of the state, and of the exclusivist legitimating principles on which the state was founded. An argument phrased in a formally non-sectarian manner – in terms of protecting law and order and the constitution – in substance sacrificed Catholic liberties in order to protect Protestant interests in the survival of the state. Certainly some unionists were dismayed at the sectarianism of other of Brooke's comments and the forms of repression and discrimination thus justified.[60] However Brooke's stance was backed by Craig, and the formal argument was constantly repeated and, as far as I am aware, not seriously challenged within unionism during the Stormont years.

Politicians and churchmen consistently noted that they had not sought partition. The 1921 General Assembly of the Presbyterian Church noted that 'This change in the government of Ireland was not sought by the members of the Presbyterian church. . . . But our people . . . are prepared to loyally carry out its provisions, so as to bring about settled government and establish law and order in our land.'[61] But while this expressed the feelings of some, quickly adaptation and acceptance of the new state turned into positive regard. As armed threat retreated, the process of building the new society for which unionists had fought proceeded. A pride, and even a patriotism, with respect to their own state developed, furthered by the unionist emphasis on the distinctiveness of the Northern Irish or Ulster people within Ireland, and within Britain. In 1936, for example, the *Belfast Newsletter*'s radio correspondent wished

> that whatever our political associations with the rest of Great Britain may be, the BBC would try to think of Northern Ireland culturally,

not as a kind of smaller and more backward England, but as a country, like Scotland, with some articulation of its own.[62]

The very survival of the state added to regional patriotism. So too did the favourable comparisons with the Republic – with respect to economics, education, religion and the compulsory learning of the Irish language – constantly made by politicians and in unionist newspapers.[63]

Just as unionists built the society they had fought for, so they resisted any intrusion into their state of the Irish society they had fought against. Their patriotism was one which consistently differentiated their 'Ulster' from the Free State, and was wary of any reference to the wider island or Irish culture which might blur that distinction. BBCNI experienced the potentially contradictory imperatives: its regional radio programmes were at once welcomed by unionists and scanned for any conflation of Ulster with Ireland, or any acceptance of the Irish cultural interests of the nationalist minority; the broadcasting of Gaelic Athletic Association results in 1934 led to such protests from unionists that such reports were banned until 1946 (and even then they were not broadcast on Sundays, when the matches were played, in deference to Protestant sabbatarianism).[64]

The divided, dualistic nature of Northern Ireland society was taken for granted, even by those of benign intent, and the assumption made, for example by liberal unionist civil servants like John Oliver, was that in voluntary affairs and social life, Catholics, 'who had their own point of view on such matters', should be allowed to go about their business, without attempt to 'press', 'cajole' or integrate them into Protestant-organized social activities.[65] In such areas, unionist liberal principles often triumphed over more authoritarian tendencies; in 1943, for example, proposals by the Orange Order and Prime Minister to forbid the teaching of Irish in schools were dropped after opposition from the Minister for Education.[66] With respect to expression of opinion, censorship and social activity, *laissez-faire* principles were usually followed and if Catholic social organization was not facilitated, neither was it forbidden. To this extent, unionists were right to insist that Northern Ireland followed liberal democratic norms. But this was liberalism in the private, not the public sphere. The unspoken assumption was that unionists would organize the public sphere, that a unionist, British and Protestant ethos should predominate in public, and that Catholic social organization should not intrude into public space. When it did, informal sectarian and formal state means of repression were used to reaffirm the unionist and British nature of Northern Ireland. Nationalist resistance to the public dominance of British symbols and authority was seen as an insult, even by the liberals.

In this period, the dominant strand of unionist thinking on social and economic issues was conservative, resisting redistributive measures, taking no active policy to combat unemployment, protecting existing social, political and economic hierarchies, and inactive on regional planning. Politicians themselves were overwhelmingly landed gentry or businessmen. Deference to the leadership was encouraged – Brooke's main plank on his initial election was loyalty to Craig. Where there was a choice between more stringent security measures and more respect for individual rights, security and the strong state won. The government's and state's identity was with the Conservative government in Britain – the Liberals had now faded, and Labour was considered suspect on the Irish question, as well as overly radical. But this was qualified by the government's need, and habitual tendency, to court popular Protestant support. The Unionist government was pressured by working-class agitation, and gave in to Orange and independent loyalist pressures on issues of Protestant working-class interest, just as it gave in to local unionist pressures. But it did this without incorporating the demands within its own rhetoric. Instead, unionist politicians attempted to deny the seriousness of class tensions: unionist politicians praised the situation in Northern Ireland where the class polarization typical of Britain did not occur. In 1929, Brooke noted that 'In our towns are many industrial workers who to their credit instead of being mostly socialist as in England are as strong unionists as you or I.'[67] Leaders like Craig blithely promised everything to everybody when under pressure, while their inclinations and initial policies remained conservative. Others tried to resist such government overspending.[68]

MODERNIZING UNIONISM 1946–70

The post-war period saw a greater confidence and even expansiveness in unionism. An emphasis on the liberties offered in Northern Ireland and the United Kingdom predominated over the more defensive emphasis on unionist rights. The pan-nationalist Anti-Partition League of the late 1940s provoked a series of articles and pamphlets justifying the unionist position to a British and American audience. These speeches and statements continued throughout the 1950s, appealing to the moral capital Northern Ireland had earned by its participation in the Allied war effort. A modernizing and technocratic rhetoric entered unionism, together with a new confidence. Comparisons with the Republic – economically stagnant and internationally marginal – were at their starkest. The Labour governments in Britain, and the development of a Butskellite consensus on economic and social issues, allowed unionists to go beyond the conservatism of the inter-war period and restore themes which had been recessive in that period.

This was a change of emphasis, rather than a change in direction of unionism. Unionist solidarity was still based on a perception of a nationalist threat. In 1949 unionist election material announced that 'the country is in danger, its people's heritage at stake'. In most other post-war elections, similar themes were dominant.[69]

Protestant solidarity remained a crucial concern for unionist leaders; the Orange Order remained a central institution within unionism, serving to unite different social classes and regions; *causes célèbres* – the refusal to open children's swings on Sundays, the naming of the new bridge in Belfast and the new city of Craigavon – showed a continuing Protestant exclusivism within unionism.

Old arguments and values appeared in new guises. Sir Basil Brooke reaffirmed a two-nations view: 'The border between Northern Ireland and Eire exists because of the ideological gulf which divides the two peoples. There are differences of racial origins, of religion and of political allegiance, and the three combined have made the separation of the two areas inevitable.'[70] Others denied any racial or national content to partition.[71] Settler themes, relatively common before partition, seldom surfaced in this period of global decolonization.

G. B. Hanna, Minister for Home Affairs in 1956, did not include such a two-nations argument in his list of the six principles at the basis of the Union.[72] In order, he mentioned (i) defence interests of the western alliance, (ii) the backward-looking policy of the South, e.g. in terms of language policy, (iii) the liberal ethos, and lack of subservience to authority in Northern Ireland, (iv) the traffic in ideas and lack of censorship in Northern Ireland, (v) the economic benefits of the union, and (vi) 'royal allegiance'.

Hanna's list is indicative of unionist priorities, at least as stressed to interested outsiders, in the 1950s. At the height of the Cold War, the need for Northern Ireland as part of the western defence alliance and as a potential base for NATO troops, was stressed. But the broader historical context was even more important for unionists, both at home and abroad. They emphasized the part Northern Ireland played in the Second World War, in contrast to the neutral Southern Irish state, the moral credit they had thus amassed, and their rightful participation in the victors' post-war world. W. Douglas, the secretary of the Ulster Unionist Association, wrote that

> Ulstermen have shared in the enterprise and adventures of their fellow-subjects across the narrow sea, have with them borne the burdens and reaped the triumphs of many a hard-fought campaign, and, by their labours freely undertaken in fulfilment of a common destiny, have won a just claim to be joined in the direction of the great Empire which they have helped to build.[73]

What was emphasized especially in the 1950s and 1960s was the modernizing character of Northern Ireland as compared to the backward South, with modernization seen in terms of liberal, cultural and social values, not simply of economic development. Three of Hanna's principles fall under this category. W. Brian Maginnis, then Minister of Finance, in the same publication as Hanna, developed the theme: Ulster people are guided by the belief in the right of the individual to think and speak for himself, the right to knowledge, the right of mental liberty. And Maginnis makes clear that these values, embodied in Ulster social life, are made possible by the Union and Northern Ireland's participation in the broader British world and western alliance: in the present 'war of ideas', 'Ulster stands on the side of freedom' and can 'show that free men with minds unhampered by authoritarian restrictions can build a better and fuller life for mankind than can ever be done by a dictator ridden world'.[74] Northern Ireland, perhaps more than before or since, was seen as a microcosm of the British and western macrocosm.

The obverse of this liberal modernizing self-image was a belief that nationalists and the South of Ireland were backward, reactionary, incapable of or uninterested in free thought. It was the pre-partition stereotype of progressive North vs. backward South, easily assimilable to loyalist stereotypes of backward and superstitious Catholics. When stated bluntly, the caricatures are clear.

> There is only one Ireland, but there are two distinct races, two distinct psychologies, two different outlooks and two different perspectives. There are those people who believe they have the supreme and heaven sent duty of trying to breathe the breath of life into the dry bones of a dead nationalism that can serve no effective purpose. . . . There is the other section of the Irish community who recognise world intelligence and who believe that . . . the best way of implementing all that is best in the human race is to strengthen and enlarge the British Commonwealth.[75]

In the 1950s and 1960s, however, liberal unionists consistently made the same points, in a somewhat more sophisticated manner.[76]

Traditional religious themes continued to be central to unionism. Reverend Leahy, of the National Union of Protestants, made clear that he was 'firmly convinced that Roman Catholicism is destructive of a nation's greatness, a people's freedom, and an individual's rights'.[77] M. W. Dewar's *'Why Orangeism?'* of 1959, which sold 40,000 copies on first printing, emphasized the religious principles of Protestantism, their consistent challenge by a Roman Catholic Church which 'has kept the Bible from its people everywhere for centuries',[78] and the repetitive pattern of trial of Protestants by Catholics throughout Irish history:

> That the overwhelming majority in the Irish Republic are Roman Catholics, and opposed to any connection with Great Britain, makes it inevitable that the overwhelming majority inn [sic] Northern Ireland are in favour of maintaining, in the twentieth century as in the seventeenth, 'the Protestant Religion and the Liberties of England'.[79]

But the emphasis on modernity and freedom affected even the traditional Protestant loyalist organizations. J. M. Andrews, unionist Prime Minister, stated the Orange position in 1950:

> The Orange ritual lays it down that it is the duty of Orangemen to support and maintain the laws and constitution. It is fundamentally important that we should continue to do so, for if we lost our constitutional position within the United Kingdom 'civil and religious liberty for all', which we are also pledged as Orangemen to support, would be endangered.[80]

The economic benefits of the union were consistently mentioned in the unionist speeches of the 1940s and 1950s. The welfare state in particular was seen as a major benefit of the Union. The contrast between Northern Ireland prosperity and Southern economic stagnation was made explicit during the 1958 election.[81] Regional planning, infrastructural development and economic modernization in Northern Ireland in the 1960s highlighted the contrast between Northern Ireland and the Republic. Terence O'Neill made economic development a central theme in his speeches.[82] In response to riots in 1964, he stressed that

> Those of us responsible for the Industrial Development of the Province can only deplore the world-wide publicity being given to events of this character when we have laboured to convince the world that Ulster is an ideal place in which to build a factory and give employment to our people.[83]

In part, however, this economic focus was a function of the new political need for unionists at least to appear to take account of Catholic interests and concerns. Brian Faulkner, writing in 1971, claims that 'economically, the case for unionism has been proven in practice'.[84] He portrays unionism as a realistic politics able to bring a prosperity and progress 'to which all men and women, regardless of political or religious affiliations, can reach out'.[85]

British patriotism, or as Hanna put it 'royal allegiance', remained of importance. Often, as for the Reverend J. Macmanaway, this was presented as a broad indeterminate patriotism, confirmed in the experience of war. At this period there was no conflict between British and Northern Ireland patriotism, or between British nationalism and contractualism. With the advent of the welfare state and parity for Northern Ireland in welfare provisions, unionists at once enjoyed the benefits of being British and of relative autonomy from central British control. The survival of the state, the lack of conflict with the central British government, and indeed the appearance of stronger British support for Northern Ireland than before in the aftermath of war and of the South's declaration of a Republic, precluded any conflict between unionist self-interest and wider British affinities, and let contractual loyalty to the Crown merge into a form of British nationalism. Many unionists came to see the state, the social order and the British connection as natural: as the New Ulster Movement put it in 1972, 'to a large majority in Northern Ireland, British nationality seems as natural as the air they breathe'.[86]

In this period especially, the values of liberty, democracy and modernization were emphasized, identified with 'western freedoms', and conjoined with a British patriotism. But this sat uneasily with the continuing discrimination and repression in Northern Ireland. Unionists justified the latter in terms of the instability of the state and the rights of unionists to a state in Ireland – the older exclusivist argument for partition. Indeed one can see the Northern Ireland state as relying on such an exclusivist sense of unionist political community for its survival, while aiming towards a more normal liberal democratic system.

All unionists to some extent saw both aspects of their state – the emergency and the normal, the exclusivist and the liberal-democratic. Those connected with the repressive apparatuses of the state were conscious of the extent of repression, and tended to accept its necessity; those in professional or service occupations might be more oblivious of its extent and more hopeful of the prospects of reform.[87] Some openly advocated reform, others openly excluded nationalists – and often also Catholics – from the political community. For example, in the 1959 controversy over whether Catholics should be allowed to join the Unionist party there were liberals (Sir Clarence Graham, and Brian Maginness) and die-hards (Sir George Clark, Grand Master of the Orange Order). But most did not see an irreconcilable contradiction between liberal principles and Northern Ireland reality, at least until the late 1960s. In 1959, most unionist politicians supported the principle of Catholic membership while believing the change was better introduced gradually and quietly, and not made a public issue.[88] Most, in short, held both the liberal ideals and the belief that some degree of exclusionary and repressive measures were necessary. Thus the different strands of unionism, the religious and the liberal, the modern and the traditional, could be held together.

At this stage, at least among unionist party politicians, it is mistaken to posit a sharp division between Ulster British liberals – British patriots who seriously held to liberal democratic principles – and Ulster loyalist reactionaries, with a contractualist sense of political obligation and a belief in Protestant power.[89] Unionists held both that their state was necessary to protect Protestant interests (implicitly a contractualist position) and that it lived up to liberal democratic British norms. Politicians did their best to prevent these two sets of principles from coming into conflict. Full equality was refused to Catholics and nationalists on the grounds that they might undermine the very basis of liberal democratic rights – membership of the United Kingdom. The distinction between Ulster British and Ulster loyalist was becoming clear in this period. But it was clearer among the unionist public than among political leaders, and even among the public it was expressed in different life-styles, social networks, cultural identities and political ideologies, and had few practical political consequences.

In the 1960s, conflict between the liberal modernizing rhetoric of Captain Terence O'Neill and the loyalist religious rhetoric of Rev. Ian Paisley became public. Initially, however, this was not seen as a source of potential unionist disintegration. Recent research suggests that the internal unionist power-struggles of this period were between local populist unionists and centralizers, rather than between liberals and traditionalists.[90] The liberal vs. traditionalist conflict, however, became politically crucial when the Civil Rights Movement brought newly assertive Catholics into the political arena and put the issue of reform on the political agenda. It highlighted the exclusivist principles at the foundation of unionism and forced unionists to choose between their liberal ideals and the protection of the unionist state. At this stage, some unionists unambiguously chose the liberal ideals and argued for reform – the O'Neillite Unionists, some of whom later moved to the Alliance party. Some unambiguously chose the protection of the state and the maintenance of unionist and Protestant power – the Protestant Unionists, later to become the Democratic Unionist Party. Most, under the leadership of Chichester Clark and later Faulkner, tried to keep the old unionist unity of perception and purpose. For Faulkner, the commitment to the union remained unchanged, but he also identified with the new, post-war unionist political confidence.[91] He defended the history of unionist rule and gave a commitment to equal citizenship and complete justice and equality for all in Northern Ireland.[92]

With the fall of Stormont in 1972 the cause was lost. British priorities and unionist interests no longer coincided, and conflict between them became increasingly apparent. In reaction, unionist political thought at once splintered and developed. It is no longer possible to reconcile the liberal modernizing ideals of the Campaign for Equal Citizenship with the pluralism of Alliance, with the Ulster nationalism of the Ulster Defence Association, with the conservatism of sections of the Official Unionists, with the Protestant loyalism of Ian Paisley. Unionist unity today is merely strategic. But this is a function of the failure of the original unionist project. Now much hangs on whether unionist loyalty is contractual, patriotic or based on liberal principle. Unionists had tried to create a polity where all three motivations were compatible, and a mode of political thought where the three sets of concepts were mutually informative and supportive.

The real problem for unionism was always partly occluded within its own self-understanding – the existence of Catholics and nationalists within the unionist state. Once Catholics asserted themselves, the contradictions between the exclusivist foundations of Northern Ireland and its liberal ideals became clear. Unionism, as a political theory, relied on a quiet, or quietist, Catholic population. In a stable political situation, unionism might have developed a more systematic self-justification – but in a stable situation, unionism would not have needed such a distinctive political theory.

NOTES

I wish to thank the British Council for a grant which facilitated research for this chapter, and the editors for comments and suggestions on an earlier draft.

1 D. W. Miller, *Queen's Rebels: Ulster Loyalism in Historical Perspective*, Dublin, Gill & Macmillan, 1973, 4–6. P. Gibbon, *The Origins of Ulster Unionism: The Foundations of Popular Protestant Politics and Ideology in Nineteenth-century Ireland*, Manchester, Manchester University Press, 1975, 136. J. Loughlin, *Gladstone, Home Rule and the Ulster Question, 1882–1893*, Dublin, Gill & Macmillan, 1986, 153–61. A. Jackson, *The Ulster Party: Irish Unionists in the House of Commons, 1884–1911*, Oxford, Clarendon Press, 1989, 4–17.

2 For examples of the historical divisions within unionism, see P. Bew, P. Gibbon and H. Patterson, *The State in Northern Ireland 1921–1972: Political Forces and Social Classes*, Manchester, Manchester University Press, 1979. 8–9, 150–1, 190.

3 T. MacKnight, *Ulster As It Is, or Twenty Eight Years Experience as an Irish Editor*, London, Macmillan, 2 vols, 1896. R. McNeill, *Ulster's Stand for Union*, London, John Murray, 1922. H. D. Morrison, *Modern Ulster: Its Character, Customs, Politics and Industries*, London, Allenson, 1920.

4 A. J. Balfour *et al.*, *Against Home Rule: The Case for the Union*, London, Frederick Warne, 1912.

5 Lord E. Hamilton, *The Soul of Ulster*, London, Hurst & Blackett, 1917. J. Logan, *Ulster in the X-Rays*, London, Arthur H. Stockwell, 1923. J. B. Woodburn, *The Ulster Scot: His History and Religion*, London, Allenson, 1914. G. Birmingham, *The Red Hand of Ulster*, Belfast, Smith, Elder & Co, 1912.

6 R. L. McCartney, *Liberty and Authority in Ireland*, Derry, Field Day, 1985. A. Aughey, *Under Siege: Ulster Unionism and the Anglo-Irish Agreement*, Belfast, Blackstaff, 1989. J. Oliver, *Working at Stormont*, Dublin, Institute of Public Administration, 1978.

7 Miller, *Queens Rebels*, 15–16.

8 T. Brown, *The Whole Protestant Community: The Making of a Historical Myth*, Derry, Field Day, 1985.

9 P. Orr, *The Road to the Somme: Men of the Ulster Division Tell Their Story*, Belfast, Blackstaff, 1987, 29.

10 Morrison, *Modern Ulster*, 99. Compare Sir E. Carson in Balfour, *Against Home Rule*, 26.

11 M. W. Dewar, *Why Orangeism?* Belfast, 1959, 15.

12 Balfour *et al.*, *Against Home Rule*, 170–1.

13 MacKnight, *Ulster As It Is*, II, 334.

14 Balfour *et al.*, *Against Home Rule*, 165.

15 MacKnight, *Ulster As It Is*. II, 392.

16 H. Patterson, *Class Conflict and Sectarianism: The Protestant Working Class and the Belfast Labour Movement 1868–1920*, Belfast, Blackstaff, 1980, 86, cf. 48–51, 56.

17 McKnight, *Ulster As It Is*, II, 385. Compare Morrison, *Modern Ulster*, 75.

18 J. Killen, *John Bull's Famous Circus: Ulster History through the Postcard*, Dublin, O'Brien, 1985, 50, 53.
19 J. Anderson, 'Ideological variations in Ulster during Ireland's first home rule crisis: an analysis of local newspapers', in C. H. Williams and E. Kofman (eds), *Community Conflict, Partition and Nationalism*, London, Routledge, 1989, 152.
20 E. J. Saunderson, *Two Irelands: Loyalty versus Treason*, London and Dublin, 1884, preface.
21 R. F. G. Holmes, *Our Irish Presbyterian Heritage*, Publications Committee of the Presbyterian Church in Ireland, 1985, 136.
22 Patterson, *Class Conflict*, 49.
23 Balfour *et al.*, *Against Home Rule*, 22.
24 MacKnight, *Ulster As It Is*, I, 219.
25 J. Loughlin, 'The Irish Protestant Home Rule Association and nationalist politics, 1886–1893', *Irish Historical Studies*, XXIV (1985), 343–4.
26 Miller, *Queens Rebels*, 91–2.
27 For example, Jackson, *Ulster Party*, 87.
28 Hamilton, *Soul of Ulster*, ch. 1, ch. 10, 171–4.
29 Jackson, *Ulster Party*, 14.
30 Anderson, 'Ideological variations', 163.
31 McNeill, *Ulster's Stand*, 13.
32 ibid., 31, 33, 116–17.
33 Morrison, *Modern Ulster*, 99–100.
34 McNeill, *Ulster's Stand*, 15.
35 ibid., 4.
36 ibid., 140–1.
37 ibid., 40.
38 See note 1.
39 St J. Ervine, *Craigavon: Ulsterman*, London, Allen & Unwin, 1949, 383.
40 Jackson, *Ulster Party*, 17.
41 ibid., 86.
42 MacKnight, *Ulster As It Is*, I, 299.
43 ibid., II, 185, 380.
44 Morrison, *Modern Ulster*, 100.
45 J. Whyte, 'Interpretations of the Northern Ireland problem', in C. Townshend (ed.), *Consensus in Ireland: Approaches and Recessions*, Oxford, Clarendon Press, 1988, 33.
46 B. Barton, *Brookeborough: The Making of a Prime Minister*, Belfast, Institute of Irish Studies, 1988, 70.
47 H. M. Hyde, *Carson: A Biography*, London, Heinemann, 1953, 449.
48 James Craig, *Belfast Newsletter*, 8 February 1921, in D. Kennedy, *The Widening Gulf: Northern Attitudes to the Independent Irish State 1919–1949*, Belfast, Blackstaff, 1988, 59.
49 Barton, *Brookeborough*, 127.
50 Craig, September 1921, in D. Harkness, *Northern Ireland Since 1920*, Dublin, Helicon, 1983, 16.
51 Holmes, *Presbyterian Heritage*, 145.
52 P. Buckland, *The Factory of Grievances: Devolved Government in Northern Ireland 1921–39*, Dublin, Gill & Macmillan, 1979, 231.
53 ibid., 72.
54 Kennedy, *Widening Gulf*, 79–81.
55 ibid., 211.
56 M. Farrell, *Arming the Protestants: The Formation of the Ulster Special Constabulary 1920–1927*, London, Pluto, 1983, 41.

57 Kennedy, *Widening Gulf*, 198.
58 P. Buckland, *A History of Northern Ireland*, Dublin, Gill & Macmillan, 1981, 42.
59 Barton, *Brookeborough*, 81.
60 ibid., 79.
61 Holmes, *Presbyterian Heritage*, 145.
62 R. Cathcart, *The Most Contrary Region: The BBC in Northern Ireland 1924–1984*, Belfast, Blackstaff, 1984, 76.
63 For example, Kennedy, *Widening Gulf*, 179.
64 Cathcart, *Most Contrary Region*, 66, 141–2.
65 Oliver, *Working at Stormont*, 47.
66 Report on Northern Ireland Cabinet papers by Eamon Phoenix, *Irish Times*, 1–2 January 1988, 4.
67 Barton, *Brookeborough*, 70.
68 Bew, Gibbon and Patterson, *The State in Northern Ireland*, ch. 3.
69 D. P. Barritt and C. F. Carter, *The Northern Ireland Problem: A Study in Group Relations*, London, Oxford University Press, 1962, 44–6.
70 Ulster Unionist Council, *Ulster is British: A Reaffirmation of Ulster's Political Outlook with Report on General Election of 10 Feb. 1949*, UUC, March 1949.
71 Rev. J. G. MacManaway, *Partition, Why Not? A Review of the Partition of Ireland*, UUC, n.d. (*c.* 1949).
72 Lord B. Brookeborough *et al.*, *Why the Border Must Be: The Northern Ireland Case in Brief*, Government of Northern Ireland Publications (PRONI 1726/0), 1956.
73 W. Douglas, 'The impossibility of Irish union', *The Bell*, 14, 1 (1947), 35.
74 Brookeborough *et al*, *Why the Border Must Be*.
75 G. Walker, *The Politics of Frustration: Harry Midgley and the Failure of Labour in Northern Ireland*, Manchester, Manchester University Press.
76 Brookeborough, *Why the Border Must Be*.
77 Rev. F. S. Leahy, 'Fears and convictions of Ulster Protestants', *The Bell*, 16.3 (1950), 10.
78 Dewar, *Why Orangeism?* 17.
79 ibid., 22.
80 M. W. Dewar, J. Brown and S. E. Long, *Orangeism: A New Historical Appreciation*, Belfast, T. H. Jordan, 1967, 188.
81 Barritt and Carter, *The Northern Ireland Problem*, 45.
82 T. O'Neill, *The Autobiography of Terence O'Neill*, London, Rupert Hart-Davis, 1972, 52.
83 O'Neill, *Autobiography*, 63.
84 B. Faulkner, 'Ireland today', *Aquarius*, 1971. Reprinted in David Bleakley, *Faulkner: Conflict and Consent in Irish Politics*, London, Mowbrays, 1974, 156.
85 ibid., 158.
86 New Ulster Movement, *Two Irelands or One?* NUM, Belfast, 1972, 5.
87 See, for example, the very different attitudes to what came to be seen as abuses of the Stormont system in the following: Sir A. Hezlet, *The 'B' Specials: A History of the Ulster Special Constabulary*, London, Tom Stacey, 1972, 64, 80. 177–8. W. Clark, *Guns in Ulster: A History of the B Special Constabulary in Parts of Co Derry*, Belfast, Constabulary Gazette, 1967, 9. Oliver, *Working at Stormont*, 71–9.
88 Report on Northern Ireland cabinet papers by Eamon Phoenix, Anne Flaherty and Mark Brennock, *Irish Times*, 1–2 January, 1991, 6.
89 J. Todd, 'Two Traditions in Unionist Political Culture', *Irish Political Studies*, 2, 1987, 3–11.

90 Bew, Gibbon and Patterson, *The State in Northern Ireland*, 155, 195.
91 Faulkner, 'Ireland today', 156.
92 B. Faulkner, Paper on the Northern Ireland crisis read to the Conservative Bow Group, 1972, in David Bleakley, *Faulkner: Conflict and Consent in Irish Politics*, London, Mowbrays, 1974, 162–5.

Index